The American Finances
of the Spanish Empire

Dedicated to
Nicolás Sánchez-Albornoz

© 1998 by the University of New Mexico Press
All rights reserved.
First edition

Library of Congress Cataloging-in-Publication Data

Klein, Herbert S.
    The American finances of the Spanish empire: royal income and expenditures in
colonial Mexico, Peru, and Bolivia, 1680–1809 /
Herbert S. Klein.—1st ed.
        p.   cm.
    Includes bibliographical references and index.
    ISBN 0-8263-1832-0 (cloth)
    1. Taxation—Mexico—History.   2. Taxation—Peru—History.   3. Taxation—
Bolivia—History.   4. Mexico—Appropriations and expenditures—History.
5. Peru—Appropriations and expenditures—History.   6. Bolivia—Appropriations
and expenditures—History.   7. Finance, Public—Spain—Colonies—America—
History.   I. Title.
HJ2466.K54   1998
336.09171'246—dc21   97-34093
                                                                              CIP

The American Finances of the Spanish Empire

Royal Income and Expenditures in Colonial Mexico, Peru, and Bolivia, 1680–1809

Herbert S. Klein

University of New Mexico Press
Albuquerque

Contents

Illustrations

Maps

Tables

Graphs

Preface

The present book began as a research project in Argentina in 1971, when I encountered my first royal treasury materials in the Archivo General de la Nación. Faced by these enormous tomes and curious as to what they contained, I began my long quest to determine what they meant and what one could do with them. Almost immediately I became perplexed by the arcane terminology and complex accounting practices I encountered. It was at this early stage that I wrote to Marcello Carmagnani and John TePaske to ask for their knowledgeable help in interpreting what I had found. Their assistance made possible my first successful penetration of these materials.

In these first efforts, I was forced to confine myself to just one year, because of the quantity of the materials which I encountered.[1] But when I returned to the United States and talked over my results with John TePaske, we decided that the time had come to begin a more systematic investigation in this area, which he himself had just begun to think about in his collection of Mexican materials. The introduction of modern computers into historical research in the late 1960s had finally provided the tools to begin the processing of these massive royal treasury accounts. In the mid-1970s we organized a major project to gather together the extant royal treasury records for the Viceroyalties of New Spain, Peru, and the Río de la Plata, as well as the allied zones of Chile and the Audiencia of Charcas, which we eventually published.[2]

But the publication of the available archival materials in a readable and usable format was just the beginning of the project. This work is the next stage in understanding royal finances; it uses the data TePaske and I assembled, along with my own reconstructions, to analyze the evolution of royal incomes and expenditures in the premier American colonies in the eighteenth century. In preparation for this analytical phase, I began working closely with Jacques Barbier on the contemporaneous Spanish metropolitan fiscal accounts, which gave me an entirely new perspective on the colonial American materials.[3] I also had an opportunity to discuss my initial findings with the late Germán Colmenares and with Hermes Tovar, when I was working in the Archivo General de Indias, and with Carlos Marichal and his students, when I was teaching at the Colegio de México. Both John TePaske and I have published together and separately a series of preliminary analyses on various aspects of these accounts.[4] But the current work is my own effort to pull many of the disparate themes I have analyzed into a coherent analytical framework. In addition the numbers used are based on my own reconstruction of the accounts for the principal colonial zones of Mexico and the Andean region.

This book is divided into several sections. The first two chapters provide an introduction to the problems of analyzing these themes and to the general trends that emerge from the study of these treasury records. The following three chapters then detail the evolution of the royal tax revenues and expenditures within each of the three major colonial zones—Peru, Charcas (Upper Peru, later Bolivia), and Mexico (New Spain). Following a conclusion that brings together all the basic themes discussed in the study and offers suggestions for future research, the book ends with a series of technical appendixes. These include a discussion of how the numbers were generated, why current prices were used, and how the grouped categories of taxes were created.

In undertaking this study I have been aided by a number of scholars and friends aside from those I have already mentioned. At an early stage of this work, I had the technical assistance of Eli Grushka and Jacob Metzer, of Hebrew University, as well as the support of Richard Garner. My friend Nicolás Sánchez-Albornoz has been a constant guide to me in colonial and economic history. Without the assistance and encouragement of John TePaske, neither this book nor the numbers upon which it was based would have been completed. Initial funds for the collection of these materials were granted to me and John TePaske by the National Endowment for the Humanities and the Tinker Foundation (1975–77). Subsequent grants provided the support for my analysis of this material. Of fundamental importance were the awards I received from the Banco de España of a "V Centenario del Descubrimiento de América" commemorative fellowship in 1988 and a "Catedra Patrimonial" fellowship granted by the Consejo Nacional para Ciencia y Tecnología of Mexico, in the spring of 1992. Both these grants permitted me to complete the analysis of these materials.

Finally I would like to thank Stephen Haber for his critical reading of the final manuscript, as well as the two anonymous readers for the University of New Mexico Press who provided an unusually detailed reading of this work.

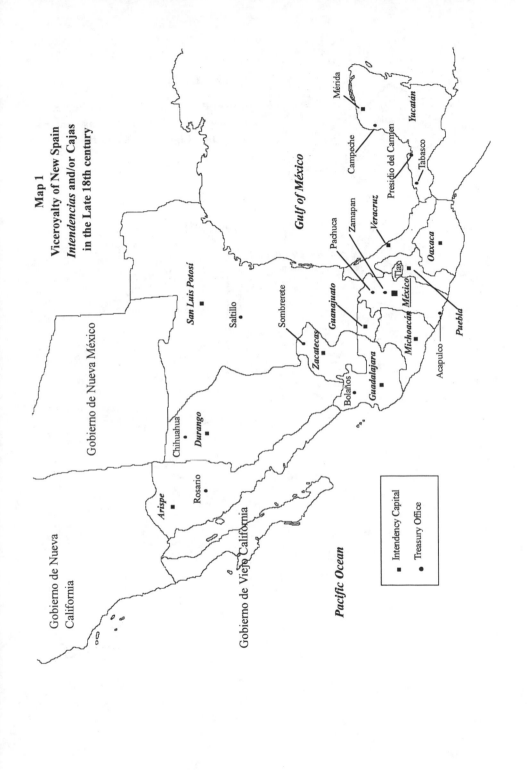

Map 1
Viceroyalty of New Spain
Intendencias and/or *Cajas*
in the Late 18th century

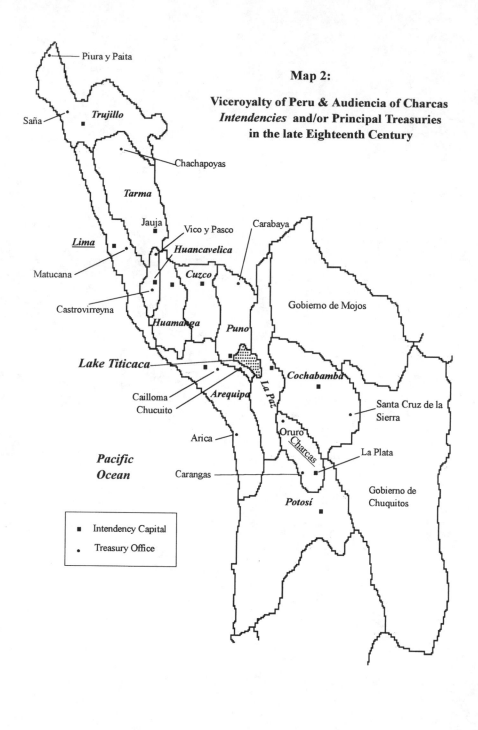

Map 2:

Viceroyalty of Peru & Audiencia of Charcas
Intendencies **and/or Principal Treasuries**
in the late Eighteenth Century

Piura y Paita

Saña

Trujillo

Chachapoyas

Tarma

Jauja

Vico y Pasco

Carabaya

Lima

Huancavelica

Matucana

Cuzco

Castrovirreyna

Gobierno de Mojos

Huamanga

Puno

Lake Titicaca

Cochabamba

Cailloma

Arequipa

Chucuito

Santa Cruz de la Sierra

La Paz

Arica

Oruro

Charcas

La Plata

Pacific Ocean

Carangas

Potosí

Gobierno de Chuquitos

■ Intendency Capital

• Treasury Office

1

Colonial Fiscal History

Although death and taxes are always with us, it has only been in recent years that historians have become deeply concerned with either of these two universals in human history. While social historians are now studying the nature of death and dying, economic historians have finally taken seriously the history of taxes. In fact the modern system of taxation by the states of western Europe is intimately tied to the growth of both modern cash economies and the rise of representative governments. The type of taxes collected, their manner of collection, and the use of authoritarian or consensual means to extract these revenues can each tell us important things about the nature of a government, its relative development, and even its popularity.[1] Tax revenues can also tell us about the economy that is being taxed. For periods prior to the existence of modern national accounts, taxes are the leading source of economic statistics about a national economy.

Yet for all their undoubted historical importance, tax records have been used in only a limited fashion by historians. Interpreting the meaning of taxes is a complex and difficult task, which first must be resolved before such records can be used effectively. Their often enormous size has meant that they could not be efficiently analyzed in any systematic way until the advent of the modern computer. With this tool now available, and with an ever growing concern with understanding the economic evolution of the less developed countries, such an analysis is well worth undertaking. The present work thus falls within a limited but growing series of studies attempting to define the colonial economies of Latin America through the use of these extraordinary sources.[2]

Taxing systems, of course, existed in the Western tradition from time immemorial. But for the states of western Europe, the conquest of America and the establishment of colonies in the Western Hemisphere provided an unparalleled opportunity to modernize their tax systems. The New World offered not only new grounds for experimenting with social utopias, but it also gave governments the potential to rewrite their tax systems unfettered by historical rights and privileges that had their origins in the medieval past and their fervent defenders in the present. Perhaps no other imperial power took such advantage of this opportunity as the Spanish crown.[3]

All the colonies of Europe developed imperial bureaucracies and empirewide tax systems, but there is little question that the most complete and efficient such system was that maintained by Spain in its American colonies. Neither the Portuguese nor the English even came close to keeping the detailed records needed to tax their subjects efficiently, nor were the French or Dutch much better. Even the critical observer Alexander von Humboldt was impressed by the efficiency of the Spanish imperial government in its role as a taxing agent.

From the very beginning of its New World conquest, the Spanish crown set about establishing as modern a fiscal system as it was possible to develop in the context of contemporary European administrative organization and knowledge. The prime concern of the crown was to establish royal control over taxation and strict accountability for those who administered the fiscal system. It was obvious that in this case, as with so many other royal institutions transplanted to America in the fifteenth and sixteenth centuries, the crown tried to create a more modern and rational structure than existed in Spain itself. Thus from the beginning the evolution of the Spanish American treasury took on a completely different shape from its European counterpart and at the same time was at the forefront of the implantation of Spanish administration in the empire. It was no accident that the first officials the crown required the conquistadors to take with them in their various expeditions were royal tax officials.

Nor was the crown at all hesitant in reorganizing its economic districts, which it carried out even faster than the reform of its political divisions. The crown made the jurisdictions of the individual treasury offices (known as *cajas reales*) coterminous with a coherent economic region. Unlike the overlapping treasury offices of the metropolis, those of Spanish America were unique to a given geographic area. As each political unit was established, it received a corresponding treasury office. The more important the district, the higher in rank was the treasury office, and clear lines of authority and hierarchy were established. In each viceroyalty, *audiencia*, or captaincy general, one treasury office was declared a head or central office (*caja principal*) and was made responsible for a group of regional treasuries. These were central treasuries, to which all the subordinate treasuries of the district sent their records and surplus revenues and whose senior officials were sent to oversee the local treasuries.

Unlike the rigid metropolitan arrangements, the Castillian crown in its American possessions was quick to disband as well as establish new treasury districts. If a new mining region was discovered, a treasury office was quickly established, and the local region was removed from the jurisdiction of its old treasury. The opposite occurred if such a region went out of production or the focus of economic activity shifted to a new zone. This process of updating and rationalizing the treasury districts guaranteed that there would not be overlapping jurisdictions and that each office reflected as closely as possible coherent local political and economic districts, as the sole representative of the royal treasury. This at least was the ideal, and it was generally carried through in practice. There were, of course, cases in which some delay occurred. In New Spain, for example, the very powerful central treasury of Mexico City continued to collect some regional taxes long after local regional offices were set up, to which those taxes should have been transferred. But in the end, even Mexico City had to concede its claims in the face of the rationalizing tendencies inherent in the organization of the colonial government.

Given the sophistication of their bureaucracy and organization and the extensive nature of their local control, the Spanish American treasuries have left an enormous historical record. The state archives of almost all the Spanish American republics are stocked with enormous volumes (*tomos*) of tax information, from daily accounts and monthly summaries to final annual account books (*libros mayores*). Yet the very quantity of this material has intimidated historians who might have been interested in examining these volumes in a systematic fashion. Only in the last twenty years has systematic research been undertaken on the numbers generated by the royal accountants (*contadores*) whom Spain maintained in America.

Despite recent increased research interest in the colonial fiscal records, the study of colonial taxation is not a new subject. The crown itself was interested in the study of its own taxing system. As early as the middle decades of the sixteenth century, there was a major effort to recreate the fiscal history of the preconquest states in order to better tax the Indian peasants whom the Spaniards had seized. In both Peru and Mexico, detailed studies were undertaken of the nature of the precolonial tax systems. Also for quite pragmatic reasons, the crown in the colonial period was always concerned with the changes in revenues occurring in the individual tax districts and often requested retrospective studies of colonial tax records. At the same time, in adapting colonial taxing districts to changing economic conditions, the government in Madrid was forever eliminating or creating treasury offices, or even changing district hierarchies. This in turn led to the need to review the evolution of the taxes and the monies they had generated in all the eliminated or reorganized districts. Many of these reports have survived and have often been cited by historians.

Finally the tax burdens of the Indian and Spanish creole populations created constant friction between the central state and its various subjects over the nature and quantity of taxes collected. Many of the colonial rebellions contained declarations listing long-standing grievances against all types of taxation. This conflict was a vital part of colonial politics, but one that few scholars have seriously attempted to integrate into a coherent overview of popular and official views on taxation, despite a very extensive literature on individual incidents and local protest movements.

While the colonial period was rife with discussion and debate, the nineteenth and early twentieth centuries were marked by a relative lack of interest in studying colonial fiscal history. It was only in the later twentieth century, as scholars began to fully elucidate the nature of the colonial governmental system in Spanish America, that interest once again concentrated on the colonial tax system. Numerous institutional studies of very high quality appeared, and some very preliminary statements of quantities were assayed.[4]

Since serious examination of extant treasury records began in recent decades, there has occurred a debate about the quality of the materials being used. Though historians had cited the summary statistics for generations, and they had formed the basis for Humboldt's influential essay on the political economy of late colonial Mexico,[5] a few recent scholars have felt compelled to deny their validity as tools for analyzing economic realities or trends.[6]

Given these criticisms, it should be stated at the beginning what these records consist of and what problems exist in their interpretation and use. First of all it must be recalled that these were not public records, designed for public consumption. They only became public records in the republican period, as the colonial royal treasury records have passed under the control of the national archives of each country. These tax books were the king's private source of information and his guarantee that his taxes were being collected and his accounts were being paid. As such these records were intended by the crown to give it the best picture available of its fiscal resources. Account books were solely designed to show that no theft or other misappropriation of funds had taken place and were subjected to repeated audits. Although interpreting accounts can present problems, standardized bookkeeping practices provide some guarantee that they are a privileged source of relatively accurate and consistent treasury information.

This is not to say that the documentation is without problems. The crown did not adopt double entry bookkeeping until the very end of the colonial period. Although all income accounts were carefully kept on an annual basis, this was not the case on the expenditure side. Also, though it rigorously divided its accounts into different types, or branches (*ramos*), of taxes, it did not always guarantee the autonomy of these accounts, with funds flowing into some ramos that belonged to others. This is especially evident in the question of such nonspecific ramos as the Real Hacienda en Común or Extraordinarios, which could at times contain quite large sums.[7]

There also existed the problem of tax farming, which occurred rather systematically in the collection of the tithes (*diezmos*) for much of the colonial period, and also in the case of several other taxes until the end of the seventeenth century. Since these were taxes auctioned off to private investors (usually individuals, but sometimes corporations such as local *consulados* or merchants associations) who collected them over a multiyear period, the quality of the annual recordings of income are affected. Two factors should be stressed, however, regarding this problem. The first is that in contrast to Castile, tax farming in the colonies was always secondary to direct collections by royal officials. As Sánchez-Bella has noted, while tax farming was "the preferred system in the administration of taxes" in Castile until well into the eighteenth century, in the Indies from the beginning, "the fundamental characteristic is the direct collection of the principal taxes by royal officials, with renting being reserved for the lesser taxes."[8] This is borne out by the fact that even at the height of tax farming in the seventeenth century, for example, only a third of the royal taxes in Peru were farmed to private individuals rather than being collected directly by royal officials.[9] The second factor is that even though such rented tax income was based on the auction (*remata*) figure agreed upon between crown and private tax farmer, rather than being an immediate reflection of output, over time, these multiyear contracts would reflect changes in the local tax base. As Carmagnani and others have shown with seventeenth and eighteenth century tithes, such tax-farmed revenues can still provide a reasonable estimate of long-term trends in agricultural production, though they are less sensitive to annual variations.[10]

More significantly, tax laws changed and exemptions to taxes varied over time and place, so that the amount of taxes collected is not always immediately correlated with changes in the local economy or in the tax base. There were even variations in the capacity of the state to collect taxes efficiently. In 1633 the Olivares Ministry in Madrid forced the Council of the Indies, against its wishes, to begin the sale of royal treasury offices, a category of government position that had hitherto been exempt from such sales.[11] Though most of these offices were purchased by Spaniards and were not as sensitive to local elites as most commentators have suggested, this practice did introduce a group of totally inexperienced officials into what had been the most selective of royal bureaucracies.[12] The result was a late seventeenth century decline in the quality of both record keeping and possibly of collections, probably with a corresponding increase in corruption.[13] So negative was this experience that the crown determined to end the practice in the early eighteenth century.

While these various changes and problems do not cancel each other out, over the long term there is a tendency for the level of income in the various taxes to match changes in the level of economic output. Moreover the use of an average estimate of income and expenditure by decade, as is undertaken in the following pages, helps to smooth out some of the more specific local variations.[14]

It is also essential to recognize that not all taxes bear the same direct relationship to the economy being taxed. Some taxes, such as those on mining, were directly based on production and contained few exemptions. The crown rather carefully taxed silver production and had a good idea of actual production, through its monopoly control over mercury sold for refining silver. Although tax evasion in mining occurred, most scholars agree that it was minimal and that royal mining taxes closely measured actual output. Tribute taxes were also linked to the economy: they tended to follow demographic changes among the rural Indian peasant population being taxed. But *alcabala* and *almorifazgo* taxes on local trade and international commerce were less tightly related to volume of output and sales, because of exemptions, changing rates, and/or fixed evaluation of goods that sometimes lagged far behind changes in prices. Monopoly consumption taxes were even less tied to basic movements in the economy because of various exemptions, the often inelastic demand for these goods with respect to income, or even noneconomic considerations. Though even in this category, mercury sales (here included with monopoly taxes and incomes) was both a significant part of these incomes and directly related to mine output. Finally there are a host of taxes (those for example based on sale of papal bulls, or on government salaries) that are only remotely related to changes in the economy.

Properly accounted for, however, none of these problems prevents one from using the tax income figures to analyze long-term trends in the economies being taxed. All the evidence that has been accumulated to date suggests that with proper consideration for many of the problems related to these accounts, they can be used to characterize general trends in government revenues by region as well as broad-range changes in the taxed economy, if not exact totals for any given year. The evidence, for example, from zones that experienced long-term depression shows that the tendency was for all taxes (even if they sometimes lagged by a decade) to follow the basic movements of production in the base economy. Equally, all local royal expenditures correlate highly with movements in local tax incomes, suggesting a coherence of government response to changes in tax collection levels.

There was, of course, one major area of the local economy that was exempt from taxes and therefore is not recorded in the tax receipts. This was the large subsistence and exchange economy of the Indian peasant population. This parallel economy, along with most Indian-produced goods that entered the market economy, remained exempt from direct royal taxation during most of the colonial period. Nevertheless these local exchange economies are reflected in the rise and fall of the tribute head taxes paid by Indian heads of families. Moreover some of the commercially produced goods of these Indian communities, such as coca leaves, were taxed and thus even provide some direct indices of changing fortunes among Indian producers and consumers.

Finally there was, as is to be expected in any economy subject to relatively heavy taxation and mercantilistic trade and production restrictions, a portion of the economy that escaped taxation because it was illegal. Everything from exports of unminted silver and gold to contraband imports of English manufactured goods and French luxury items was part of the colonial system. But the size of this illegal system is impossible to measure, and historians have often exaggerated its importance and denigrated official statistics, without providing any justification for doing so.[15] Moreover, as Sempat Assadouran has argued, most of the northern European contraband trade with colonial Latin America represented the luxury end of the market and had little impact on the overall productive capacity of the local economy.[16] In addition some of these illegal imports eventually did get taxed as they moved into the interior markets, in the form of alcabala taxes, even if they escaped the almorifazgo charges.[17] In short the inability to capture the taxes lost to contraband trade does not mean that the data we have at our disposal cannot tell us about the movement of the colonial economy.

The fact that most taxes were uniform across all units and that all tax income data was usually registered in the same annual units is crucial in establishing a common time frame and essentially uniform tax base across the entire American empire of Spain. There exist no other economic data for colonial Spanish America that are of this range, depth, quality, or utility. Although estimating the growth and change of the local economies through the use of royal taxes has evident problems and limitations, it still remains true that these official statistics are the very best sources we have for analyzing long-term trends in everything from government revenues and expenditures to the growth and decline of regional economies. These accounts can and will be critiqued by other scholars through more fine tuning of these gross numbers and more detailed analyses of local accounts. Nevertheless once the proper safeguards are in place and the limitations of the results are recognized, using these tax income numbers affords an enormous potential for defining the economic evolution of Spanish America and for understanding the colonial state created there by Spain.

The crown also modernized its expenditures, especially in contrast to metropolitan practices. Accounts payable were carefully controlled items. The local treasury was supposed to pay for local expenses out of clearly defined incomes. Income from other ramos was not to be spent locally, but was to be shipped on, first to the capital cities and sometimes even on to Spain itself. Any special payments which the crown wished to make out of treasury accounts were taken from its surplus revenues. As much as possible, the crown attempted to keep these funds free and did not mortgage such accounts to outside lenders. Nor did it issue script payments to its debtors, collectable on local treasury offices (the so-called *data formal*, or *entrada por salida*), a major activity within Spain itself that made accounting an extremely complex task.

In its definition of taxes, the crown carefully distinguished between monies that were to be spent locally and those that were to be shipped to Spain. It also tried to guarantee that it would have autonomy of choice in these matters. This especially distinguished its American treasuries from its Spanish ones. In the metropolis historic *fueros* and customs often meant that the crown had very limited access to the funds it collected, and most of these funds were spent locally. In the American case this was not so. The crown reserved considerable funds for its metropolitan expenses and allowed itself much more discretion in handing local expenditures.

But the crown did not think of expenditures on an annual basis, thus making it very difficult to calculate net income per annum. It was also the custom to accumulate monies in individual ramos over many years and then to expend them all in one year, even though income in that year might well be minimal. Given this accumulation of funds in local accounts, the crown often permitted its officials to borrow from these accumulated funds and apply them to other ramos where the income was too low for the expenditures required. Moreover the crown would require the repayment of these borrowed funds, often years after the fact. Thus low-income ramos would suddenly have their income artificially increased with funds not based on the products taxed for that year, when such borrowed treasury funds were distributed. Fortunately any annual funds not shipped to Spain or expended locally were listed in a separate ramo known as *Existencia del año anterior*, which in effect was carry-over income; the sudden extra incomes appeared in this ramo. These nonexpended funds were held in this account in the new fiscal year and were usually not added to the income accounts for the new year, thus guaranteeing that in the overwhelming majority of cases, these income figures reflect only annual income.

Given the nonannual nature of the expenditure side of the ledger, it is very difficult to estimate annual net rates of income for the crown in individual treasuries and to closely relate annual expenditures with annual changes in local, regional, and imperial economic trends. This does not mean that such expenditures cannot be related at all to income trends. With some accounting for lag, such expenditures in fact do follow changes in royal income over time. Finally the expenditure materials give the historian excellent insight into government policy decisions and where the crown was spending its funds and to what purpose.

There is, however, an especially complex problem with both income and expenditures in the Viceroyalty of New Spain, beginning in 1780 and becoming a major factor after 1790. This was the rise to extraordinary importance of new voluntary and forced loans and donations, which were collected in this wealthiest of colonies to help pay for imperial war expenditures in the late eighteenth and early nineteenth centuries.[18] At the same time, the crown expended some of its colonial and metropolitan funds in new types of debt instruments, above all the so-called *vales reales*.[19] These "were interest-bearing bonds that were declared to be legal tender for [some] private and [most] public debt," and were first emitted in Spain under Charles III in the 1770s.[20] The repayment of these bonds would eventually lead to some profound changes in Europe and America, as the crown took over the incomes from pious foundations and the church to pay for these state debts.[21] Along with an ever increasing issuance of such bonds, the government made emergency expenditures for the exigencies of war and other special events, assigned large amounts of colonial revenues for special war loans, and in general greatly increased the complexity of expenditures, which seems to have led to some serious problems of proper assignment of funds in the principal Mexican treasuries by the early nineteenth century.[22]

In examining these royal accounts, I have decided to concentrate on tax incomes and expenditures of the royal government in the three principal colonies that were consistently producers of surplus revenue for the crown and were considered the most economically important of its American colonies throughout the colonial period. These were the viceroyalties of Peru and Mexico (until well into the eighteenth century the only two such viceroyalties in the Americas) and the audiencia district of Charcas (also known as Upper Peru, later Bolivia). Only these colonies sent funds to Spain, were its premier mining districts, and were the major source of subsidy funds for almost all the other colonies in America, the majority of which produced less revenue than expenditures. Funds from these three treasuries went to pay for most of the governmental expenses in other New World colonies of Spain, from Buenos Aires to California and the Caribbean islands.

How the income and expenditures were estimated is discussed in detail in appendix 1, and the numbers themselves are presented in the standard colonial currency of account, which was *pesos a 8*, or a peso valued at eight *reales*.[23] I have not deflated these numbers to account for changes in prices, which would be a standard exercise in this type of study. The problem is that the requisite price indices have not been reconstructed for the colonial period, despite a number of partial attempts at examining local market prices or those for a particular product over time.[24] I have, in fact, gathered together all the major price indices collected for Mexico, Peru, and Spain in the eighteenth century, but have found that they do not correlate with each other in any significant way (see appendix 2). Nor is there any reason to choose one over the other, since these series are limited as to geographic zone and/or the number of products analyzed and often are not even coherently related within the same series. Moreover the biases created by inflation would not change the discussion of the relative importance among types of taxes, though it would affect trends. The most recent attempt to create a price series is that undertaken by Garner on the basis of the maize price series from a limited set of regions in Mexico. He finds that inflation ran at around half a percent per annum in the eighteenth century.[25] Using this rate, for example, would not change the direction of the trends discussed for Mexico, though it would change the volume. In any case, not revising the tax data by correcting for inflation or deflation at this time is not a severe problem, since once such a complete price series exists, the treasury numbers (here given in current rates) can be properly adjusted.

Because taxes often lagged in reflecting local economic changes, and also because of the rather abrupt shifts in growth that occurred in the various regions, I have decided to cover almost a century and a half of royal receipts to take fully into account the changes I wish to analyze. The selection of 1680 as a starting point reflects special problems related to the Peruvian treasuries. The data gaps are especially problematic for Peru in the seventeenth century. Major treasuries such as Arequipa, Cailloma, Cuzco, and Huancavelica are missing accounts for most of the period up to 1680. This means that starting earlier than 1680 would have biased the results against Peru in all comparative analyses. The choice of 1809 as an end point is due to the deteriorating quality of local records after that date. Because of the political upheavals that began in the Americas in 1810, the consistency and quality of treasury records for many regions no longer reached their pre-1810 levels.

While my primary interest is the eighteenth century because of the profound changes that occurred in this last colonial century, I am also interested in the differing evolutions of the two major centers in the Andes and Mesoamerica. Both Mexico and the two Perus were approximately the same size in terms of fiscal income and expenditure by the end of the seventeenth century, yet both would have different trajectories from this common base over the next several decades. The late seventeenth century changes also embody some of the Mexican and Andean repercussions of the generalized western European economic turning point that has become known as "the seventeenth century crisis." As for the eighteenth century records, they reflect very well the profound economic changes experienced by the American colonies in the age of the Bourbon Reforms, changes that were the crucial background of the emergence of these regions as republican governments.

It is thus my aim to cover as many of the basic trends as can be ascertained from these fiscal records in the two central regions for one of the most important periods of change in Latin American history.

2

Major Trends in Tax Revenues in Eighteenth-Century Spanish America

Which of these three crucial colonies were the most important for total royal treasury income in this 130-year period, and how did they evolve over time? What were the major components of that income in each zone, and did they change in similar or different ways? Finally what happened to both surplus incomes generated by the crown and the relationship of its expenditures to its income over time and from place to place? These are the major themes of this chapter.

The Three Zones and Changing Contributions to Income

There is little question that this period was of crucial importance in defining a major shift in the relative contribution of each of these zones to the royal exchequer. Of the 9.8 million pesos generated by the three zones in an average year in the 1680s, two-thirds still came from the Andean colonies of Peru and Charcas, reflecting their historic role as the leading centers of royal revenue in the sixteenth and seventeenth centuries. The former produced 3.1 million pesos per annum and the latter 3 million pesos. The entire Viceroyalty of New Spain at that time generated only 3.7 million pesos.

This Andean dominance appeared not only in terms of total gross revenues collected, but also in the amount of "surplus" revenues (monies left over from tax revenues after all local expenses were deducted) the crown was able to extract from these two Andean centers. Between half and two-thirds of total government silver exported to Spain or its Philippine colony came from the Peruvian viceroyalty until the decade of the 1660s (see table 2.1).

By the end of the seventeenth century, this Andean dominance was already being challenged by the rapidly growing Viceroyalty of New Spain. As of the first decade of the eighteenth century, total gross revenues in Andean zones had declined to an annual 3.5 million pesos, while New Spain had increased its estimated total annual income to 5.5 million per annum; this amount did not stop growing until the end of the century.

The share of total gross revenues coming from New Spain climbed to 56 per-

	REMITTED TO SPAIN from		REMITTED TO PHILIPPINES from	TOTAL REMISSIONS to all	PERCENTAGE OF TOTAL FROM	
Decade	Peru	Mexico	Mexico	REGIONS	PERU	MEXICO
1591-99	19,957,476	9,333,073	466,016	29,756,565	67%	33%
1601-09	17,249,406	10,016,003	1,174,782	28,440,191	61%	39%
1611-19	11,025,487	6,072,134	2,541,652	19,639,273	56%	44%
1621-29	11,037,808	5,782,816	3,620,573	20,441,197	54%	46%
1631-39	16,577,813	7,201,026	3,672,874	27,451,713	60%	40%
1641-49	14,847,713	2,981,421	2,206,810	20,035,944	74%	26%
1651-59	10,812,749	4,333,383	1,508,388	16,654,520	65%	35%
1661-69	2,973,745	3,991,220	1,379,509	8,344,474	36%	64%
1671-79	2,089,103	9,967,125	1,628,439	13,684,667	15%	85%
1681-89	307,387	4,770,990	1,952,190	7,030,567	4%	96%
1691-99	432,021	2,741,057	1,661,385	4,834,463	9%	91%
1701-09	1,658,007	5,233,621	1,248,873	8,140,501	20%	80%
1711-19	77,411	7,811,117	1,010,868	8,899,396	1%	99%
1721-29	1,034,400	5,586,811	1,339,403	7,960,614	13%	87%
1731-39	1,427,272	8,509,817	1,510,826	11,447,915	12%	88%
1741-49	545,000	5,325,510	1,761,649	7,632,159	7%	93%
TOTAL	112,052,798	99,657,124	28,684,237	240,394,159	47%	53%

Table 2.1   Estimate of Government Silver Shipped to Spain and Philippines from Peru and Mexico, 1591–1750. (Source: John J. TePaske, "New World Silver, Castile and the Far East (1590–1750)," in John F. Richards, ed., *Precious Metals in the Later Medieval and Early Modern Worlds* (Durham, N.C., 1983), tables 1 & 2a.)

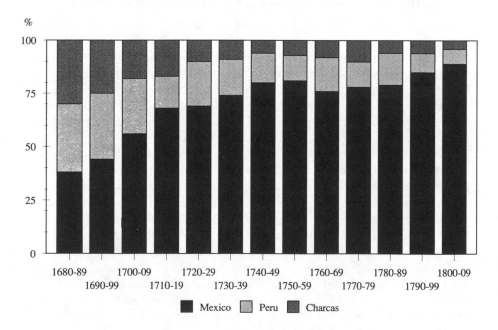

Graph 2.1   Ratio of Total Income from the Viceroyalties of Peru, New Spain, and the Audiencia of Charcas, 1680–1809. (Source: Tables 3.2, 4.1 & 5.1)

cent (see graph 2.1), although total revenues from the three zones tended to stagnate at 8 million pesos per annum until 1720, because of the severe declines in the Andean treasuries. But the modest recovery of the Peruvian viceroyalty and the continued growth of Mexico sent the total revenues upward again to reach an annual total of 22.5 million pesos by the 1770s; by then New Spain accounted for 78 percent of these revenues.

This fundamental shift in the relative importance of the three zones was due to profound changes in the regional economies and their differential response to international crises and economic change. It also reflected major new developments in their crucial local export industries.

From its conquest in the 1530s until the last half of the seventeenth century, the Viceroyalty of Peru and its associated Audiencia of Charcas had been the dominant economic force of the Spanish American economy. The dynamic growth of tax income from the Andean treasuries was based on the extraordinary silver production of the mines of Potosí, which were found in Charcas (Upper Peru). These high Andean mines were the single most important source of silver in the Western World in the sixteenth century, accounting for 57 percent of world output, a figure that grew to 61 percent in the following century, despite declining output. By that time it was also producing 60 percent of total world gold output, unqualifiedly surpassing any other source of mineral production in America.[1]

The output of the mines of Potosí peaked in the 1590s (at a volume of output not achieved again until the late nineteenth century), and after 1620 experienced a secular decline that did not end until the 1750s (see graph 2.2). Though smaller Andean mines initially compensated for the reductions at Potosí, the long-term trend was for Andean silver bullion production to decline. Total silver output in the Peruvian viceroyalty and in Charcas peaked in the decade of the 1630s. Production thereafter declined in a slow but steady manner until the trough of the 1720s. It was only in the 1790s that Andean production finally surpassed that of the 1630s. At the same time, Mexican bullion production, which had increased slowly in the first half of the seventeenth century, took off in the decade of the 1670s. In that same decade its output finally passed Andean production for the first time, beginning a long-term secular growth that would end with Mexico producing over three times as much silver as the Andean mines by the end of the eighteenth century.

Total royal revenues followed the path of silver production. The crown saw its gross tax revenues from the two Andean regions seriously decline in the middle decades of the seventeenth century. This decline in total revenues led to a decline in "surplus" funds generated from these treasuries. But here there was a surprising development. Although the Andean zone was still producing greater "surplus" funds than the Mexican viceroyalty, the monies they shipped to the metropolis declined faster and more dramatically than the actual available "surpluses" did. Thus by the 1660s, long before Mexican revenues surpassed those of the two Andean colonies, Mexico had become Spain's dominant generator of surplus tax funds. What had happened was that the local

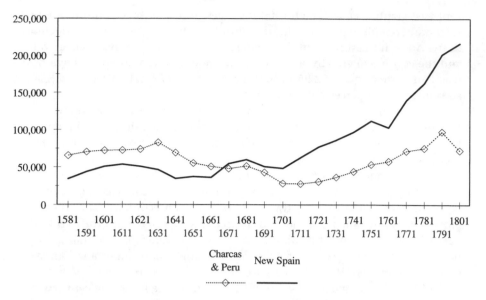

Graph 2.2 Value of Bullion Production in Charcas and Peru (combined), and New Spain, 1581–1810 (in millions of pesos). (Source: J. TePaske, "Bullion Production," loc cit)

American demands on Peruvian resources had escalated by the second half of the seventeenth century, as dependent zones such as Chile and the Río de la Plata became important regions of Spanish settlement. These treasuries were deficitory from the beginning and thus relied on Peruvian surpluses to support their settlement. Thus more and more Peruvian "surplus" funds were being expended in other American regions and far fewer funds were shipped to Spain.

Mexico thus become dominant in government silver exports to Europe by the 1660s, but it was still the lesser economic zone as measured by total royal tax monies generated. The long-term decline in bullion production in the Andes and the concomitant rise in Mexican production, however, guaranteed that Andean dominance in total tax revenues would not continue. In fact the first decade of the eighteenth century marks the definitive shift of dominance in total silver production and royal revenue from Peru and Charcas to the Viceroyalty of New Spain, as the later finally produced over half the total income generated by the taxes in these three colonies (see graph 2.1).

To analyze the relative growth of royal incomes from Mexico and the Andean centers, it is useful to break down that growth into its component parts. For this reason, I have selected for analysis the largest tax categories and those most closely related to local patterns of production and consumption. These groups consist of taxes on mine production, taxes on local and international trade (from which only Indian consumed goods were exempt), receipts from the sale of government monopoly products, and finally the head tax on Indian landowners and workers. These taxes account for over 90 percent of the income received in Charcas and over half of the taxes in the two viceregal centers of Peru and Mexico.

Mining

The driving force behind the economies of both Mexico and the two Perus was the silver mines. These provided the bulk of exports to Europe and generated the means of payment to import European goods. In turn the mining centers promoted the development of powerful regional markets that could supply the basic necessities to their workers as well as the raw materials for carrying out the mining.[2] While accounting for a large share of the economy, mining absorbed only a minor share of the economically active population.

Although no detailed breakdown exists for the two Perus of the shares of the economy controlled by the various producers and markets, there is an estimate by Humboldt for Mexico at the end of the colonial period (see chap. 4). It can be assumed that the two zones were roughly similar in that agriculture was more important in terms of total value and of number of workers employed than the mining industry, and that both were well ahead of manufacturing, which tended to consist of small units concentrated in production for the popular end of the market, with little ability to export beyond regional markets. Moreover, in the Andes as in Mexico, it was the mining industry that accounted for over three-quarters of the value of exports and paid for the bulk of imports of European textiles, manufactured goods, and comestibles to America.

While mining played such a predominant role in international trade, it was less important as a source of income from royal taxation. Throughout most of the eighteenth century, mining income (excluding income generated from sales of mercury) made up only 20 percent to 27 percent of total royal revenues. Even moving these mercury sales from the monopoly category (which is how they are treated in this volume) and including them here increases the average to only about a third of total revenues until the 1780s, when even this combined total drops below 20 percent of the gross tax revenues generated for the three colonies. By the early decades of the eighteenth century, the combined taxes on commerce, on consumption of monopoly goods and on Indians had equaled the total revenues derived from mining, even with mercury sales included. By the last fifth of the eighteenth century, these other tax categories finally equaled or outdistanced mining in importance for the royal treasury. Though great fortunes were to be made in mining, the crown evidently was unwilling to tax this industry too heavily, as an examination of the Mexican industry will show.

Of the three colonies, Charcas was the most influenced by silver receipts, which until midcentury made up half or more of total tax income.[3] Next in relative importance was Mexico, where it represented between a fifth and a quarter of gross tax revenues; Peru was last at around 10 percent.[4] But in the course of the century, there were some interesting changes (see graph 2.3). Whereas

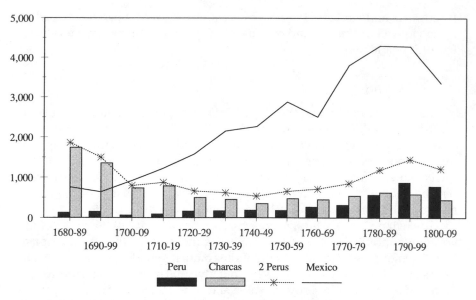

Graph 2.3   Comparative Growth of Mine Income in Charcas and Peru
(combined), and New Spain, 1680–1809 (in thousands of pesos). (Source:
Tables 3.3, 4.2 & 5.2)

Mexican treasury receipts maintained a relatively steady ratio until 1780 (indicating that such receipts kept pace with all tax incomes), those of Peru slightly
increased their share, and those of Charcas experienced a steady relative decline
from the 1730s onward. Moreover while Mexican receipts irreversibly passed
those of the two Andean regions in the first decade of the eighteenth century,
Andean receipts took until 1750 to begin growing again. Even so their peak in
the 1790s did not attain the total output that had been generated in the last two
decades of the seventeenth century. In addition the decline of Charcas and rise
of Peru shifted the relative importance of the two regions, with Peru now producing the dominant share of taxes. This relative and absolute growth of Peruvian mine taxes occurred despite the continued crises of the mercury mines of
Huancavelica, thanks to the impressive mining development at Vico y Pasco
and the increase in receipts collected from the interior mines by the Lima treasury.[5] That such royal revenues from mining taxes grew despite the halving of
the tax rate for the Andean colonies early in the eighteenth century is impressive evidence for the importance of the small but dynamic element of the Peruvian mining sector. But the fact that Peru and Charcas received tax relief much
later than the Viceroyalty of New Spain[6] goes a long way toward explaining
why the combined Andean treasuries produced more income from mine taxes
until the first decade of the eighteenth century, some four decades after Mexican bullion production had surpassed the Andean output.
    In contrast to the other two zones, mining tax revenues in the Audiencia of

Charcas were the single most important source of government income until the last quarter of the eighteenth century. Accounting for two-thirds of all revenues at the end of the seventeenth century, mine tax revenues continued to account for at least 40 percent of incomes until the 1760s, but then dropped significantly in importance as other sources of income began to grow more rapidly. As with Peru, one of the fastest growing accounts was tribute income, which was to take the lead from mining and all other taxes by the last two decades of the century.

Trade

The second major tax category that most influenced total revenues, taxes on trade and commerce, showed similar patterns in the three major regions. Trade, agricultural, and commercial taxes tended to grow in quite close harmony with total revenues, at least until 1790, for Mexico, Peru, and Charcas. Regional variation in these trade taxes, however, was quite pronounced. Because of its booming international commerce, Mexican trade revenues tended to grow at a faster pace than in the Andean colonies. In the decade of the 1780s, trade and commerce taxes in Mexico already had passed mining taxes in total value. Then in the 1790s, as mining tax revenues stagnated, trade and commercial tax income doubled, so that in this decade it generated 1.2 million pesos more for the crown than did mine income and was eight and a half times greater than it had been in the decade of the 1680s (see graph 2.4).

In the case of Peru, Lima (both as a regional center and port, as well as the capital city) tended to account for a more significant percentage of total trade and commerce receipts than the Mexico City Treasury. Lima alone generated on average over four-fifths of all viceregal trade tax receipts, with Cuzco a distant second (averaging just 6 percent) followed by Arequipa (with just 3 percent). Growth in trade revenues had been rather flat from the last quarter of the seventeenth century until the middle decade of the eighteenth century. Thereafter trade tax income expanded quite rapidly, almost doubling in the 1760s and maintaining high levels until the 1780s. It is probable that these levels were sustained or increased in the 1790s, and then probably suffered from decline because of the negative impact of the English wars of the late 1790s and beginning of the first decade of the 1800s. But it is impossible to study this trend. The failure to list both the alcabalas reales and the almorifazgo tax incomes for Lima for any year after 1789 invalidates the numbers not only for Lima but for the viceroyalty as a whole during the last two decades of this study, since their combined total averaged over 90 percent of all trade receipts for the entire viceroyalty. Even the second most important treasury in terms of trade, that of Cuzco, stopped recording either *aduana* or alcabalas income after 1799. But from the Cuzco numbers for the decade of the 1790s, it would appear that interior trade remained high until the end of the century.

As for Charcas, trade and commerce taxes varied little in their relative importance throughout the period (see graph 2.4). Averaging between 5 and 10

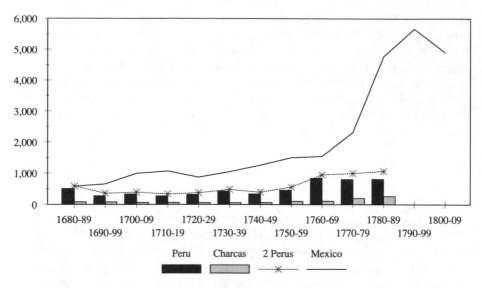

Graph 2.4   Comparative Growth of Trade Income in Charcas, Peru (combined), and New Spain, 1680–1809 (in thousands of pesos). (Source: Tables 3.4, 4.3 & 5.3.) Note: Trade data for Peru & Charcas are missing for the last two decades.

percent of total revenues, commercial and trade tax revenues tended to move in close association with total revenues and thus hardly changed in relative importance over the course of the century. Though Charcas probably suffered from the crisis in trade due to the international wars that began in the 1780s, here too the lack of relevant data from the Potosí materials makes it impossible to estimate how the regional trade crisis affected royal receipts in Charcas.

Monopoly

Monopoly tax revenues also showed important differences among the three colonies. The range of products taxed as monopolies or regarded as government products was amazing, ranging from standard European monopoly items such as stamped official paper and playing cards to cockfights, snow, and gunpowder.[7] But the most important income-generating monopolies were the sale of mercury to silver miners and of liquor and tobacco sales to the general public. Though varying from region to region, there is little doubt that mercury sales were the single largest generator of income in Charcas and Mexico, though less so in Peru. In all regions liquor sales were important, and the tobacco monopoly was of such importance that in the second half of the eighteenth century, it formed a separate monopoly with its own accounting system, independent of the royal treasury.[8]

The movement of monopoly consumption income in Mexico closely paralleled that of gross revenues (see graph 2.5). There was little growth until the

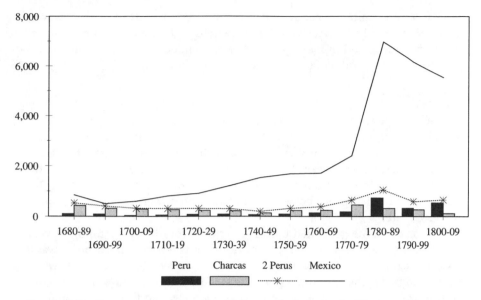

Graph 2.5 Comparative Growth of Monopoly Income in Charcas, Peru (combined), and New Spain, 1680–1809 (in thousands of pesos). (Source: Tables 3.5, 4.4 & 5.4)

1730s, when suddenly such taxes passed the million peso mark. Growth was impressive for the rest of the century and ended up at over 5 million pesos by its end, having passed mining taxes in importance by the 1780s and more or less keeping pace with trade incomes.[9]

Within each treasury district in New Spain, the mix of incomes was quite different. Overall traditional *estancos* (monopolies) accounted for about half of all monopoly incomes, mercury about 30 percent and liquor sales about 20 percent, though the mix would vary considerably between mining and nonmining districts. What is most interesting, however, is the steady and almost universal nature of monopoly incomes. In all but four of the twenty-three Mexican treasuries, monopoly consumption taxes provided important and steady royal incomes. Thus along with commercial and trade taxes, monopoly consumption taxes were the most widely distributed in the viceroyalty.

In Peru monopoly taxes grew at a pace consistent with total revenues, and on average accounted for 7 percent of total revenues. Only in the 1770s and 1780s did monopoly revenues outpace growth in total income, but they fell back into line at the end of the period. As was to be expected, mining centers were important in mercury sales, while Lima alone accounted for half of all incomes and participated in all types of monopoly revenues.

In the case of Charcas, monopoly incomes fell less rapidly than did total revenues and thus tended to increase their share of total revenues, rising by the 1720s to 25 percent of total incomes. But then their growth slowed considerably, as total revenues expanded. In contrast to conditions in Peru, however, mercury income in Charcas was the overwhelmingly predominant producer, and thus mining and monopoly tax revenues tended to move in tandem, especially in the second half of the eighteenth century.

Tribute

Since tribute taxes on Indian heads of households were relatively fixed, being based on initial assessments of the value of the land held in each free Indian landowning community, growth and decline in tribute income tended to reflect the natural growth of the Indian population. After 1730 landless Indians working on the estates of non-Indians, as well as those residing on the Indian communal lands but possessing no land rights, were also taxed, though at a lower rate.[10]

Thus tax income generated by this discriminatory head tax followed very general demographic trends within the dominant Indian population. It was a tax on a segment of the population that was in considerable flux. Thus while New Spain had by far the largest population of the three colonies, and its economy and tax rates grew to far outdistance those of Peru and Charcas combined, income from tribute taxes in the Andean region was the only major category to keep pace in terms of total receipts with that of New Spain throughout the colonial period (see graph 2.6). This situation was due to the progressive growth of the mestizo population in New Spain at the expense of the Indian peasant population and the surprising resiliency of the Indian masses in the Andean region to this type of status loss.

Unlike the other major taxes so far examined, the tribute tax was much more highly concentrated in all the regions, since it was exclusively linked to a clearly defined rural population living in free communities. By the end of the seventeenth century, for example, the northern regions of the Viceroyalty of New Spain were socially rather complex, with mestizos and landless and noncommunity Indians making up the majority of the population. They therefore paid little in the way of tribute taxes. It was only the central and southern zones, the old core area of the Aztec empire, where the majority of the settled Indian peasant communities were found, that provided the bulk of royal tribute monies.

The surprising sensitivity of Indian population figures to general economic trends is well revealed in the high correlation between tribute income and total revenues. Until the 1780s, Indian tribute monies in New Spain averaged between 5 and 8 percent of total income. However, the tribute tax proved immune to the crises in international trade and regional mine production and continued to grow until the Hidalgo rebellion of 1810.

Tribute taxes were also highly unevenly distributed in Peru. These taxes in the case of Lima accounted on average for only 18 percent of total revenues, whereas in such southern highland centers as Puno and Cuzco, they accounted for almost half of all income. In contrast to all other revenues, tribute income declined less in the initial decades after the 1680s, though experiencing an un-

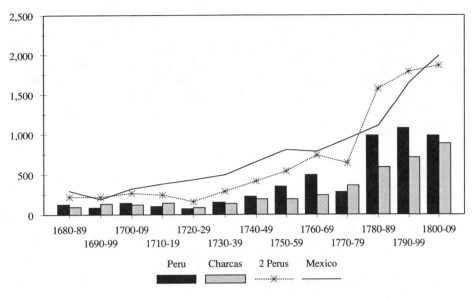

Graph 2.6   Comparative Growth of Tribute Income in Charcas, Peru (combined), and New Spain, 1680–1809 (in thousands of pesos). (Source: Tables 3.6, 4.5 & 5.5)

usual new decline in the 1720s. This drop of revenues was also experienced in neighboring Charcas, and clearly reflected a pan-Andean crisis in the Indian peasant communities, which was due to the shift of more and more Indians out of the taxed *originario* class of communal members to the nontaxed and nonlanded class of *forasteros*, or *agregados*. It was probably this decline that encouraged the royal government in Peru and Charcas to revise the tax base in 1734 and include these landless communal Indians, as well as Indians on the private estates of the Spaniards and mestizos, in the tax base.[11] This expansion of the tax base, even at the quite low rates charged, had an immediate effect on increasing total tribute income in the 1730s. Thereafter growth was steady in the two colonies, with Peru actually taking the lead from Charcas by the end of the period. This growth meant that tribute income in Peru as early as the 1750s had begun to surpass mining income (even when mercury sales were added to the mining taxes) and was the audiencia's largest single source of government income by the second half of the eighteenth century (see graph 2.6). So dramatic was this growth that tribute was almost ten times greater in the 1790s than in 1680s.

In this as in so many other areas, the Audiencia of Charcas followed a path similar to that of the Peruvian viceroyalty. In contrast to the other two regions, however, tribute revenues were more evenly distributed and were an important aspect of all local treasury incomes. This was due to the rather uniform spread of Indian peasant communities throughout the audiencia. Charcas, like Peru, also experienced an unusual and sharp drop in tribute revenues in the 1720s but thereafter experienced relatively steady growth throughout the period. This growth meant that tribute income by the 1790s had even surpassed mining income and, as in Peru, was the audiencia's largest single source of government income. In contrast to Peru and like New Spain, however, Charcas tribute income continued to grow in the first decade of the nineteenth century—the only major tax category to do so.

Special War Taxes and the post-1790 "Boom"

The changes in the post-1790 period, especially in total Mexican receipts, deserve more thorough explanation, because of their controversial and special nature. Most of the growth came from a previously insignificant tax category of loans (see chap. 4). In the late eighteenth century, these forced and voluntary loans rose to prominence in the overall picture of royal revenues in the Viceroyalty of New Spain. Forced and voluntary loans and other special emergency taxes were used to support a debt-ridden and increasingly bankrupt imperial treasury incapable of prosecuting a series of late eighteenth century international wars on the basis of normal tax revenues.[12] With the onset of almost continuous warfare, beginning in 1793, these special loans and exactions become the single most important source of revenues from Mexico, if not from the Andean treasuries (though no zone escaped these exactions). Clearly not all of these forced loans were fully collected, but there is little question that they fell heavily on the American populations.

For Mexico these new taxes caused a fundamental shift in the relative importance of the components of royal tax incomes. Production, trade, monopoly consumption, and tribute revenues, which had formed the basis of royal income prior to 1780, were replaced by loans and new miscellaneous special taxes after that date as the single largest source of income. What the costs of these exploitative taxes on private capital accumulation were is difficult to assess. But in Mexico and Peru they came at the same time as an international trade crisis caused by the European wars, which blocked off traditional incomes and foreign capital investments. Combined with the scarcity of mercury imports, this meant that mining halted in many Andean and Mexican zones even before the outbreak of fighting in the nineteenth century wars of independence.

In the case of Peru, some special subsidies and war taxes existed, but clearly the economy could not support the type of capital extraction that the crown developed in Mexico. In fact such taxes produced little revenue, and such miscellaneous incomes had little impact in increasing overall revenues. For this reason such basic taxes as those on tribute, monopolies, and mining income actually increased their relative rates of participation in the last three decades of the period. Royal officials seemed to recognize that Lima and its allied treasury offices were incapable of supplying the quantity of funds needed by Spain and were therefore uninterested in applying the tax pressures they put on Mexico and its treasury offices.

Nor was Charcas used by the crown as a source of new funds in the post-1780 period. There were the special war taxes and new *censos*, just as could be found in Peru, but these added only small amounts to the income ledger and hardly changed the relative weight of the other major income sources. Thus the experience of both Perus would seem to suggest that the crown concentrated all of its special energies on its richest colony and made no serious attempt to extract extra resources from its other colonial American possessions.

General Trends in Expenditures

A look at the long-term movements in expenditures shows two clearly defined patterns. The first and most obvious is that total expenditures moved closely with total income figures in terms of growth and decline over this 130-year period. In all regions this correlation was consistently very high and significant. Obviously the crown spent only what it had, and if that income disappeared, it did not "invent" new incomes or go wildly into deficit financing. Thus when income declined drastically, so too did expenditures (see graph 2.7).

Secondly it is evident that expenditures never fell below income levels in New Spain, though they certainly did so in both Andean zones. It would appear that the crown had more of an expectation of growth or was more willing to gamble with accumulated debt in New Spain than it was in the Perus. This could mean that it actually anticipated long-term growth in New Spain, as opposed to long-term decline in the Perus.

Examining the major components of expenditures in the three treasuries, we find some marked differences. In Mexico and Peru war-related expenditures for army and naval affairs were the single most important item of government concern (see graph 2.8). In Mexico such expenses varied considerably, but on the whole they averaged overall just under half of all expenditures, ranging from a low of 15 percent to a high of 55 percent (in the 1770s). In the case of Peru, they averaged over a third of all expenses, from a low of 22 percent in the 1760s to a high of 47 percent in the 1780s.

In contrast the essentially interior colony of Charcas needed few of its resources for local military expenditures. On average it spent only about a tenth of its revenues on local military affairs, except in the crucial period of the Tupac Amaru rebellions of the 1780s, which absorbed as much as 48 percent of total expenditures.

Neither Peru nor Mexico spent much on administration: Peru spent about 15 percent of its budgetary expenses on this category, while Mexico averaged only some 5 percent. But Charcas averaged some 40 percent for such expenses overall, and only began to reach the low Peruvian and Mexican levels in the last quarter of the century. Moreover the actual amount of spending on administration in the two Perus was considerably higher than in Mexico (see graph 2.9). This finding is difficult to explain. Mexico was the more populous and richer zone, with as wide an administrative coverage from the geographic

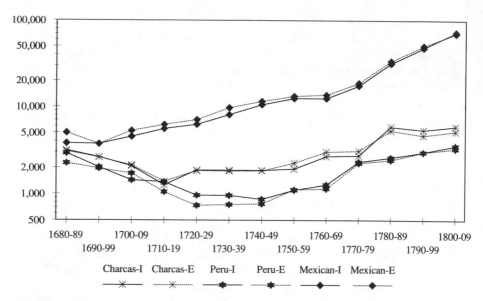

Graph 2.7 Comparative Growth of Expenditure (E) and Income (I) in Charcas, Peru, and New Spain, 1680–1809 (in thousands of pesos). (Source: Tables 3.2–3.9, 4.1–4.7, 5.1 & 5.9)

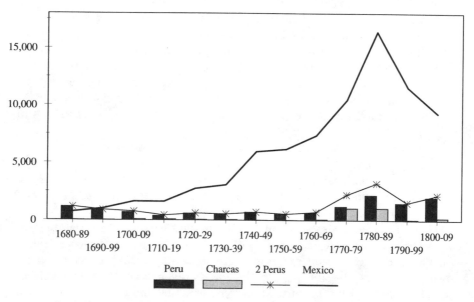

Graph 2.8 Comparative Growth of War Expenditure in Charcas, Peru (combined), and New Spain, 1680–1809 (in thousands of pesos). (Source: Tables 3.10, 4.8 & 5.11)

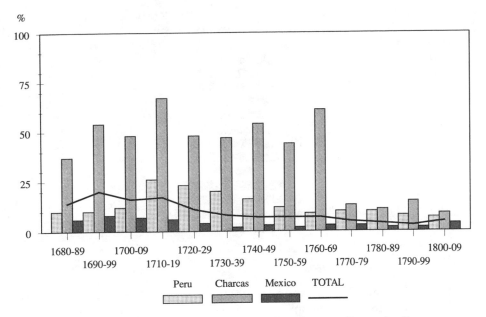

Graph 2.9   Ratio of Administrative Costs to Total Expenditures for Peru, Charcas, New Spain, and Combined Total, 1680–1809. (Source: Tables 3.9–3.11, 4.8–4.9 & 5.9–5.11)

point of view as the two Perus, yet it expended less on administration in absolute terms until the 1750s. Its administrative expenses only surpassed the combined Peruvian costs in the 1790s. Does this mean that Mexico was more efficient and better administered than the two Perus? This would seem to be the logical conclusion.

The surplus revenues category in all three regions well reflects the varying fortunes of the local economy (see graph 2.10). The ability of New Spain to send large sums of specie to Spain and the Philippines throughout the period contrasts sharply with the inability of Lima to produce excess revenues after 1750.[13] In contrast Charcas was able to supply both an important subsidy to Lima (not reflected in the figures in graph 2.10) until the 1710s. This subsidy had peaked at half a million pesos in the 1680s. Charcas also maintained a steady supply of excess funds for the deficitory operations in the Río de la Plata. These Buenos Aires subsidies, known as the *situado*, tended to reflect the highs and lows of Altoperuvian royal income. Thus they dropped to dramatically low levels in the middle decades of the century and then rose again as mining production and the general economy boomed, at the end of the colonial period. Reaching almost 1.7 million pesos in the 1790s, such excess funds shipped from Charcas formed the single most important source of government revenues for the Buenos Aires viceroyalty.[14]

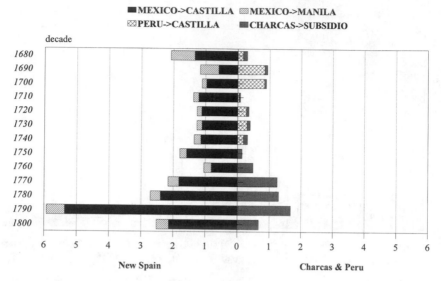

Graph 2.10   Remittances and Subsidies from New Spain, Charcas, and
Peru, 1680–1809 (in millions of pesos)

Conclusion

Excluding the special incomes in the period from 1780 to 1809, what can the
changing pattern evident in total revenue flows and the movement of revenues
in various categories of taxes tell us about general trends within the viceregal
economies of New Spain and the two Andean colonies? To begin with the numbers do reflect, however imprecisely, changes in the local economy as well as in
the fiscal health of each of the colonial governments. This was also the opinion of Humboldt and almost all later commentators. It is entirely possible that
new tax collection procedures may have suddenly generated new income in
the place of stagnant receipts, but this could only have occurred for a short period of time without causing severe economic crisis, if in turn the economy
was not expanding. In sharp contrast to the Spanish metropolitan tax structure at the time, American taxes tended to be collected directly by royal officials,
were immediately related to quite local economies, and were systematically collected and reported on an annual basis.[15] Also the fact that royal expenditures
were so highly correlated with income trends meant that the crown obviously
responded in a reasonably rational way to declines in revenues, by severely reducing expenditures rather than by any imaginary deficitory financing.

Accepting then that tax flows did reflect basic economic changes, the question is what these flows tell us about the history of the Spanish American economies in the period between 1680 and 1809. Some very broad patterns are
apparent. There was obviously a late seventeenth century period of growth, fol-

Decade	Peru	Charcas	Andean*	Mexico	Mexico-B**
1680-89	100	100	100	100	100
1690-99	84	69	77	98	80
1700-09	66	49	58	119	114
1710-19	40	47	43	146	142
1720-29	59	33	47	164	155
1730-39	59	33	46	212	198
1740-49	59	30	45	278	230
1750-59	61	38	50	329	278
1760-69	85	43	65	330	264
1770-79	87	80	83	463	382
1780-89	186	89	140	842	694
1790-99	171	102	138	1274	718
1800-09	188	122	156	1929	638

Table 2.2   Index of Growth of Total Income in Charcas, Peru, and Mexico (1680–89=100).

Notes: *Andean totals is the combined income of Peru & Charcas.

**The column "Mexico-B" comes from "Totals B" column of table 5.1 and excludes the loans and miscellaneous incomes.

lowed by an early eighteenth century period of intense depression.[16] Evidently the Mexican economy was only temporary slowed by this crisis, whereas for both Peru and Charcas, it was a crisis of such profound proportions that recovery was only moderate (see table 2.2). It would seem that the fundamental decline of Potosí mining output put severe strains on both Andean economies. The further blow of the withdrawal of Charcas funds and their transfer to Buenos Aires, along with an eventual political union in the 1770s, meant that the economy based on Lima and its associated zones never really recovered its seventeenth century position of leadership. The recovery of Upper Peruvian mining through government subsidies and the discovery of new silver deposits in Oruro and other zones guaranteed that by midcentury Charcas would once again begin to grow at a more than reasonable rate. Peru also experienced a late eighteenth century growth in mining output, but together these new developments still did not match the spectacular growth of the northern viceroyalty.

Mexico in contrast never looked back. It had a small boom between the 1720s and the 1750s, with another pause in the 1760s, though the economy was at a higher level of output than during the previous seventeenth century peak. This mid-eighteenth century pause was followed by its greatest period of sustained growth, which probably lasted from the late 1760s until the early 1790s. There was then another leveling of output, if not actual decline, in the late 1790s and early 1800s.

Tax revenue data also give us some reasonable ideas about Spanish royal fiscal policy toward the American colonies. It seems that the crown tried throughout most of the period not to burden the crucial mining sector with taxes that would cripple its ability to produce. The major productive zones of Mexico early had their taxes reduced, while the poorer mining zones of Charcas and Peru received this support much later. Thus mining taxes provided a considerably lower ratio of total revenues in Mexico then they did in Charcas. But once the crown decided to support Upper Peruvian growth, the relative importance of mine income declined.

The rapid growth of tribute income in all three colonies was impressive and clearly reflected the demographic growth of the Indian peasant population in America. But however important such revenues became in Mexico, they never surpassed the other major categories of funds. The relative weakness of the two Andean economies was evident in the fact that such regressive tax income by the end of the colonial period became their single most important source of government revenue.

The special development within Mexico of the new war-related taxes and exactions, which produced such enormous sums for the royal coffers in the post-1780 period, presents a special problem. The crown apparently concentrated its special loan efforts exclusively on Mexico because Mexico was the single source of royal "profits"—remittances of specie from the royal treasury. This special taxation creates two problems for the analyst. The first is the masking of actual economic conditions (the beginnings of a cycle of depression) through this sudden taxation of individual and institutional savings, which was in effect a tax on local wealth.

At the same time, the sums became so extraordinarily large in the 1790s and 1800s (reaching 48 million pesos per annum in the first and 73 million pesos in the second decade) that a severe accounting problem must have suddenly been emerging. Both royal generated summaries of total taxes in the 1790s and Humboldt's estimates for this period are in harmony and place New Spain's total average annual tax income at over 20 million pesos. The crown generated very large amounts from these special taxes, shipping out of the colony some 26 million pesos in an eighteen-month period between 1795 and 1796[17] and raising another 10 million just from the consolidation of church lands in New Spain in 1805–1808.[18] Nevertheless some part of the extra 20 to 50 million pesos supposedly collected may have been the result of improper accounting procedures.[19] Though only a very careful analysis of the post-1790 account books can resolve this issue, there is little doubt that the crown did raise very extraordinary sums from New Spain in these special loans, which far outpaced normal tax incomes. The question then remains as to how this special extraction of wealth affected the viceregal economy. Was this the beginning of a "Malthusian" crisis, as one more extreme position holds,[20] or was this an extraction that the local elite and local economy could survive, because of the extraordinary growth of the economy in the preceding century? The answer to this question would have major implications for the history of Mexico in the nineteenth century. The resolution of this question would also determine if the crown's special taxing policy was a desperate attempt by a metropolitan government willing to sacrifice its colonies to its European interests, or if it was instead a sophisticated policy of using the crisis of European war to effectively tax the hitherto unexploited wealth of the Mexican elite, without really destroying the colonial economy upon which it depended. Some support for the latter hypothesis is found in the fact that the crown did not attempt such monumental new tax extractions in either of the other two colonies. But most historians now seem to feel that the sacrificial and negative impact model is the correct one.[21] At this point the terms of the debate can only be suggested, not resolved, on the basis of these tax materials.

The expenditure patterns of the royal treasuries within America show relatively few surprises. As in Spain itself, the major category of expenses was that of war, with little left over for social overhead. The actual administration of the colonial government was rather a small part of the crown's expenditures, usually representing less than 10 percent of total expenditures. Thus in the decade of the 1750s, when war costs absorbed 41 percent of the combined royal expenditures of 16.6 million pesos in the three colonies, administrative costs for these zones was but 7 percent. By the 1780s actual administrative costs were approximately the same as they had been thirty years before, but as expenditures now totaled 41.6 million pesos, their relative importance declined to but 4 percent. The only surprising result here is the consistently lower administrative costs of Mexico compared to the other two zones until the very end of the colonial period.

War expenditures on the other hand had surpassed even the growth in total disbursements, and in the 1780s accounted for 47 percent of this larger sum. Though shipments of "excess" funds outside America had risen from 1.8 to 2.7 million pesos per annum in this period, this growth was less than total expenditure increases and thus actually declined in relative importance, from 11 percent to just 7 percent of the total for these three colonies. Moreover, even as far as the Mexican surpluses were concerned, over half, or some 7.9 million pesos a 8 were spent in America, versus 6 million pesos sent to Spain. Of the surplus spent in America, some 5 million pesos went for subsidies to help sustain the economies of the Caribbean islands, the frontier provinces along the Pacific and Atlantic coasts, and the famous northern mission frontier.[22]

Finally it is quite obvious that in America as well as in Spain, the Atlantic wars of the late eighteenth and early nineteenth century were fatal for the imperial system, whatever the long- or short-term impact may have been on the local colonial economies.[23] The ill-conceived and poorly financed participation of Spain in these wars, especially the two against England, clearly was the major factor ushering in a new crisis in the Spanish American colonial system in the early nineteenth century. It was this crisis that provided the background to the wars of independence. Moreover this was a crisis that now affected New Spain as profoundly as it did the two Andean colonies.

3

The Viceroyalty of Peru

Given its early importance, the Viceroyalty of Peru is the colonial center that initially attracted the most attention from royal treasury officials. The Spanish conquest of Peru in the 1530s brought with it an estimated 9 million Indians and one of the world's great mineral regions.[1] Already an advanced metallurgic society before the conquest, the Incas and their various subject and allied populations provided Castile with vast supplies of silver and a population knowledgeable in mining and smelting. Though European disease and social and economic disruption associated with the conquest would reduce the native population to only 1 million persons by the 1570s, this region was without question Spain's premier colony in the sixteenth and seventeenth centuries. Although New Spain contained more Indians and would ultimately produce more precious metals, initially it was not as wealthy as these lands opened up by Pizarro's armies. In these first two centuries, it was Peru that produced the largest quantities of precious metal and tax revenues for the crown to remit to the metropolis or use for further conquests and colonies in the Americas.

To effectively exploit these newly discovered resources for itself as well as its citizens, the Spanish crown rapidly organized the Andean region into a series of political and fiscal districts, based on the economic reality of the time, and appointed paid royal officials to administer this empire. After intense local civil wars among the first Spanish settlers over the spoils of the conquest, the crown moved in to establish its authority. The central administrative city of Lima was established in 1533, and by 1542 it was the seat of a viceroyalty, with a host of other provincial Spanish-dominated cities scattered along the coast and throughout the Andean highlands to control the production and commerce of these rich agricultural and mineral lands.

After the discovery of the mines at Potosí in the southern Peruvian highlands in 1546, this southern zone was separated from the viceroyalty in 1559 and became its own regional government, known as the Audiencia of Charcas, popularly Upper (or Alto) Peru.[2] Despite this administrative autonomy, Charcas was dependent upon the Peruvian viceroyalty until the 1770s, and its district treasury offices reported to the Principal Treasury of Lima. Most historians have considered Charcas as a vital part of the "Peruvian space," a term used by Sempat Assadourian to describe the enormous regional market associated with the dynamic centers of Potosí and Lima.[3] Thus I have considered Charcas as an integral part of what I am calling the Andean treasuries. Given its distinctive economy and its ultimate detachment from Lima, however, I have treated it separately for the purpose of analyzing its treasury districts (see chap. 4).

The growth of Potosí was matched by the development of the mercury mines in the central Peruvian highland district of Huancavelica, which were opened in the 1570s. This was a fortuitous development, since the decline of the purity of silver in the Potosí mines by the last quarter of the seventeenth century forced Spanish miners to abandon traditional Andean open hearth smelting procedures and to adopt the mercury amalgamation process to extract ever declining grades of silver from other minerals.[4] This guaranteed a booming local economy in the city and mines of Huancavelica, with a population of around five thousand persons, until these royal mines went into decline in the late eighteenth century.[5]

There was also a serious silver mining industry within Peru itself. Although in the sixteenth and seventeenth centuries it produced only a tenth of the silver mined in Upper Peru, local silver taxes were an important factor in viceregal revenues. Major mines in the districts of Castrovirreyna (which went out of production in the 1660s) and Cailloma (which started producing in the 1630s), along with numerous lesser mines near Cuzco and Lima, together generated about 11 million pesos worth of silver at the peak of seventeenth century Peruvian production, achieved in the 1630s. Cailloma, which extracted 6.8 million pesos in its first decade of activity, never again reached such heights, but it remained a source of silver until the end of the colonial period.

Though Peruvian silver production declined steadily from the 1640s until the decade of the 1710s, it picked up considerably thereafter, not only surpassing seventeenth century levels by the 1730s, but doubling by the 1770s and doubling again by the 1790s, when it reached a value of over 43 million pesos. Given that the late seventeenth century Peruvian decline was less dramatic than the late seventeenth and early eighteenth century crisis in Upper Peruvian mining, the recovering Peruvian mines reached half the output of Upper Peruvian silver centers by the 1730s and by the 1790s succeeded in equaling output from the Audiencia of Charcas. This post-1710s boom was based on production from the mines of Cerro de Pasco, which entered into production in the 1670s but did not became a major mining center until the second half of the eighteenth century, and the mines at Huaygloc (Trujillo district), which began in the 1770s and quickly followed Cerro de Pasco as Peru's second most important eighteenth century mining zone.[6]

Aside from its mercury production and the increasingly important silver mines, Peru developed a complex agricultural, grazing, and manufacturing economy, based on the labor of its dense Indian peasant populations, along with African slaves. The collection of regions making up the Peruvian economic zone stretched from Quito in the north to Santiago de Chile in the south and stretched inland into the eastern Amazon and northern Argentina, in what by the late sixteenth century had already become a rather self-sufficient and highly integrated market.

The core of this enormous region were the southern highlands, which had been the heartland of the traditional pre-Columbian Andean agriculture and grazing industries. This ancient center of the Incan empire, with its capital at Cuzco, was the most densely populated zone of the viceroyalty (with still over half a million persons by the 1570s) and the home of the dominant Quechuan population.[7] Cuzco in the sixteenth century, though clearly not the great metropolis it had been in the preconquest period, nevertheless equaled Lima in size and importance in the sixteenth century. It housed some three thousand to four thousand Spaniards and some thirteen thousand Indians by the end of the century.[8] Traditional grains, root crops, and such artisanal products as textiles, in addition to minerals, were the dominant exports of these central and southern highlands.

In many of the valleys of the Pacific coast, commercial European crops were planted (above all sugar and grapes), and these were produced by both Indian and imported African slave labor. These newer regional producers made the viceroyalty almost self-sufficient by 1600, in everything but high quality textiles and finished steel products. These valleys also produced large quantities of foodstuffs for transport by sea to the major Spanish towns. One of the most important of the valley economies was that of Lima itself, which was a major producer of wheat and maize and was thus able to sustain the viceroyalty's premier city. This new city of Lima by the 1590s had some fourteen thousand persons, over 90 percent of whom were either of European or African origin.[9] Just before the devastating earthquake of 1687, that population had risen to almost eighty thousand persons and the city had become an enormous market for the consumption of European and traditional Andean products.[10]

Though the Peruvian regional economy was a relatively limited and fragile market, it covered an enormous area and was anchored by two key poles of development: Lima, with its port and administration, and the mining zone of Potosí in Charcas, which could produce few of its own needs from the surrounding barren highlands. Both of these centers created enormous backward linkages, from the wheat fields of Chile to the *obrajes* (textile mills) of Quito.[11]

The viability of this economic region depended upon the continued exports of the mines, for which all Europe and most of Asia were the principal market. Any decline in production would have an immediate impact on the backward linkages to all the local economies, leading to increasing disarticulation and fragmentation of this system. This is in fact what happened beginning in the second half of the seventeenth century, when Charcas's mineral output began to go into severe decline because of the exhaustion of the richest deposits. This phenomenon led to a fall in population at Potosí and several of its associated centers and a subsequent retrenchment of regional production.

The late seventeenth century crisis in Potosí mine production had a profound impact on the Peruvian viceroyalty, inasmuch as it was accompanied by the decline of local Peruvian mining centers and a general failing of international trade as a result of the decline of metropolitan Spain at the end of the century. It was also matched by a profound downturn in royal treasury receipts in every category and in most regions.[12]

But some have argued that there was at the same time a maturation of the colonial economy as capital, diverted from trade and mining, went into local artisanal manufactures and new agricultural production to substitute for Spanish imports and help develop marginal zones such as Quito, Buenos Aires, and Chile. These developments, together with the expansion of the European population and its market; the increasing legal and illegal Pacific trade with other American colonies and even Asia; and finally, the retention of more treasury funds for expenditure in America despite declining overall collections, may have attenuated the crisis in many regions.[13]

Although there obviously was some reorganization of local regional economies and more local government spending, there is no question that there was a profound local recession in Peru and Charcas that can be clearly defined as a "seventeenth century crisis." Much of the growth described by "dependency" critiques had occurred already in the late sixteenth century, and as Sempat Assadourian and others have shown, the enormous "Peruvian space" severely contracted, and most regions experienced declining exports and imports, while many withdrew from interregional markets.[14]

However the "crisis" of the seventeenth century is measured and however deep it was in any given region, it is evident from the royal treasury records that the secular decline in royal revenues only came to an end in the first quarter of the eighteenth century. Differing in timing from region to region, growth of treasury income in most areas was evident by the last quarter of the eighteenth century. Beginning with moderate growth in the second and third quarters of the century, the final quarter was to witness a rather spectacular boom, based mostly on local developments of the regional economies of Peru and an allied expansion of international trade. It was in fact the late eighteenth century crisis of international trade that was probably the single most important factor that would bring this last colonial growth to a halt and usher in the late eighteenth and early nineteenth century period of crisis.

Given the constant shifts of population, changing mining fortunes, and regional variations in growth and decline during this period, the crown and its royal officials responded by constantly redrawing the fiscal map of the viceroyalty. Over the course of three centuries, in fact, the viceroyalty went from a high of sixteen treasuries to a low of seven at the end of the colonial period. In the seventeenth century it terminated two failing mining districts (Castrovirreyna and Chachapoyas), and another followed in the eighteenth century (San Juan de Matucana). In a major attempt at rationalization in the late eighteenth century, the northern treasury of Trujillo absorbed the two smaller districts of Sana and Piura y Paita; while Arequipa absorbed the previously booming but now declining mining caja of Cailloma.[15]

The general evolution of the Peruvian economy, at least as seen in the royal treasury accounts, during this period of 120 years thus can be seen as a long economic decline that began in the second half of the seventeenth century and lasted until the first decades of the new century. There would then follow an eighteenth century period of growth, driven by silver production from new mines and new commercial agricultural activity and trade, which would last until a late eighteenth century crisis brought on by Spain's European wars.

Tax Income of the Viceroyalty of Peru

How did royal income reflect the general changes experienced in the viceregal economy in this long century of change? To answer this question, I will examine the total income and expenditure of the viceroyalty and its constituent regions and treasury districts, as well as the major components of both royal income and expenditure.

In examining the patterns of income-producing revenues of the Spanish Crown in this and all other colonies, I will use the total estimated average revenues per decade, as well as taxes related to major sectors of the economy and population.[16]

To account for the very strong regional differentiations that defined the viceroyalty, I have grouped the treasuries (cajas) into three major regions (graph 3.1 and table 3.1). In this categorization I have adopted the regional divisions employed by Slicher van Bath when using these materials, which combine specific regions of the coast with their associated highland districts. The patterns of growth of total revenues did in fact vary from region to region within the viceroyalty (see graph 3.1). The north and south suffered less variation than the central region, but given their lesser weight within total revenues, they did not influence the trends of royal revenues.

The center accounted on average for four-fifths of total income. Next in importance was the southern coastal and highland area, which accounted for an average 14 percent of incomes, and the north, which took in some 5 percent of total income. Dominating the center was the Principal Treasury of Lima, which alone averaged 85 percent of the central region's income and an impressive average of 69 percent of the total viceregal income during this whole period.[17]

Given its dominant position and the lack of records for most of the other local treasuries, the Lima caja and its growth can be used as a proxy for the pattern of change that occurred in the Peruvian viceroyalty prior to the 1680s.[18] From this analysis (see table 3.1), it is clear that the late sixteenth century and the first half of the seventeenth century was a period of steady and rather spectacular growth for the Peruvian colony. Total revenues grew at a steady pace until the 1640s. Though a secular decline set in after the middle decade of the seventeenth century, there were periods of relative stability, such as the last quarter of the century. But from the 1690s onward, the trend was steeply downward, with an extraordinary crisis registered in the 1710s.

Thus the taxes collected in Lima were already in decline by the 1680s, when we are able to assess the total revenues for the entire viceroyalty. This secular de-

Decade	INCOME	INDEX
1580-89	2,611,612	100
1590-99	3,364,704	129
1600-09	3,566,557	137
1610-19	3,503,698	134
1620-29	3,304,022	127
1630-39	3,656,878	140
1640-49	3,966,377	152
1650-59	3,683,912	141
1660-69	2,798,604	107
1670-79	1,799,219	69
1680-89	1,842,181	71
1690-99	2,249,024	86
1700-09	1,793,360	69
1710-19	960,921	37
1720-29	1,320,343	51
1730-39	1,288,613	49
1740-49	1,333,382	51
1750-59	1,550,713	59
1760-69	2,144,378	82
1770-79	1,946,273	75
1780-89	4,112,584	157
1790-99	2,960,461	113
1800-09	3,260,675	125

Table 3.1   Estimated Average
Annual Total Income of Lima
Caja by Decade (1580–89=100).
(Source: John TePaske and
Herbert S. Klein, *Royal Treasuries
of the Spanish Empire in America*
(3 vols.; Durham: Duke University Press, 1982), Vol. I,
pp. 284ff.) Notes: Monies in
this and all subsequent tables
are given in pesos of 8 reales.

cline in total revenues continued until the 1710s. Thereafter modest growth in
viceregal tax revenues continued until the 1780s, when a major spurt in revenues in all three zones, but especially the center, saw total income reaching
double its previous peak in the 1780s. Lima, by the 1780s, even exceeded its
previous high income registered in the decade of the 1640s.

Until 1700 the center collected almost 90 percent of total revenues, but the
eighteenth century saw the steady growth of the south, dominated by the two
highland agricultural and grazing centers of Cuzco and Arequipa, and to a
lesser extent, of the farming zones of the north, whose dominant centers were
Trujillo and Piura y Paita (see table 3.2). For most of the century, changes at
the center had determined total revenue flows. But starting in the eighteenth

Thousands of pesos

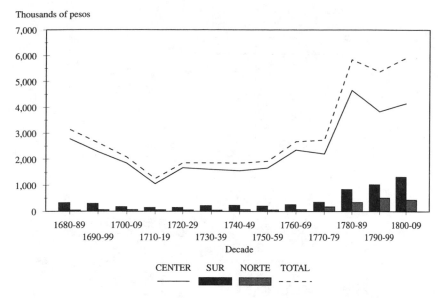

Graph 3.1   Total Income by Region in the Viceroyalty of Peru,
1680–1809 (in thousands of pesos)

century, the southern agricultural zones began to account for an ever greater percentage of total viceregal income revenues, growing from an average of 7.12 percent of total viceregal income per decade to a quarter of total income after 1780. Less spectacular (but in close correlation with the south) was the growth of the north, which after 1770 accounted for between 6 percent and 9 percent of total revenues.

There was also some change in relative importance of the Lima treasury within the central zone. The last major growth of the Huancavelica mines occurred in the period from 1720 to 1740, which reduced Lima's relative weight to between two-thirds and one-half of total revenues in the zone and to just half of viceregal income by the decade of the 1730s. But the definitive decline of Huancavelica once again gave extraordinary prominence to Lima in regional income flows. The rise of the new silver-mining centers in the treasury district of Vico y Pasco, however, especially after 1790, again reduced Lima to two-thirds of total regional incomes and just half of total viceregal royal incomes in the 1790s and the first decade of the nineteenth century.

Given the initially modest mining zones contained within its borders, it is not surprising that mining taxes represented only 1 percent of royal revenues in 1680. But mine taxes grew rather dramatically during the century. First there was the midcentury growth of production at the mercury-mining center of Huancavelica (see table 3.3), which created new sources of mine income, and this was followed by the growth of new silver mines at Cerro de Pasco. The

I - CENTRAL REGION   II - SOUTHERN REGION   III - NORTHERN REGION

Decade	Lima	Humanga	Vico-Pasco	Huancav.	Jauja	Matuncana	Puno	Cuzco	Arequipa	Cailloma	Carabaya	Trujillo	Piura-Paita	Sana	TOTAL
1680-89	2,759,345		15,892					169,810	22,994	133,113		37,830			3,138,984
1690-99	2,249,024		29,021					146,700	21,824	118,521	5,031	33,133	23,107		2,626,360
1700-09	1,793,360		50,023					107,334	22,301	41,516		35,523	21,512	4,078	2,075,647
1710-19	960,921		30,545	67,019				80,255	18,116	44,055		34,900	14,383	3,307	1,253,501
1720-29	1,320,343		45,266	286,156		15,679		37,960	22,788	71,531	9,058	25,269	17,928	4,499	1,856,477
1730-39	1,288,613		45,210	247,310	25,311			97,007	28,035	77,550	8,244	20,821	17,786		1,855,887
1740-49	1,333,382		37,367	160,641	29,524			119,971	30,280	59,041	13,702	41,743	17,100	4,966	1,847,717
1750-59	1,550,713		50,623	36,111	26,240			118,423	37,842	27,702	17,067	32,728	17,525	6,607	1,921,581
1760-69	2,144,378	48,585	87,344	39,706	29,899			120,008	65,168	29,164	41,035	29,076	29,204	8,902	2,672,469
1770-79	1,946,273	15,597	128,821	71,126	46,087			155,140	76,542	51,435	64,320	117,278	46,249	11,772	2,730,640
1780-89	4,112,584	158,942	207,334	126,750	52,616			338,297	367,146		137,730	344,605			5,846,004
1790-99	2,960,460	312,359	561,040					504,864	390,999		130,423	512,932			5,373,077
1800-09	3,260,675	329,807	556,168				388,060	507,472	426,513			438,666			5,907,361

Table 3.2   Estimated Annual Average Total Income by Caja and Region in the Vice-royalty of Peru, 1680–1809 (in pesos of 8 reales). (Source: John TePaske and Herbert S. Klein, *Royal Treasuries of the Spanish Empire in America* (3 vols.; Durham: Duke University Press, 1982), Vol. I.) Notes: In this and all subsequent tables "0" indicates no income was obtained, though the caja was open, and a blank indicates a lack of documentation on the caja.)

REGIONS

I - CENTRAL II - SOUTHERN III-NORTHERN

Decade	Lima	Humanga	Vico-Pasco	Huanca.	Jauja	Matucana	Puno	Cuzco	Arequipa	Cailloma	Carabaya	Truillo	TOTAL
1680-89	3,455		4,542					34,367	4,941	75,444		766	123,514
1690-99	16,158		12,980					16,979	0	96,332	4,331	225	147,005
1700-09	8,952		16,011					4,962	1,398	27,214	999	1,033	60,570
1710-19	29,984		13,290	16,622				1,938	636	24,308	999	1,237	89,015
1720-29	32,296		19,334	47,674		6,682		973	3,362	44,393	6,444	0	161,158
1730-39	42,801		19,357	43,879	5,989			2,522	6,061	42,757	4,283	0	167,649
1740-49	73,834		23,458	37,861	5,671			1,186	7,467	28,905	4,930	0	183,312
1750-59	80,754		34,790	17,803	6,430			0	8,563	26,318	3,780	0	178,438
1760-69	138,589	0	58,432	10,033	12,496			388	9,166	27,044	4,464	0	260,612
1770-79	99,943	0	79,162	6,515	11,390			0	17,253	33,544	0	62,036	309,843
1780-89	319,661	15,040	93,456	11,288	9,251			242	38,327			75,659	562,924
1790-99	447,455	20,332	251,475					0	35,847			112,110	867,219
1800-09	321,548	16,832	278,827				44,919	0	33,644			75,357	771,127

Table 3.3   Estimated Annual Average Mining Income by Decade for the Treasuries
of the Viceroyalty of Peru, 1680–1809. (Source: Same as table 3.2)

growth of the latter was impressive, and the receipts collected in other interior mines by the Lima treasury also were highly significant. Thus by the last decades of the century, taxes on mining were ranging from 10 percent to 16 percent of total royal receipts and were beginning to approximate the relative weight of such taxes in total Mexican income (see chap. 5).[19] The fact that royal revenues from taxes grew despite the halving of the tax rate in the eighteenth century is impressive evidence for the importance of the relatively small but dynamic Lower Peruvian mining sector.[20]

The other major tax categories that influenced total revenues followed similar patterns in all the regions in the viceroyalty. For most regions in Peru, trade, agricultural, and commercial taxes tended to grow in quite close harmony with total revenues, at least until 1790. Regional variation in these trade taxes, however, was quite pronounced. Lima, both as a regional center and port as well as the capital city, tended to account for a significant percentage of total trade and commerce receipts. It generated over 80 percent of all receipts during the entire period, with Cuzco a distant second at an average of just 5 percent, followed by Arequipa with just 3 percent during the entire period (table 3.4).

Nevertheless there were important shifts of such income over time. In the heart of the southern Andean agricultural and grazing zone of the Quechuan Indians, Cuzco was, of all the major treasuries, the one to have experienced the most steady growth for most of the eighteenth century. It lost little income from its late seventeenth century figures and only experienced a serious crisis in the 1720s, which was quickly overcome in the following decades. In contrast Lima went through several periods of sharp growth and decline. In the second half of the seventeenth century, Lima trade revenues reached unprecedented heights. There followed a collapse in the period from 1690 to 1719, however, which left revenues at a tenth of their level during the late seventeenth century boom. Lima revenues then stagnated until midcentury, though the more rapid growth of Arequipa, Cuzco, and Trujillo meant that total trade revenues recovered more quickly. Then until the end of the 1780s there was rather impressive growth. The lack of trade tax information for Lima after 1790 and for Cuzco after 1800 make it difficult to assess late colonial trends in this important tax category. The surviving data from Cuzco and the smaller treasuries would suggest a pause in growth if not an actual decline of these trade receipts, which had always provided the single largest source of government income in the viceroyalty (or a third of total revenues at its height in the 1760s).

Monopoly tax revenues also showed important regional differences, ranging from standard European monopoly items such as stamped official paper (*papel sellado*) and playing cards (*naipes*) to cockfights, and gunpowder. Among the largest of such monopolies (estancos) were the provisioning and sale of mercury for use in the amalgamation process whereby silver was liberated from mineral impurities. Equally important was the sale of tobacco products. Given the enormous funds generated by these consumer products, the crown in the 1750s created a separate administration (*renta*) in Peru outside the framework of

	I - CENTRAL REGION						II - SOUTHERN REGION				III - NORTHERN REGION			
Decade	Lima	Humanga	Vico-Pasco	Huancav.	Jauja	Matucana	Cuzco	Arequipa	Cailloma	Carabaya	Trujillo	Pirua	Sana	TOTAL
1680-89	453,754		1,800				25,365	8,084	400	0	11,209			500,612
1690-99	223,251		2,909				23,744	8,009	400	0	10,156	4,135		272,605
1700-09	273,755		3,907				25,268	10,658	193		7,846	4,184	1,004	326,816
1710-19	214,982		2,273	1,855			21,258	10,570	227		12,247	3,507	1,007	267,926
1720-29	259,175		3,252	3,094		1,794	16,490	10,586	200	210	8,611	6,908	2,379	312,699
1730-39	356,426		4,034	3,171	1,752		22,632	16,287	310	150	8,211	8,081		421,054
1740-49	264,972		2,850	3,805	2,222		23,777	15,488	385	0	11,246	5,618	1,382	331,745
1750-59	375,047		3,389	4,662	2,903		33,440	16,802	502	0	8,080	7,181	1,716	453,722
1760-69	719,356	22,684	4,204	10,277	4,458		34,242	23,771	720	3,418	7,147	6,016	2,520	838,813
1770-79	648,007	8,865	7,605	23,503	6,825		38,959	27,429	1,374	4,750	13,105	10,522	3,675	794,619
1780-89	596,796	19,287	11,250	21,216	15,962		54,810	35,756		6,722	36,215			798,014
1790-99*		4,386	7,733				55,989	11,749		4,069	12,080			
1800-09*		4,009	4,844					11,380			7,415			

Table 3.4   Estimated Annual Average Trade Income for Viceroyalty of Peru, 1680–1809. (Source: Same as table 3.2.) Notes: *From 1789 onward there are no recordings of "Alcabalas Reales" and "Almorifazgos" for Lima, and from 1799 onward there are no recordings either for "Aduana" or any type of "Alcabalas" for Cuzco. For these reasons no totals are given for the viceroyalty in the last two decades because the income for these two treasuries accounts for most of the income for the viceroyalty.

the royal exchequer, a decade before the creation of New Spain's renta. The autonomous administration of the Renta de Tabaco produced cigarettes and other tobacco products for monopoly sale to the colonial population. The crown generated an average gross of between 1 and 2 million pesos from the sale of tobacco products in the three regions of Peru, Chile, and Río de La Plata in the 1750s and early 1760s, a figure double the estimated 300,000 to 500,000 pesos generated from monopoly income in these three zones.[21] Thereafter tobacco monopoly profits were never included in the royal accounts and were sent separately to Spain by the administrator of the renta.[22]

Monopoly taxes grew at a pace surprisingly consistent with total revenues, of which they accounted for 7 percent on average. Only in the 1770s and 1780s did monopoly revenues outpace growth in total income, but they returned to their slower growth at the end of the period. As was to be expected, the mining centers were important in mercury sales, while Lima (which alone accounted for half of all incomes) had the largest nonmercury monopoly income, as would have been expected of the viceregal capital (table 3.5).

The final major category of tax income is the tribute tax on Peru's Indian population. This tax dated back to the beginnings of the Spanish conquest in America. Initially applied to Indian male heads of household of eighteen to fifty years of age who owned land, in the early eighteenth century it was extended to all landless Indians as well. Since the rates of taxation were relatively fixed, being based on initial assessments of the value of the land held in each free Indian community, growth and decline in tribute income tended to reflect the natural growth of the Indian population.

In the case of Peru, this pattern of population growth was quite marked by change over the course of the colonial period. The initial contact population, whatever its number (9 million is the current estimate) suffered a major crisis and experienced only negative growth rates for most of the first two centuries of European contact. Reconstruction of the Indian population of Peru from 1570 to 1620 suggests a long-term secular decline, from an estimated 1.3 million Indians in the former year to 589,000 in the latter.[23] This decline continued into the eighteenth century. A census of the viceroyalty in 1754 listed only 401,000 Indians.[24] Sometime in the late seventeenth and early eighteenth centuries, however, the native populations began to achieve a basic immunity to European diseases, as such diseases moved from an epidemic to an endemic level of impact on the local population. By 1774 the Indian population was up to 456,000, and by the census of 1792 the Indian population had climbed back to 609,000 in a total viceregal population of just over 1 million persons.[25]

Unlike the other major taxes so far examined, the tribute tax was much more highly concentrated in the specific regions in which rural Indian peasant communities predominated, since it was a tax exclusively confined to this group of persons. Lima in this case generated on average only 18 percent of such viceregal tribute revenues, whereas such southern highland centers as Puno and Cuzco accounted for almost half of all such income (see table 3.6). Also in contrast to all other revenues, tribute income declined less from the

ESTIMATED ANNUAL AVERAGE
MONOPOLY TAXES INCOME IN THE VICEROYALTY OF PERU, 1680-1809

Decade	I - CENTRAL REGION						II - SOUTHERN REGION					III - NORTHERN REGION			TOTAL
	Lima	Huamanga	Vico-Pasco	Huancav.	Jauja	Matucana	Puno	Cuzco	Arequipa	Cailloma	Carabaya	Trujillo	Piura-Paita	Saña	
1680-89	31,874		3,737					7,028	428	57,148	0	1,874			102,090
1690-99	55,665		1,358					4,880	1,142	21,429		592	1,071	0	86,138
1700-09	9,165		5,544					4,005	838	12,536		783	819	0	33,690
1710-19	7,248		4,458	15,552				1,698	918	17,432		593	585	0	48,484
1720-29	7,977		11,898	19,159		5,085		2,538	769	25,282	0	394	904	0	74,006
1730-39	8,620		11,339	19,366	7,148			2,460	696	32,556	0	1,521	400		84,106
1740-49	9,896		247	14,098	5,654			1,088	814	28,928	0	347	812	394	62,278
1750-59	74,433		132	1,729	4,457			1,160	1,429	62	0	322	876	230	84,830
1760-69	135,179	465	230	761	242			1,309	1,689	51	4	461	1,492	372	142,255
1770-79	119,014	570	15,201	770	9,266			2,154	1,566	14,839	684	20,831	1,323	233	186,451
1780-89	534,816	40,680	55,687	496	14,598			4,214	27,192		2,785	49,383			729,851
1790-99	158,859	13,397	87,739					5,417	22,964			34,161			322,537
1800-09	328,111	11,869	110,446				29,088	11,208	17,323			29,921			537,966

Table 3.5 Estimated Annual Average Monopoly Taxes Income in the Viceroyalty of Peru, 1680–1809. (Source: Same as table 3.2)

Decade	I-CENTRAL REGION						II-SOUTHERN REGION					III-NORTHERN REGION			TOTAL
	Lima	Humanga	Vico-Pasco	Huancav.	Jauja	Matucana	Puno	Cuzco	Arequipa	Cailloma	Carabaya	Trujillo	Piura-Paita	Saña	
1680-89	69,556		2,733					44,998	1,226	0		7,134			125,647
1690-99	21,629		7,055					40,912	2,778	0	1,572	6,264	4,740		84,949
1700-09	65,197		21,096					28,501	1,202	0		7,274	7,537	13,454	144,262
1710-19	44,708		8,301	2,304				30,344	613	0		6,854	8,218	0	101,341
1720-29	35,047		7,895	1,867		2,085		9,080	415	0	2,173	7,597	5,320	1,820	73,299
1730-39	63,305		7,500	3,839	8,959			47,242	2,222	0	3,863	8,610	6,228		151,768
1740-49	90,964		7,351	4,617	17,159			65,172	2,846	0	8,739	16,243	7,746	2,820	223,657
1750-59	231,292		7,044	4,412	12,908			55,908	1,840	0	10,788	16,320	5,142	4,556	350,210
1760-69	335,751	696	10,472	11,061	11,159			55,918	10,496	0	27,281	15,512	12,730	5,251	496,327
1770-79	35,661	65	14,401	24,402	12,970			76,241	14,136	2,198	43,641	23,324	24,543	7,313	278,895
1780-89	217,200	112,409	38,708	88,519	4,866			197,436	86,483		94,439	142,970			983,030
1790-99	263,703	123,125	61,233					281,197	82,777		119,236	144,926			1,076,197
1800-09	90,680	130,151	46,926				221,879	269,374	88,416			133,343			980,769

Table 3.6   Estimated Annual Average Tribute Tax Income in the Viceroyalty of Peru, 1680–1809. (Source: Same as table 3.2)

	I -CENTRAL REGION			II -SOUTHERN REGION					II - NORTHERN REGION	
Decade	Lima	Humanga	Vico-Pasco	Puno	Cuzco	Arequipa	Cailloma	Carabaya	Trujillo	TOTAL
1680-89	86,671		0		0	0	0		1,633	88,304
1690-99	56,234		692		1,811	2,022	0	469	444	61,673
1700-09	154,600		335		1,308	1,415	1,199		0	158,857
1710-19	36,654		0		2,468	512	0		0	39,634
1720-29	27,800		1,080		0	0	0	0	0	28,880
1730-39	92,330		512		400	200	0	0	200	93,642
1740-49	87,177		0		800	666	0	0	0	88,643
1750-59	611		0		521	400	0	0	0	1,532
1760-69	8,663		0		667	0	0	0	0	9,330
1770-79	332		0		0	0	0	0	0	332
1780-89	35,295	0	216		100	3,376		1,500	0	40,487
1790-99	86,504	3,219	0		7,196	12,810		2,930	9,178	121,837
1800-09	118,370	8,865	0	2,740	5,763	20,766			5,785	162,289

Table 3.7   Estimated Annual Average Loans, Etc., Incomes in the Viceroyalty of Peru, 1680–1809. (Source: Same as table 3.2.) Notes: Cajas with "0" income have been deleted from the table.

1680s peak, recovered more quickly. and then went on to increase at a steady pace. Much of the initial recovery had to do with the recovery of the Indian population, but it was even more dependent on the expansion of the tax to previously exempt Indians. Beginning in 1734, Indians living on the estates of Spaniards were required to pay a tribute tax, and all nonoriginal members associated with Indian communities (the so-called agregados or forasteros) were also now taxed.[26]

This may explain the doubling of income from tribute in the 1730s, but it does not quite explain the very dramatic rise in the following decades. Though the Indian population grew from its especially low levels of the first half of the eighteenth century, it did not grow at the same rate as these tribute tax receipts. This would suggest that either the seventeenth century census estimates (based on using a multiplier to arrive at total population from just the lists of tributary males) are too high, or that the tax in the late eighteenth century was being collected with an efficiency never before noted. Tribute income was almost three times greater in the 1790s than in 1680s, and from the 1750s to the 1790s, tribute income grew twice as fast as population. So dramatic was this growth that by the 1780s (even before the crisis in international trade reduced taxes on commerce to a secondary rank), tribute had become the single largest source of royal revenues, a position it maintained to the end of the colonial period.

Toward the end of the eighteenth century, the Spanish crown committed the empire to expensive international wars with the two leading European imperial powers, first with England (1779–83, during the American Revolution), then with Revolutionary France (1793–95), and then two long naval wars again with England (1796–1802, 1805–8). The result was a crisis in metropolitan state finances that resulted in new tax exactions from the American

	I - CENTRAL REGION						II - SOUTHERN REGION					III - NORTHERN REGION			
Decade	Lima	Humanga	Vico-Pasco	Huancav.	Jauja	Matuncana	Puno	Cuzco	Arequipa	Cailloma	Carabaya	Trujillo	Piura-Paita	Sana	TOTAL
1680-89	8,879		454					13,505	1,873	299	163	5,186			30,197
1690-99	14,269		2,698					4,848	865	245		0	6,069	738	29,156
1700-09	21,319		1,735					8,552	1,324	541		2,263	2,621		39,093
1710-19	23,601		523	616				4,147	682	1,615		1,199	1,429		33,813
1720-29	99,480		1,256	700		310		1,639	5,683	1,656	221		330	1,362	112,637
1730-39	19,978		2,940	1,064	726			10,626	1,002	631		1,924	3,098		41,989
1740-49	52,505		2,087	2,657	645			17,644	1,800	668	232	9,337	5,187		92,762
1750-59	104,807		2,538	1,518	169			15,105	1,785	295		6,245	5,266		137,728
1760-69	78,490	378	4,786	2,415	549			8,733	1,657	220	4,639	3,113	7,166		112,146
1770-79	21,269	548	4,844	5,992	6,453			8,417	1,984	150	8,680	14,148	8,043	268	80,796
1780-89	978,816	2,397	2,181	384	8,693			7,719	7,749		19,288	9,152			1,036,379
1790-99	57,560	295	2,046					17,004	2,250		959	1,026			81,140
1800-09	12,473	196	980				2,024	7,725	1,054			752			25,204

Table 3.8 Estimated Annual Average Total Miscellaneous Taxes by Caja and Region in the Viceroyalty of Peru, 1680–1809. (Source: Same as table 3.2)

colonies. While the war with France was fought with temporary loans, voluntary contributions, and special war taxes, all such sources had been exhausted by the late 1790s. The crown was forced to take new measures to tax personal and institutional savings, first in the metropolis and then in the colonies, including even an attempt to nationalize the properties of the American church.[27] Though these new loans, taxes, and sales of offices and honors increased royal incomes in the next two decades, such a policy could not go on indefinitely. The protest of the local elite and, probably even more importantly, the rapid depletion of resources in the relatively thin capital market of Peru, led the crown to abandon this new taxing resource in the last two decades of the period. In addition the beginnings of independence revolts in South America after 1808 turned Peru into a bastion of royal power that in turn would draw more local resources into local activity and provide even less capital for special taxes related to metropolitan income needs.

Even at the height of their importance, special subsidies and war taxes in Peru could not support the type of capital extraction that the crown developed in Mexico. In fact such loans and special taxes, except in the decade of the 1780s, produced little revenue and had only a modest impact in increasing overall receipts (tables 3.7 and 3.8). For this reason such basic taxes as those on tribute, monopolies, and mining income actually increased their relative rates of participation in total revenues in the last three decades of the period, especially as trade suffered disastrously as a result of the international wars. Why Peru and Upper Peru were spared these special royal taxing efforts is difficult to understand, except insofar as the crown may have consciously recognized the limitations of the resources from which it could extract such income. Though individuals were offered incentives to provide special loans and numerous sales occurred of such special "gifts" as *mayorazgos*, or entailed estates, the Andean region was only moderately affected by the imperial financial crisis in terms of extra capital extraction.

General Trends in Expenditures

A look at the long-term movements in Peruvian expenditures shows two clearly defined patterns. The first and most obvious is that total expenditures moved closely with total income figures in terms of growth and decline over this 130–year period. In all regions there was an obvious, very high correlation between the movement in income and resulting expenditures.[28] Thus when income declined drastically, so too did expenditures, in quite close correlation. This pattern is a very significant proof that the so-called "fiscality" argument has little factual basis in regard to royal treasury activities; the crown clearly spent only what it had. In fact, in most periods, spending was below estimated income (see graph 2.7), and in the few periods where it exceeded income, the discrepancy was quite modest.

The regional breakdown of expenditures closely parallels that of income, again with Lima originally accounting for 87 percent of expenditures (and dropping to half by the nineteenth century), and the treasuries of the central region again being the primary zone of expenditure and accounting for between 72 percent and 91 percent of all government expenses (table 3.9). As with the income figures, the role of Lima and the center declined with the rise of the southern cajas, which by the first decade of the nineteenth century accounted for 22 percent of expenditures, and those of the north, which now accounted for 7 percent of overall expenditures.

From an examination of the major components of expenditures, it is evident that in Peru war-related expenditures for army and naval affairs were the single most important item of government costs. Lima and its regional treasuries had relatively high military costs, because of the need to maintain a Pacific armada in the seventeenth and early eighteenth centuries to defend against pirates, because of having to put down several major armed rebellions and civil wars throughout the period, and finally because of the role it played as the major outpost of imperial government in the Southern Hemisphere. The cost of supplying and paying for troops, ships, forts, and armaments averaged over a third of all expenses, though in times of internal rebellions (such as that of Tupac Amaru in 1780) this category could account for almost half of all expenditures (table 3.10). As could be expected, the basic expenditures came from the central treasury of Lima, which averaged 92 percent of viceregal expenditures in this period. Some districts in fact spent no funds on war-related expenses, and others were only sporadically forced to expend their income in this way.

In contrast all treasuries were required to expend funds for local administration of the treasuries, salaries, and tax collections. Surprisingly, by contemporary standards, Peru spent modestly on administration, which accounted for only about 15 percent of its budgetary expenses (table 3.11). Though Lima spent considerable sums on administration, because of the large number of royal officials employed in the capital city, it spent slightly below the average treasury expenditure in the region, roughly 10 percent.

The variation of expenditures was quite dramatic from year to year, yet Lima always had relatively fixed costs because of its need to send surplus revenues to Europe and/or to subsidize all the Southern Hemisphere outposts of the Spanish empire, from the cities of Chile, to the interior forts of the Chaco, to the government in Buenos Aires.[29] Though Lima had been the leading American producer of excess revenues for the Spanish crown for the sixteenth and most of the seventeenth centuries (see table 5.1), its surplus funds were no longer sufficient to both satisfy local American needs in all the deficitory colonies and also to supply the mother country with government silver. These increasingly conflicting demands show up in the declining export of government silver to Spain at the same time as surpluses remained high.

Given the decline of total revenues by the end of the seventeenth century, it was inevitable that surplus revenues would follow suit. This meant not only the elimination of the Peruvian viceroyalty as a source of surplus funds for the metropolis, but also a decline in the crown's ability to maintain colonial outposts. This became even more severe after the 1710s, when the crown ordered Potosí to send its surplus funds directly to Buenos Aires, to maintain that colony's bureaucracy.

I - CENTRAL REGION   II - SOUTHERN REGION   III - NORTHERN REGION

Decade	Lima	Humanga	Vico-Pasco	Huancav.	Jauja	Matucana	Puno	Cuzco	Arequipa	Cailloma	Carabaya	Trujillo	Piura-Paita	Saña	TOTAL
1680-89	2,671,554		12,510					172,277	23,002	133,113	4,675	41,434			3,058,565
1690-99	2,240,024		31,237					143,781	22,691	118,521		26,872	23,528		2,606,655
1700-09	1,851,162		44,657					107,076	22,300	41,527		34,239	19,277	5,136	2,125,374
1710-19	1,048,567		31,038	95,880				81,896	18,232	44,065	9,342	31,013	19,104	1,840	1,380,977
1720-29	1,358,712		48,008	256,814		16,230		999	21,873	75,018	8,243	25,512	19,993	4,541	1,835,943
1730-39	1,286,331		47,328	219,371	25,360			82,343	28,064	77,573	13,783	17,177	18,983		1,816,313
1740-49	1,328,848		37,892	150,455	30,390			116,327	30,770	59,201	18,115	35,088	17,782	4,953	1,829,821
1750-59	1,738,405		52,909	136,539	26,453			113,946	42,985	27,841	44,880	40,747	14,231	6,606	2,245,542
1760-69	2,344,239	29,672	95,166	36,110	37,562			178,323	62,170	29,155	112,388	36,746	40,079	8,926	3,010,536
1770-79	2,118,583	2,446	137,972	47,000	60,162			215,014	111,220	61,434	78,860	194,328	50,579	11,806	3,089,404
1780-89	3,381,024	136,378	224,282	104,823	80,165			350,933	399,058		146,741	454,010			5,277,414
1790-99	2,439,660	270,806	544,242	162,292				432,099	361,531			443,258			4,653,888
1800-09	2,905,647	276,295	532,547				339,435	424,061	354,219			359,594			5,191,798

Table 3.9   Estimated Average Annual Total Expenditures by Decade, Viceroyalty
of Peru, 1680–1809. (Source: Same as table 3.2)

Decade	Lima	Humanga	Vico-Pasco	Jauja	Puno	Cuzco	Arequipa	Cailloma	Carabaya	Trujillo	Piura-Paita	Saña	TOTAL
1680-89	1,114,502		0			20,125	0	0	0	2,639	10,693	0	1,147,959
1690-99	866,050		0			0	0	0	0	764	14,443	0	881,257
1700-09	655,528		0			0	0	121	0	0	13,524	3,246	672,419
1710-19	344,979		0	0		0	1,903	121		0	11,154	0	358,157
1720-29	467,768		18,122	0		0	3,285	70,035	0	3,940	3,227	0	566,377
1730-39	434,489		14,399	0		0	3,560	47,333	0	0	2,827	999	503,607
1740-49	630,059		21,643	23,318		0	0	0	0	0	8,894	0	683,914
1750-59	480,132		32,000	19,756		0	180	0	0	0	0	0	532,068
1760-69	582,896		35,313	14,193		0	480	0	0	0	4,393	370	637,645
1770-79	1,117,970		37,639	14,170		0	0	0	0	0	0	0	1,169,779
1780-89	1,891,597	231	25,829	15,385		109,761	93,814		23,027	0			2,159,644
1790-99	1,317,387	0	18,483			89,423	23,468		704	16,735			1,466,200
1800-09	1,820,190	0	29,916		7,135	61,508	20,239			37,553			1,976,541

Table 3.10 Estimated Annual Average War Expenditures for the Viceroyalty of Peru, 1680–1809. (Source: Same as table 3.2)

I-CENTRAL REGION   II-SOUTHERN REGION   III-NORTHERN REGION

Decade	Lima	Humanga	Vico-Pasco	Huancav.	Jauja	Matucana	Puno	Cuzco	Arequipa	Cailloma	Carabaya	Trujillo	Piura-Paita	Saña	TOTAL
1680-89	180,108		4,623					87,233	5,692	8,332		25,733			311,721
1690-99	169,378		4,321					69,198	8,068	8,052		6,825	4,529		273,634
1700-09	155,448		6,171					64,371	9,139	4,545	3,263	8,022	2,196	2,838	252,730
1710-19	165,963		8,099	97,193				50,038	9,452	4,547		16,546	2,179	1,841	355,859
1720-29	212,139		13,002	156,024		2,582		0	6,606	11,761	4,533	14,174	1,680	1,831	424,332
1730-39	205,428		8,160	97,920	5,035			13,600	7,334	4,094	4,848	10,087	2,238		358,744
1740-49	181,976		2,821	33,852	13,888			0	9,929	6,145	3,470	29,638	1,884	2,003	285,606
1750-59	208,535		8,933	2,060	9,710			741	10,932	4,146	3,000	20,884	1,803	1,973	272,717
1760-69	196,034	0	3,970	1,726	8,228			12,383	8,304	3,042	3,098	19,876	3,019	1,857	261,537
1770-79	223,594	0	13,312	1,931	14,729			14,251	8,232	11,189	3,208	13,000	1,968	2,414	307,828
1780-89	326,988	9,181	15,459	158	22,376			55,024	52,349		3,228	65,264			550,027
1790-99	248,694	14,085	11,918					55,943	38,826		778	17,106			387,350
1800-09	224,318	11,604	12,243				20,602	56,493	25,531			15,361			366,152

Table 3.11 Estimated Annual Average Administrative Costs in the Viceroyalty of Peru, 1680–1809. (Source: Same as table 3.2)

Conclusion

What do these tax flows tell us about the history of the Peruvian viceregal economy in the period from 1680 to 1809? Some very broad patterns are apparent. Clearly Peru was already experiencing a crisis in royal income in the decade of the 1680s. This long-term secular decline did not end until the second decade of the eighteenth century. Peru clearly suffered an intense depression as a result of the so-called seventeenth century crisis. For Peru it was a disaster of such profound proportions that recovery was slow and took almost a half century to complete. It would seem that the fundamental decline of Potosí mining output put severe strains on the Peruvian economy as well. The further blow of the withdrawal of Upper Peruvian funds and their transfer to Buenos Aires (along with an eventual political union in the 1770s) meant that the economy based on Lima and its associated zones never recovered its seventeenth century position of even regional leadership.[30]

This relative decline showed itself as early as the middle decades of the seventeenth century, when Mexico would replace Peru as the chief supplier of surplus royal revenues to the metropolis. By the first decade of the eighteenth century, Peru, even with its associated revenues from Charcas, had been replaced by Mexico as America's largest producer of royal income. Though Peru obviously recovered after the 1720s, and by the end of the century was in fact ahead of its seventeenth century highs, it no longer was the dominant player within America. Although its actual revenue by the end of the colonial period was higher than at any time previously, its relative position had profoundly declined.

At the same time the comparative growth of the rest of Spain's South American colonies redirected the flow of Peruvian surpluses to the maintenance and growth of this expanding empire. For all their subsequent rivalry, there is little question that it was Peru that paid for the effective establishment of the viceregal government in the Río de la Plata region.

The categories of income also support the recent reinterpretations of the relative importance of the Peruvian mining sector in this period. Though the Huancavelica mercury mines collapsed in the middle of the eighteenth century, silver mining went from rather modest proportions to becoming a relatively important part of the Peruvian economy by the end of the colonial period. By the end of the eighteenth century, mining taxes had doubled their share of total revenues, to almost 10 percent of the total.

But the prime economic sector for the production of tax revenues for almost the entire period was trade. Peru was obviously the entrepot for international trade to South America, and its role as primary supplier to the Upper Peruvian mines guaranteed that this sector was the principal source of royal revenues until the late eighteenth century crisis of European wars brought international commerce to a halt.

The most surprising finding, given the relatively slow growth of the rural Indian peasant population in the eighteenth century and the concurrent rise of a large mestizo population (and their withdrawal from tribute payment), was the rapid growth of tribute income. In the relatively weakened Peruvian economy, this regressive tax became the second most important source of revenue after trade by the 1740s and finally passed the trade figures in the 1780s. That this essentially regressive head tax became the crown's dominant source of income by this decade implies a growing crisis in the Peruvian economy that was further revealed by the collapse associated with the nineteenth century wars of independence.

In terms of regional growth, it was evident that the central coast and sierra region dominated the Peruvian economy. But both the southern region, and more especially the northern coast and highlands, grew at impressive rates and reduced the importance of the central coast and sierra by the end of the colonial period. As measured by tax incomes, the south was double the size of the northern coastal-sierra economy. Mining, an increasing peasant population, and the growth of local grazing and the woolens industry explain this remarkable difference and increasing importance of this region. But even more impressive is the growth of the north, some twelve times larger in 1800 than it had been in 1680. This, the smallest of the regional economies, was the fastest growing region and in fact moved at a different rhythm from the rest of the viceroyalty. Though it experienced a decline in revenues after 1700 and recovered like the other regions after the 1740s, it never dipped below 1680s revenues in any period under consideration here.

The expenditure patterns show relatively few surprises, especially in the light of earlier studies of Spanish metropolitan expenditures.[31] As in Spain itself, the major governmental costs were related to war (absorbing on average a third of expenditures), with little left over for social overhead expenditures. The actual administration of the colonial government was rather a small part of the crown's expenditures, usually representing less than 15 percent of the total. Thus in the decade of the 1750s, when war costs absorbed 25 percent of the 2 million pesos in viceregal expenditures, administrative costs were just 13 percent of that amount. By the 1780s administrative costs accounted for just 10 percent, while total expenditures now reached over 5 million pesos. War expenditures on the other hand had surpassed even the growth in total disbursements, and now accounted for 41 percent of this larger sum.

Between falling revenues in the formerly primary tax category of commerce and the concurrent rising expenditures for the military, it is evident that the late eighteenth century colonial wars had a profoundly negative impact on the economy of the Viceroyalty of Peru. Though revenue and expenditure growth in the last quarter of the century had surpassed all previous records for the region, the colony began the nineteenth century in a precarious state, which the wars of independence (beginning in the region in 1809 and not ending until 1825) further exacerbated.

4

The Audiencia of Charcas

Located in the highlands some 12,000 feet above sea level, to the south of Lake Titicaca, the plateau (*altiplano*) region of what would become the Audiencia of Charcas (modern-day Bolivia) is one of the most mineral-rich zones on earth. In the pre-Hispanic period it was the primary home of the Aymara Indian kingdoms, which had only recently been conquered by the Quechuan Indians of Cuzco, to the north. For this reason there were Quechua-speaking military colonies throughout the high plateau and associated tropical agricultural valleys that made up this region. The region was a very rich zone of animal husbandry (of American cameloids) and both highland root crop and tropical valley agriculture; it was one of the most densely populated regions in the Andes. In spite of its agricultural dominance, it was a zone that initially attracted relatively few conquerors, and in the early sixteenth century it contained an estimated 730,000 Indians and only 7,000 Spaniards.[1]

But in 1545 this situation changed, with the discovery of silver mines at Porco, a barren and poorly populated region, which would suddenly become one of the worlds greatest known mineral deposits.[2] By 1546 the new town of Potosí was founded, and so quickly did it grow that by 1547 the crown had already granted it the title of "imperial" and a coat of arms.[3] Very quickly the crown moved to control this extraordinary wealth, which was attracting both Spaniards and Indians in such large numbers. In 1561 the region was separated from Lima and given its own autonomous government, ruled by a high court, and became known as the Audiencia of Charcas, or sometimes as Alto (Upper) Peru.

From its establishment, Potosí was the economic motor of Charcas. Within a generation of its founding, the city become one of the largest in America and may have passed the 100,000 population mark.[4] Given the barren zone in which it was established, the need to supply the city and its mines with workers, food, and goods of all kinds created one of the great interior regional markets of Spanish colonial America. This market stretched from northern Argentina and the Chilean coast to Quito.[5] From the 1540s to the 1570s, the silver content of the ores was so high that traditional Indian open-hearth methods could be used to extract the pure metal. But the rapidly declining content of the ores led to the necessity to use new extraction methods. The mercury amalgamation process totally transformed the industry, bringing with it Spanish control over refining and smelting. It also turned mercury into so fundamental a necessity in silver production everywhere in the New World that the state was forced to provide credit for its sale, even as it created a monopoly over its distribution. Also in the 1570s, the crown decided to subsidize the faltering Potosí silver mines by providing labor in the form of several thousand forced draft workers per annum, who were paid less than a standard wage—the so-called Indian *mita* laborers.[6] Whereas free wage labor was relied upon in all the rest of Spanish American mining, except for the unique case of the Huancavelica mercury mines in Peru, this subsidy to the Potosí miners was instrumental in this early period in helping to revive the industry, so that silver output continued to grow into the next century and only began a long-term secular decline after the 1640s. It is estimated that between free wage laborers and the *mita* workers (*mitayos*), the town held at least 30,000 Indian laborers working in the mines and smelters by the end of the sixteenth century.[7]

From the beginning, the Audiencia of Charcas was dominated by the central treasury office of Potosí, which was founded in the city in 1560. By the end of the seventeenth century, some five other cajas had been added, all reflecting new zones of growth or new mines. There were the three mining centers of Oruro (the second most important silver mine zone in Charcas),[8] Carangas, and Chuquito, as well as two major market centers—the port of Arica (tied closely to Potosí) and the city of La Paz, the center of Upper Peru's largest concentration of free Indian peasant communities. At the end of the eighteenth century, aside from moving the Audiencia from its dependence on the viceroyalty at Lima to the new viceroyalty established at Buenos Aires, three more cajas in commercial-agricultural centers were established: those of Charcas (present-day Sucre), Cochabamba, and Santa Cruz de la Sierra. Thus in contrast to Peru, and much more in tune with what would occur in the Viceroyalty of New Spain (Mexico), Charcas actually saw a steady expansion of its treasury districts, especially as new mines opened up and agricultural activity became ever more important in the economy of the region.

But the output of the mines of Potosí peaked in the 1590s (at a volume not achieved again until the late nineteenth century) and thereafter experienced a century-long secular decline, which began in the 1640s and did not end until the 1750s (graph 4.1). Though the trend in mining production was strongly negative for this entire period, there were important cyclical variations. It was not until the 1660s that average annual output dropped significantly below 500,000 marks, still only one-third off the peak 1590s figure. But production then declined in the 1660s and hovered around 300,000 marks until the end of the century. The first decades of the eighteenth century were the worst for the Potosí mining economy, with the bottom reached in the 1740s, when average annual production fell below 100,000 marks.[9]

This decline of Potosí mineral output was directly reflected in the waning

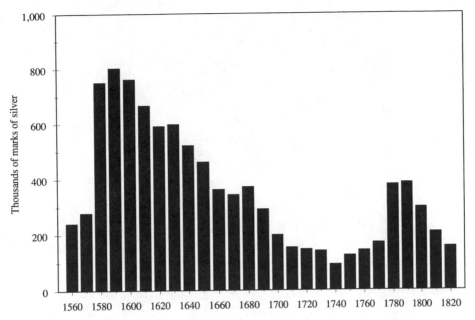

Graph 4.1   Average Annual Silver Output at Potosí, 1580–1820 (by decade)

importance of the Potosí treasury in the total receipts of the region, and of course in a reduction of total receipts as well. Whereas Potosí accounted for over 80 percent of all government incomes in the last two decades of the seventeenth century, its share progressively declined throughout the eighteenth, and by the first decade of the nineteenth century accounted for only half of total audiencia royal incomes (table 4.1).

At the same time, the receipts for the entire region, which had been a respectable 2.5 million pesos per annum in the 1680s (three-quarters of total Peruvian receipts), would decline severely in the next several decades and not bottom out until the 1740s. While growth was impressive in the second half of the eighteenth century, Upper Peru's total tax revenue output, which climbed to 3.5 million pesos per annum, now represented just 60 percent of total Peruvian receipts.[10]

Potosí was initially challenged in its dominant role by the secondary mining center of Oruro, which had come into full production at the beginning of the seventeenth century. But in its turn, Oruro could not sustain high levels of production and experienced a decline in output and in consequent royal tax revenues after the 1760s. Relying on free wage labor rather than the subsidized forced labor recruited for the Potosí mines, the Oruro mines had grown by exploiting new deposits. But declining quality of ore and a lack of worker subsidization eventually forced a sharp drop in mining output, which was also reflected in the decline in its treasury's participation in total receipts, from a

Decade	Potosí	La Paz	Oruro	Chuquito	Charcas	Cochab.	Carangas	Arica	Santa Cruz	TOTAL
1680-89	2,016,678	519,450	111,025	230,450	0	0	31,686	0	0	2,909,289
1690-99	1,707,106	103,606	175,079		0	0	30,065	0	0	2,015,856
1700-09	1,021,859	120,774	231,310	53,875	0	0	0	0	0	1,427,818
1710-19	923,571	88,517	274,568	64,323			15,604			1,366,583
1720-29	582,250	51,109	221,511	87,595			15,799			958,264
1730-39	593,379	68,148	193,240	75,812			17,614	5,160		953,353
1740-49	583,840	95,746	138,332	37,942			8,105			863,965
1750-59	672,799	124,477	188,881	72,104			15,680	22,421		1,096,362
1760-69	864,872	144,542	154,716	61,141			20,626	18,794		1,264,691
1770-79	1,471,866	234,554	282,922	106,372	89,752	66,720	42,968	22,477		2,317,631
1780-89	1,304,243	354,562	145,408	286,314	233,798	148,884	38,494	78,519	4,328	2,594,550
1790-99	1,647,904	376,903	176,520	302,558	185,384	159,626	41,980	84,961	5,777	2,981,613
1800-09	1,618,181	658,823	258,471	315,092	326,510	243,660	47,476	64,377	16,546	3,549,136

Table 4.1 Estimated Annual Average Total Income by Decade for the Treasuries of the Audiencia of Charcas, 1680–1809 (in pesos of 8 reales). (Source: John TePaske and Herbert S. Klein, *Royal Treasuries of the Spanish Empire in America* (3 vols.; Durham: Duke University Press, 1982), Vol. II.) Notes: A blank means that no data exist for that year, and a "0" means that zero income occurred in that year.

Thousands of pesos

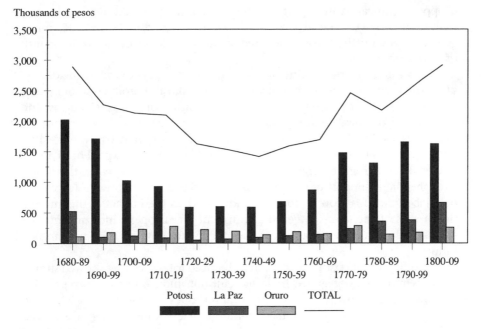

Graph 4.2   Total Income by Principal Cajas in Charcas, 1680–1809
(by decade)

high of almost one-quarter in the 1720s to under 10 percent by the last decades
of the century (graph 4.2).

Though accounting for less than 5 percent of total regional incomes at the
end of the seventeenth century, the commercial and agricultural zone of La
Paz grew rapidly in the second half of the eighteenth century. This was the
zone of coca production, traditional Andean agricultural and grazing activity,
and home to the densest populations of Aymara and Quechua peasant populations. It also contained, in the coca lands of the Chulumani (Yungas) district,
the richest Indian peasant communities in the Andes. Though La Paz also suffered a sharp decline in revenues at the beginning of the century, reaching a
low point in the 1720s, growth thereafter was continuous and dramatic (see
table 4.1). By the first decade of the nineteenth century, it accounted for almost a fifth of total regional revenues. By then the city had finally passed the
cities of Oruro and Potosí in terms of total population and had become the region's most important urban center.

In contrast to the Peruvian viceroyalty, Charcas was predominantly a mining zone, and mining taxes for most of the period were the single most important source of government income. Accounting for two-thirds of all revenues
at the end of the seventeenth century, mine tax incomes continued to account
for at least 50 percent of total revenues until the 1760s. After that time they

dropped significantly in importance, both as mining production began to stag-nate at the end of the century and as there occurred a regional shift in economic activity to the northern zone, centered in the intendency of La Paz, just south of Lake Titicaca.

The dominant zone of mine production was of course found in the district of Potosí, with Oruro following in second place. But the production of moder-ate amounts of mine income in the treasury districts of La Paz, Carangas, and Chuquito also showed that mining was rather well distributed throughout the highlands (table 4.2). The figures for these taxes show that Oruro was still a significant producer until 1780. In turn Potosí, which had experienced a pro-longed decline from the highs of the 1680s, only began to revive in the 1780s, with the major support of royal subsidies and the continued use of forced un-paid labor. But this growth would be short-lived, as the impact of the interna-tional wars of the late eighteenth century cut off European mercury supplies and also dried up new sources of capital investment for the local mining industry.

The other major tax categories that influenced total revenues showed similar patterns in the major regions. Trade, agricultural, and commercial taxes tended to grow in quite close harmony with total revenues, at least until 1790, for all regions in the two Perus. Regional variation in these trade taxes, however, was quite pronounced. We have seen that in the case of Peru, Lima (as a regional center and port as well as the capital city) tended to account for a significant percentage of total trade and commerce receipts. As for Charcas, trade and com-merce taxes varied little in their relative importance throughout the period. Av-eraging between 5 and 10 percent of total revenues, commercial and trade tax incomes tended to move in close association with total revenues and thus changed their relative importance little over the course of the century. Though Alto Peru probably suffered somewhat from the crisis in trade that affected Lima after 1790, the lack of relevant data from the Potosí materials makes it impossi-ble to estimate how the regional trade crisis affected royal receipts in Charcas. Though given the decline in mine revenues and the continued decline of the local population, it can only be assumed that Potosí revenues at least did not amount to more than 67,000 pesos for the 1780s, and they most likely declined. La Paz had already passed Potosí as the leading producer of trade revenues in the 1770s, and it probably never lost that position through the end of the colo-nial period (table 4.3).

Monopoly tax revenues also showed important differences in Charcas as compared to the Peruvian viceroyalty. The relative importance of monopoly incomes shifted, as this quintessential mining center absorbed enormous quantities of state-owned mercury. The provisioning and sale of mercury for use in the amalgamation process, whereby silver was liberated from mineral impurities, was the single largest source of estanco revenues for Charcas.

Given the use of credit for sales of this mercury, however, and the constant accumulation of debt by silver miners, who purchased these stocks on credit, it is not surprising that the income from mercury sales, if not the sales themselves,

Decade	Potosí	La Paz	Oruro	Chuquito	Carangas	Arica	TOTAL
1680-89	1,442,952	30,174	66,733	179,700	17,704		1,737,263
1690-99	1,201,362	14,168	113,893		19,405		1,348,828
1700-09	543,250	6,645	150,436	29,931			730,262
1710-19	573,121	2,368	159,530	37,296	10,036		782,351
1720-29	296,868	40	128,575	59,277	11,135		495,895
1730-39	276,166	253	103,192	55,807	12,409		447,827
1740-49	209,979	37	95,808	34,795	7,962		348,581
1750-59	289,001	1,776	108,269	60,367	13,573		472,986
1760-69	290,224	1,700	104,062	38,568	14,089		448,643
1770-79	355,398	4,681	111,822	45,901	20,736		538,538
1780-89	487,990	9,218	42,961	33,862	11,733	35,220	620,984
1790-99	408,932	17,981	61,697	39,289	13,289	36,602	577,790
1800-09	295,633	17,423	44,231	45,282	19,351	17,745	439,665

Table 4.2   Estimated Average Annual Mine Income from the Audiencia of Charcas, 1680–1809. (Source: Same as table 4.1)

is not highly correlated with silver mining taxes.[11] In the case of Alto Peru, monopoly incomes fell less rapidly than did total revenues, thus tending to increase its share of total revenues, which by the 1720s had risen to 25 percent of total incomes. But then its growth slowed considerably, as total revenues expanded (table 4.4).

The final important category of income was the tribute tax on the Indian population. As we have seen, this tax dated back to the beginnings of the Spanish conquest in America and initially applied to Indian male heads of household who owned their own lands. As noted previously the rates of taxation were relatively fixed, being based on initial assessments of the value of the land held in each free Indian community, so that growth and decline in tribute income tended to reflect the natural growth of the Indian population. Thus tax income generated by this discriminatory head tax followed very general economic trends, which were also reflected in population expansion or contraction.

Usually the tribute tax was highly concentrated in specific regions where rural Indian peasant communities predominated. The Audiencia of Charcas, however, had without question the highest proportion of Indian peasant population of the three regions being studied. For this reason, in contrast to the other two regions, tribute revenues were more evenly distributed and were an important aspect of all local treasury incomes. As with Peru, however, tribute revenues declined at a slower pace than total revenues and then grew much more rapidly, so that by the end of the colonial period they were, like those in Peru, the largest single component of government tax revenues. Although Charcas had a population smaller than that of the viceroyalty itself, it was paying almost the same amount of income in tribute payments (table 4.5). This was

Decade	Potosí	La Paz	Oruro	Chuquito	Charcas	Cochab.	Carangas	Arica	Santa Cruz	TOTAL
1680-89	70,906	7,434	4,974	0			136			83,450
1690-99	70,113	9,647	3,678				155			83,593
1700-09	50,195	8,384	3,856	400						62,835
1710-19	46,903	9,299	4,399	366			137			61,104
1720-29	44,139	9,090	3,842	443			137			57,651
1730-39	37,927	12,480	4,146	258			240	1,776		56,827
1740-49	37,813	15,459	6,315	498			131			60,216
1750-59	61,597	22,262	8,505	2,562			186	4,854		99,966
1760-69	55,525	30,337	10,486	1,822			611	5,824		104,605
1770-79	57,399	65,692	11,198	5,466	27,377	18,928	2,403	6,760		195,223
1780-89	67,150	70,002	16,208	2,796	47,979	30,419	334	22,506	265	257,659
1790-99*		84,274	25,584	3,859	44,308	31,829	448	24,488	258	
1800-09*		40,239	23,559	10,810	61,191	28,740	616	16,652	235	

Table 4.3   Estimated Average Annual Income from Trade Taxes, Audiencia of Charcas, 1680–1809. (Source: Same as table 4.1.) Notes: *Although the Potosí accounts are complete for the period 1790–1809 they are missing all information on trade taxes. Thus, a blank in these income accounts means in fact that the numbers were missing. Given their weight in the total Audiencia income, I have not calculated the total income for the last two decades.

Decade	Potosí	La Paz	Oruro	Chuquito	Charcas	Cochab.	Carangas	Arica	Santa Cruz	TOTAL
1680-89	317,513	15,747	20,253	64,512			10,895			428,920
1690-99	271,154	4,582	36,611	0			8,957			321,304
1700-09	201,385	4,283	56,173	23,854			0			285,695
1710-19	148,219	5,353	82,900	21,797			5,212			263,481
1720-29	127,812	3,411	75,007	26,795			3,812			236,837
1730-39	125,461	2,109	70,440	17,960			2,158	199		218,327
1740-49	118,987	2,163	11,380	188			15			132,733
1750-59	185,847	2,200	44,506	212			21	0		232,786
1760-69	223,494	642	16,233	189			31	474		241,063
1770-79	312,724	3,363	111,456	19,828	3,349	969	8,399	825		460,913
1780-89	97,707	15,099	40,406	140,784	3,932	2,658	4,122	14,625	565	319,898
1790-99	15,544	10,554	39,093	175,931	6,779	4,782	3,689	7,424	211	264,007
1800-09	36,043	8,730	22,320	21,351	10,467	7,991	1,439	10,583	180	119,104

Table 4.4   Estimated Annual Average Income from Monopoly Taxes in the Audiencia of Charcas, 1680–1809. (Source: Same as table 4.1)

Decade	Potosí	La Paz	Oruro	Chuquito	Charcas	Cochab.	Carangas	Arica	Santa Cruz	TOTAL
1680-89	63,145	21,323	8,957	0			0			93,425
1690-99	85,502	32,631	14,630				0			132,763
1700-09	71,109	36,079	14,277	0						121,465
1710-19	84,457	40,300	14,062	4,215			0			143,034
1720-29	60,653	18,001	9,396	0			0			88,050
1730-39	93,575	28,979	13,381	0			0	387		136,322
1740-49	119,070	50,514	17,531	4,858			0			191,973
1750-59	77,517	72,861	18,964	6,635			4,714	10,314		191,005
1760-69	99,727	94,560	16,752	17,320			5,818	7,461		241,638
1770-79	91,037	142,083	26,049	30,844	17,533	31,244	11,911	10,534		361,235
1780-89	143,192	171,575	35,878	104,239	40,616	67,176	19,646	4,719	2,940	589,981
1790-99	173,449	242,210	39,840	75,618	59,823	90,115	22,275	2,246	2,960	708,536
1800-09	153,441	260,281	44,971	232,865	68,094	80,376	24,463	15,307	3,510	883,308

Table 4.5 Estimated Annual Average Tribute Income in the Audiencia of Charcas, 1680–1809. (Source: Same as table 4.1)

Decade	Potosí	La Paz	Oruro	Chuquito	Charcas	Cochab.	Carangas	Arica	Santa Cruz	TOTAL
1680-89	7,232	21,901	0	0						29,133
1690-99	12,970	16,454	0				0			29,424
1700-09	14,809	17,440	0	0			0			32,249
1710-19	13,884	15,962	0	0			0			29,846
1720-29	4,534	5,058	0	0			0			9,592
1730-39	3,287	7,709	0	0			0	0		10,996
1740-49	3,166	8,282	0	0			0			11,448
1750-59	886	6,692	0	0			0	0		7,578
1760-69	356	1,627	0	0			0	0		1,983
1770-79	0	382	0	119	12,618	1,489	0	0		14,608
1780-89	35	4,484	4,903	1,269	40,520	2,204	30	400	0	53,845
1790-99	52	581	10,578	0	4,568	1,935	41	0	2,867	20,622
1800-09	35	277	0	0	0	1,521	30	0	31,503	33,366

Table 4.6 Estimated Annual Average Loans Income for the Audiencia of Charcas, 1680–1809. (Source: Same as table 4.1)

because the northern region of the audiencia contained some of the wealthiest free Indian communities in the Andes. This was especially the case in the coca-producing district of Chulumani, in the Intendency of La Paz.[12]

The Audiencia of Charcas (as also the case for the Viceroyalty of Peru) was not used by the crown as a source of new funds after 1780. There were special war taxes and new censos, as could also be found in Peru, but these added only small amounts to the income ledger and only minimally changed the relative weight of the other major sources of income (table 4.6). Thus the experience of both Peru and Charcas would seem to suggest that the crown in the late eighteenth century concentrated all its attention on New Spain and made no serious attempt to extract extra resources from its other colonial American possessions for financing its European wars.

General Trends in Expenditures

A look at the long-term movements in expenditures reveals two clearly defined patterns. The first and most obvious is that total expenditures moved identically with total income figures in terms of growth and decline over this period. In all regions there was a very high correlation between the movement in income and expenditures.[13] This pattern again shows that the crown in Charcas, as in the Viceroyalty of Peru, had kept expenditures tightly tied to income. Thus when income declined drastically, so too did expenditures. In fact in most periods spending was below estimated income (see graph 2.7), and in the few periods where it exceeded income, the discrepancy was again quite modest.

The Audiencia of Charcas saw expenditures equally distributed among the regional cajas (table 4.7) in the same ratio as their respective incomes. Here again the evolution of expenditures paralleled that of income. Initially Potosí was the biggest spender of royal income in the zone, on average accounting for 80 percent of total expenditures until the 1710s. In the first half of the eighteenth century, the revived Oruro dominated second place and accounted for over a quarter of expenditures, thereby reducing Potosí's share to just over half of total audiencia expenditures. Finally in the second half of the eighteenth century, La Paz replaced Oruro as the region's second biggest spender.

In contrast to Peru, the essentially interior colony of Charcas needed few of its tax revenues for local military expenditures. On average it spent only about a tenth of its accumulated government revenues on local military affairs, except in the crucial period of the Tupac Amaru rebellions, when such expenditures accounted for as much as 48 percent of the total (table 4.8).

On the other hand, Charcas spent a surprisingly high percentage of its locally spent monies on salaries and other administrative expenses. In contrast to both Peru and Mexico, which spent relatively little on administration, Charcas averaged some 31 percent for such expenses overall, and only began to reach the much lower Peruvian and Mexican levels in the last quarter of the century (table 4.9). This would seem to have more to do with mining-related expenses (such as the *Casa de Moneda*) than with ordinary expenditures. Thus the

Decade	Potosi	La Paz	Oruro	Chuquito	Charcas	Cochab.	Carangas	Arica	Santa Cruz	TOTAL
1680-89	1,746,259	108,193	115,201	246,930			32,434			2,249,017
1690-99	1,639,808	102,124	173,725				30,523			1,946,180
1700-09	1,309,545	114,021	231,370	56,313						1,711,249
1710-19	605,161	87,937	274,602	64,518			15,651			1,047,869
1720-29	366,739	49,651	213,691	87,616			16,326			734,023
1730-39	410,830	68,147	175,406	73,633			17,643	3,817		749,476
1740-49	474,782	95,746	149,836	37,947			8,425			766,736
1750-59	675,758	124,477	202,739	72,123			15,669	21,421		1,112,187
1760-69	707,376	157,845	164,849	65,885			20,669	19,902		1,136,526
1770-79	1,402,970	210,644	271,212	89,054	85,008	101,832	49,395	33,297		2,243,412
1780-89	1,267,182	277,207	162,474	199,780	254,775	153,503	36,778	80,333	4,903	2,436,935
1790-99	1,684,438	302,121	164,797	264,773	190,088	247,466	36,544	81,995	6,601	2,978,823
1800-09	1,452,146	514,027	231,582	367,722	332,131	275,700	50,966	58,280	15,904	3,298,458

Table 4.7 Estimated Average Annual Total Expenditures of the Royal Treasuries
of Charcas, 1680–1809. (Source: Same as table 4.1)

Decade	Potosí	La Paz	Oruro	Chuquito	Charcas	Cochab.	Arica	Santa Cruz	TOTAL
1680-89	9,372	0	1,070	0					10,442
1690-99	7,138	0	0						7,138
1700-09	0	143	75,320	0					75,463
1710-19	0	663	0	65,501					66,164
1720-29	0	0	0	33,226					33,226
1730-39	0	0	1,336	32,630			0		33,966
1740-49	0	0	0	14,000					14,000
1750-59	0	209	10,000	0			0		10,209
1760-69	0	0	68,530	0			0		68,530
1770-79	1,026,696	3	0	0	0	3,540	941		1,031,180
1780-89	810,012	35,156	24,754	52,304	68,145	33,717	0	4,532	1,028,620
1790-99	0	18,736	10,890	0	4,506	3,404	9,601	3,376	50,513
1800-09	62,386	22,940	5,585	2,544	38,837	39,335	6,856	11,063	189,546

Table 4.8 Estimated Annual Average Expenditures for War in the Audiencia of Charcas, 1680–1809. (Source: Same as table 4.1)

Decade	Potosí	La Paz	Oruro	Chuquito	Charcas	Cochab.	Carangas	Arica	Santa Cruz	TOTAL
1680-89	795,502	0	7,766	4,295			32,434			839,997
1690-99	994,685	1,740	32,732				30,523			1,059,680
1700-09	724,546	19,994	65,897	4,346						814,783
1710-19	376,921	51,383	244,869	21,827			6,033			701,033
1720-29	286,759	21,011	26,380	9,529			6,678			350,357
1730-39	318,442	0	19,677	4,063			5,834	3,817		351,833
1740-49	338,733	18,654	47,734	3,529			4,460			413,110
1750-59	447,706	16,860	5,087	5,723			3,906	9,508		488,790
1760-69	633,647	41,712	5,388	5,220			5,684	6,179		697,830
1770-79	245,500	13,237	8,261	8,576	4,850	8,277	5,841	5,220		299,762
1780-89	94,790	39,710	15,181	13,900	65,940	21,892	6,100	13,159	164	270,836
1790-99	277,195	44,114	8,085	590	64,099	37,604	5,622	7,016	169	444,494
1800-09	134,405	27,778	8,423	15,958	62,412	27,516	5,618	6,719	4,310	293,139

Table 4.9 Estimated Average Annual Administrative Expenditures in the Audiencia of Charcas, 1680–1809. (Source: Same as table 4.1)

commercial and agricultural center of La Paz only expended on average some 13 percent of its total royal costs on administration, as opposed to the overall figure of 41 percent for Potosí.

Again in sharp distinction to the Peruvian experience, Charcas consistently produced excess revenues for use outside the region throughout the colonial period. Charcas was able to supply both an important subsidy to Lima until the 1710s (which peaked at half a million pesos in the 1680s) as well as to maintain a steady supply of excess funds for the deficitory operations in the Río de la Plata. These Buenos Aires subsidies, known as the situado, tended to reflect the highs and lows of Upper Peruvian royal income. Thus they dropped to dramatically low levels in the middle decades of the century and then rose again as mining production and the general economy boomed at the end of the colonial period. Reaching almost 1.7 million pesos in the 1790s, such excess funds shipped from Charcas were the single most important source of government revenues for the Buenos Aires viceroyalty.[14]

Conclusion

What this examination of trends in income and expenditures in the royal treasuries of the Audiencia of Charcas makes evident is the powerful impact of the fortunes of Potosí mining on royal finances. The cajas of Charcas had obviously been in secular decline from the middle decades of the seventeenth century, due to the declining power of the Potosí mines. This decline accelerated in the last quarter of the seventeenth century and grew ever more desperate in the first decades of the eighteenth century. Nor was Charcas alone in this response, as the Peruvian trends make clear. It would seem that the fundamental decline of Potosí mining production put severe strains on both Peruvian economies. The recovery of Alto Peruvian mining through major government subsidies and the discovery of new deposits in Oruro and other zones guaranteed that by mid-century Charcas would once again begin to grow at a more than reasonable rate, so that a partial recovery could be achieved by the end of the century.

Tax revenue data also give us some reasonable ideas about Spanish royal fiscal policy as related to the American colonies. It seems that the crown tried throughout most of the period not to burden the crucial mining sector with taxes that might cripple its ability to produce. But by the late seventeenth century it was favoring Mexican miners over those of the Peruvian region. Nevertheless the eventual granting of reduced mining taxes, along with credit purchases of mercury and subsidized labor support via the reduced mita, all helped to revive mining tax income by the last half of the eighteenth century. The growth of trade and tribute income, however, meant that the relative share of mining in total revenues declined from a steady 50 percent or more in the period to 1730 to less than 25 percent by the 1780s and thereafter.

The rapid growth of tribute income is impressive and clearly reflected the growth of the Indian peasant population in America. It is also related to the weakened Spanish Andean economies of the two Perus. This is evident from the fact that by the end of the colonial period such a regressive tax as that charged on Indians could become the single most important source of government revenue in the two colonies.

How much the crown actually extracted from this complex tax structure is another interesting finding from the treasury records. There is little question that Peru, which had stopped remitting monies to Spain after the 1740s, was barely holding its own in terms of paying for local government and defense from the incomes it received; it could afford little beyond this. Charcas on the other hand, was able to send large quantities of "excess" revenues across its borders. Unfortunately for the crown, all of this money had to be directed to the maintenance of the new viceroyalty of Buenos Aires, which in turn could afford to send no significant quantities of "excess" revenues to Spain. Only Mexico could be relied upon to send massive financial support directly to the coffers in Madrid.

There is little question that everywhere in America the crown actually spent more of its tax income in the colonies than it shipped to the metropolis. This situation was even more so in these two Andean colonies, where all surplus revenues generated by the mining zones of Upper Peru were used to pay for the costs of guarding the southern Atlantic coasts, for constructing fortifications at the major ports of the Río de la Plata region, and for subsidizing the interior forts in the Chaco and along the southern Chilean frontier. While heavy taxes thus generated major surpluses, over three-quarters of those surpluses were spent in America, defending the interior peace and tranquillity of one of the world's largest free trade zones in that period.

Other expenditure patterns present few surprises. The major category of expenses was that of war, with little left over for social overhead. The only major variation for the Charcas zone was the high cost of administration, probably related to the complex government structure needed to maintain the mines, administer the mita, and handle government mercury sales and the Potosí mint.

5

The Viceroyalty of New Spain

Even before the end of the seventeenth century, the Viceroyalty of New Spain (modern-day Mexico) had become Spain's richest American colony. By the early decade of the eighteenth century, it was producing over half of the crown's gross tax revenues from its New World empire and at least two-thirds of its net imperial income.[1] Although the importance of New Spain's contribution to imperial finance was recognized at the time, it has only become possible now, through the reconstruction of these annual regional treasury records, to assess the significance, long-term trends, and origins of royal taxes in this region.

As with my study of the treasury accounts for the two principal Andean colonies, I am concerned in this chapter with using reconstructed tax series to define the major cycles of revenue growth and decline for the viceroyalty as a whole, to determine the importance of the various regions in producing royal income, and to estimate the relative significance of the categories of taxes levied by the metropolitan power on its American colony. Finally these reconstructed series will be used to describe general trends in the economy as a whole, as they can be perceived through an examination of selected tax income figures.

The extraordinary growth of the economy of New Spain from the last quarter of the seventeenth century until the first quarter of the nineteenth century is reported in all primary sources and secondary studies of this period.[2] This relatively steady expansion was fueled by a constant increase in the production of silver, both through the revitalization of older mining regions as well as the discovery of major new zones in the mid-eighteenth century. Silver production reached unprecedented levels, unique to American production in premodern times, and it did not fully peak until the end of the first decade of the nineteenth century.[3]

The growth in silver output was accompanied by a generalized expansion in all sectors of the economy. Throughout the eighteenth century, agricultural production grew almost as fast as silver output, reaching an estimated 1.3 percent per annum for the entire colony.[4] Clearly there were regional variations, and there seems to have been a general slowing of agricultural production after the famine of 1784–86.[5] But overall agricultural growth, just as mining output, surpassed population growth by a reasonable margin until the beginning of the nineteenth century. This general economic development in turn encouraged population expansion. During the course of the eighteenth century, the viceregal population of New Spain doubled, probably to close to 6 million persons.[6]

This major growth in production and population benefited the crown, and the royal exchequer experienced increased revenues in everything from mining and trade taxes to head taxes on Indians and monopoly sales of tobacco, gunpowder, and mercury. Although there was long-term growth in tax receipts throughout the viceroyalty, this growth was neither constant nor uniform across all regions during the century. Royal revenues experienced several periods of stagnation and even decline, at times confined to a few regions and at other times affecting almost the entirety of the viceroyalty. While the economies of most of the major tax-producing regions moved in an approximately equal rhythm, the medium and smaller centers often responded to quite local factors and tended to move at their own pace. But on the whole, periods of crisis and growth were to be felt throughout the majority of regions of New Spain during most of the century.

In analyzing the estimated "total income" figures for the entire viceroyalty (table 5.1), it is evident that the fourth quarter of the seventeenth century was one of moderate decline from a high reached in the 1680s. The estimated 4.9 million pesos of that period were not surpassed until the 1710s. This decline was short-lived, and royal income was on the rise again from the decade of the 1700s onward. By the 1740s average annual income was double the 1680s range and only paused in its rapid growth during the decade of the 1760s. In the 1780s this annual income figure almost doubled over the previous decade, indicating major new advances in the viceregal economy. This growth, as will be seen when the various sectors of the economy are examined, was achieved by a steady growth of taxes based on mining and a rather major increase in taxes based on commerce.

The expansion of the last quarter of the eighteenth century was fueled by the discovery and rapid development of new mining districts in Guanajuato, Catorce (San Luis Potosí), and Zacatecas; the growth of international trade due to the freeing of imperial commerce after 1778; and a general reform in the royal fiscal (*hacienda*) administration, which culminated in the implementation of the intendant system. In this and the next decade, some half dozen new treasury districts were established, and a better system for collecting the traditional incomes was instituted.

While comprehensive national price data still do not exist for the Viceroyalty of New Spain, none of the few studies available show any extraordinary inflationary trend in the last quarter of the eighteenth century or the beginning decade of the nineteenth century that could explain this growth.[7] Rather this expansion of state revenues occurred through the steady growth of the population and the economy being taxed, at least until 1790.

It is the post-1790 expansion in total receipts for New Spain that causes the

Decade	México	Veracruz	Puebla	Chihuahua	Guanajuato	Rosario	Michoacán	Zacatecas	Saltillo	Oaxaca	Guadalaj.	Durango	S.L. Potosí	Acapulco	Arispe
1680-89	1,465,621	1,022,801			95,000			318,669			175,306	129,916	73,011	221,317	
1690-99	1,822,259	773,924			121,817			184,491			161,524	90,357	90,855	220,819	
1700-09	1,939,505	1,513,323			145,513			197,207			158,089	115,389	71,831	211,257	
1710-19	2,338,248	1,681,268			178,176			391,171			175,790	181,408	64,520	281,009	
1720-29	2,573,715	1,856,945			271,360			431,826			191,410	192,232	61,645	222,609	
1730-39	3,430,459	2,743,490			387,842			373,039			225,326	224,373	72,303	221,183	
1740-49	4,525,657	4,040,121			538,980			323,240			221,570	258,998	56,869	204,893	
1750-59	5,698,698	4,112,307			444,352			324,876			296,014	260,264	191,730	217,190	
1760-69	5,894,576	4,135,159			451,889			204,534			394,997	358,353	163,496	246,271	
1770-79	7,678,278	5,961,114			795,420	222,172		349,681			502,145	485,562	355,699	340,254	
1780-89	12,310,700	11,890,288	673,843	477,663	1,056,013	463,512	423,290	510,204	408,049	397,638	805,582	509,055	916,202	404,094	287,130
1790-99	23,049,340	13,034,803	1,000,407	716,396	1,329,536	822,825	489,771	1,103,208	564,692	576,480	1,084,418	611,775	967,280	622,943	264,076
1800-09	40,444,538	19,527,251	1,509,436	733,918	1,660,950	727,970	521,025	845,251			999,916	554,583	809,538	693,848	239,473

-II-

Decade	Pachuca	Bolaños	Mérida	Tabasco	Zimapán	Campeche	Sombrerete	Pr.Carmen	TOTAL	TOTAL_B*
1680-89	102,782		18,199				163,554		3,786,176	2,473,694
1690-99	147,359		7,818				100,853		3,722,076	1,978,790
1700-09	98,376		3,861				50,630		4,504,981	2,825,758
1710-19	135,350		11,582			59,474	33,348		5,531,344	3,504,603
1720-29	241,046		15,542	4,031	25,017	61,541	21,831	44,495	6,215,246	3,822,053
1730-39	148,402		17,041	5,714	26,776	51,464	72,511	44,495	8,044,418	4,898,612
1740-49	108,276		34,331	4,886	35,511	46,604	140,796		10,540,732	5,698,999
1750-59	176,502	504,132	69,083	6,558	56,490	58,251	49,485		12,465,932	6,869,207
1760-69	200,834	172,017	58,414	9,028	49,220	118,020	29,361		12,486,169	6,529,195
1770-79	157,182	171,629	96,310	10,554	76,425	167,752	69,314	87,924	17,527,415	9,460,554
1780-89	134,970	186,819	210,052	11,961	75,360	316,427	90,233	108,474	31,861,872	17,161,931
1790-99	743,527	191,131	396,643	16,982	106,825	333,776	420,957	123,432	48,235,738	17,762,496
1800-09	817,819	49,099	475,112	21,169	82,551	407,936	597,593	177,477	73,037,625	15,791,049

Table 5.1 Estimated Average Annual Total Income for the Viceroyalty of New Spain, by Treasury Office, 1680–1809. (Source: John TePaske and Herbert S. Klein, *Ingresos y Egresos de la Real Hacienda de Nueva Espana.* 2 vols.; Mexico: Instituto Nacional de Antropología e Historia, 1986.) Notes: In this and all subsequent tables "0" indicates no income was obtained, though the caja was open, and a blank indicates a lack of documentation on the caja. *"Total-B" is the total of all the major category incomes (tables 5.2–5.5) excluding the special Miscl. taxes and Loans & Situados (tables 5.6 & 5.7).

most difficulty in the analysis of any period or region for which we have data. After 1790 the extraordinary doubling of total royal revenues was generated by a whole new set of incomes, those coming from special loans and "voluntary" gifts (*donativos*) associated with the European war efforts of the metropolitan government. It was only in New Spain that this extraordinary category of income became important. In general the growth in traditional taxes on commerce and production tended to slow down in the 1790s and decline in the first decade of the nineteenth century, although taxes generated from tribute continue to grow at steady rates. These special loans and new miscellaneous gifts, on the other hand, accelerated at an extraordinary pace.

Because of the unusually rapid expansion of these special funds, their sporadic nature, their lack of direct connection to production, trade, or population developments, and even questions as to their effective collection, post-1790 royal treasury data for New Spain have caused much debate, discussed below. In light of this debate, I have also calculated the total estimated income for the viceroyalty based only on major production, trade, and population tax categories (see "Total-B," table 5.1). Though these figures do not give the complete income for the royal treasury even in the case of production and consumption taxes, they well reflect the underlying economic and demographic trends of the viceregal economy. Clearly in terms of the post-1790 period, the economy was beginning to slow its very rapid pace in the last decade of the century. Mining stagnated from the previous decade, and incomes from monopoly sales had already begun to decline. Though income generated from taxes on trade and tribute continued to grow substantially, this was not the case in the next decade, and in fact only tribute incomes continued their growth into the first decade of the nineteenth century. But this increase was insufficient to overcome the general decline, and total receipts in these major commercial and population taxes dropped by 11 percent in the first decade of the 1800s.

Regional Treasury Participation

Before analyzing the participation of individual taxes in the makeup of the total income figures, certain general features should be noted about the geographic origin of these incomes. The most outstanding characteristic of a regionally based examination of the accounts is the vital role played by just two treasury districts: those of Mexico (here and afterwards meaning the district of the City of Mexico) and of Veracruz. The first of these treasuries was the matrix, or central, treasury for the entire Viceroyalty of New Spain, and the second accounted for the majority of all the colony's imports and exports, being the primary connecting port to Europe. Veracruz also played a crucial role as collector of revenues from other treasury districts, with some 60 percent of its income deriving from interior districts. Together the changing fortunes of these two districts determined the ebb and flow of total viceregal income. On average the two treasuries accounted for almost three-quarters of all income generated in the viceregal region, and their combined tax receipts never fell below two-thirds of total revenues in any given decade. Thus the movement of total revenues for the viceroyalty was highly correlated with the movement of revenues into these two offices.

In terms of their relative importance within total receipts, the two treasuries remained remarkably stable for most of this period. On average the Mexico City treasury produced about 45 percent of total tax revenues in all the decades between 1680 and 1799. For its part Veracruz for most of the period produced on average about one-third of total viceregal revenues. In the case of Mexico, there was no serious variation until the end of the eighteenth century. Even when new treasury districts were carved out of Mexico's jurisdiction, in the 1780s, there was no decline in its relative importance. Though more treasury offices were opened in the 1790s, the relative weight of Mexico in total revenues remained high until the crisis of the first decade of the 1800s.

An examination of the smaller treasury offices and their tax incomes shows some important variations from the pattern established for total viceregal income and for the matrix treasury of Mexico. These smaller treasuries tended to move in harmony with other treasuries that shared their basic economic characteristics. Treasuries can be roughly grouped either on the basis of their relationship to one or more primary industries, by their location, and by whether over half of their total income was determined by one major tax category (usually either mining or trade). Thus among the older treasuries, or those in existence before 1700, one can distinguish those based primary on mining centers (Guanajuato, Zacatecas, Durango, San Luis Potosí, Pachuca, and Sombrerete); those located in zones where internal trade, manufacturing, and commerce were important (Guadalajara, Mérida, and Campeche); and those dependent on international trade (Veracruz and Acapulco).

In general mining centers differed sharply from the viceregal and Mexican trends in their consistent growth in the last decade of the seventeenth century; most of them then declined in the first decade of the eighteenth century. The only variant from this pattern was San Luis Potosí, which continued its growth until the 1710s. At this point the general trends of income at these mining centers began to vary somewhat. All but San Luis Potosí and Sombrerete grew in the next few decades. In the decade of the 1740s and 1750s, either stagnation or decline characterized all mining regions but Durango, which proceeded along at its very impressive pace of 2.5 percent annual growth rate for the rest of the century. Even Guanajuato, which grew at over 2 percent throughout, and climbed even more rapidly after 1760, also experienced a period of stagnation at midcentury. Thereafter growth was rather steady, if not spectacular, for most of the provincial mining centers until the first decade of the nineteenth century.

It should be stressed that two mining treasuries departed strongly from these trends. Pachuca experienced a long-term decline from the 1720s, with only a temporary respite in the 1790s, while the *real* (mining camp) of Bolaños, which began as an independent treasury in the 1750s with half a million pesos in tax revenues, declined at almost 3 percent per annum for the rest of the century. Revenue in these centers was obviously sensitive to local company failures and to the exhaustion of easily accessible deposits of silver.

Domestic trade and production zones varied not only from the dominant Mexican and viceregal trends, but also from the trends seen in the mining treasuries. Guadalajara, the largest of the interior trade centers after Mexico itself, did not experience sustained growth until the 1730s, and really rapid growth occurred only after midcentury. Neither Guadalajara nor Campeche suffered a recession in the 1760s. Campeche showed steady growth until the 1780s and entered a long-term decline only thereafter, while Mérida tended to grow steadily from the early decades of the eighteenth century until the nineteenth century, with only a short pause (though no recession) in the 1760s.

The two ports of Veracruz and Acapulco followed their own quite unique trends until the 1770s. Royal treasury funds in Veracruz went into a sharp decline in the 1690s, but by the first decade of the eighteenth century, growth was again steady, doubling the rate of the 1680s by the 1720s. This was followed by steady growth in the next five decades and then by spectacular growth after 1780. Clearly the *comercio libre* decree of 1778 had a profound impact on this Atlantic port's revenues. Acapulco, tied in as it was to the special rhythm of the Asian trade, differed from all other New Spain treasuries in its rather long-term growth from 1680 to 1719, after which it experienced sharp midcentury fluctuations and did not recover the peak income of the 1710s until the 1800s.

In several of the smaller frontier trade and commerce cajas created in the late eighteenth century, surplus funds from the other treasuries arrived as basically needed subsidies and accounted for most of the income generated. Thus Campeche, in the southeast, and Arispe and Chihuahua, in the northwest, were most influenced by funds arriving in their *otras tesorerías* (other treasuries) accounts. In the former, intertreasury transfers were important early on. Removing these incomes reveals an unusual pattern of severe decline in local revenues occurring after a 1780s peak. Arispe was a treasury whose local income dropped by two-thirds; it was clearly an insignificant producer of local taxes. The same characterization applies to the neighboring frontier office of Chihuahua, of whose total revenues over half are accounted for by transferred funds. As was common to most viceroyalties at the time, otras tesorerías funds sent to these frontier and marginal treasuries were a crucial subsidy necessary to make them solvent.[8]

Despite these obvious local variations, it can be argued that the lesser treasuries in a general way followed the larger ones in their patterns of growth and crisis. All districts seemed to have experienced an early eighteenth century decline, a midcentury stagnation and/or decline, and a rapid growth rate in the last two decades of the century, with a sharp tapering off of growth in the first decade of the 1800s.

Components of Income

In his analysis of the basis for the extraordinary wealth of New Spain in the colonial period and its tremendous growth in the eighteenth century, the German scientist Alexander von Humboldt noted that it rested on three foundations: mining, agriculture, and manufactures. He estimated the annual volume

of mining at about 23 million pesos, agriculture at 29 million pesos, and manufacturing at between 7 and 8 million pesos.[9] Of these three pillars of the economy, agriculture, which employed most of the population and accounted for
the majority of national output, was primarily directed toward internal trade
and consumption, with only commercial dyes, together with some cotton,
sugar, spices, and other condiments being exported to Europe (representing an
average of 20 percent of exports in peacetime). As for manufactures, they too
were predominantly oriented toward local market consumption, though Mexico did export to the rest of the Caribbean such royal monopoly products as
gunpowder and some finished jewelry and minted coins. In contrast the mining industry was almost exclusively oriented toward exports, with its output of
gold and silver accounting for 80 percent of the value of exports during any
peacetime year.[10]

It was thus mining and the export of precious metals that paid for the bulk of
viceregal imports of European textiles, manufactured goods, and comestibles.
So impressive were mineral exports that they accounted for two-thirds of total
world output and guaranteed that New Spain could maintain a consistently
positive balance of trade.[11]

While mining played such a predominant role in international trade, it was
less important in terms of generating income from royal taxation. Throughout
most of the eighteenth century, mining income made up only between 20 and
27 percent of total royal revenues. Moreover this was not a consistent pattern,
as both in the 1680s and in the 1780s and afterwards, its relative importance
dropped to half that amount. By the last fifth of the eighteenth century, in fact,
taxes on trade, agriculture, and commerce outdistanced mining taxes in importance for the royal treasury. Though clearly great fortunes were to be made
in mining, the crown evidently was unwilling to tax this industry too heavily.
Humboldt, in his detailed analysis of New Spain's mining industry, in fact estimates that the diezmo, *cobo*, and minting taxes took only some 15 percent of
the value of mine output, a figure he claimed was lower than was then the norm
for European miners.[12] Garner, in his studies of individual Zacatecas mines, estimated the rate at 12 percent for taxes and another 6 percent for royal mintage
charges.[13]

Trends for mining tax income differed from those for total royal tax revenues. Total viceregal mining tax receipts in the course of the seventeenth
century had a sustained period of growth, peaking in the last decade. They
stagnated in the first decade of the eighteenth century, but picked up more
quickly than total revenues, passing the level of the 1680s by the 1710s and
sustaining reasonable growth until the 1750s. In the 1760s came a temporary
drop in total mining revenues, due to short-term mercury and labor shortages,[14]
but a boom followed for the next two decades, with income in the 1780s five
and one-half times greater than that of the 1680s. In the next two decades, mine
income dropped by over one-fifth from its 1780s peak. Each of the periods of
crisis in mine tax revenues tended to reflect either crises in the supply of mercury, labor, or capital, or problems related to trade blockages as a result of international warfare (table 5.2).

Decade	México	Chihuahua	Guanajuato	Michoacán	Zacatecas	Rosario	Guadalaj.	Durango	S.L. Potosí	Pachuca	Bolaños	Zimapán	Sombrerete	TOTAL
1680-89	100,591		62,632		182,577		80,188	83,822	66,849	50,139			126,249	753,047
1690-99	67,757		84,516		109,660		76,199	69,598	79,224	75,117			73,372	635,444
1700-09	339,156		114,650		157,466		84,418	75,827	67,207	40,226			34,103	913,053
1710-19	437,042		120,902		239,187		78,581	179,673	60,616	86,444			21,283	1,223,728
1720-29	629,204		186,438		257,766		81,216	170,346	58,043	153,724		25,017	14,802	1,576,556
1730-39	1,096,788		280,190		237,268		96,208	201,032	66,328	93,569		26,761	53,110	2,151,254
1740-49	1,123,184		386,799		185,810		89,747	228,797	52,014	67,151		35,500	92,615	2,261,617
1750-59	1,416,122		326,331		196,475		94,871	212,056	151,181	115,862	282,947	56,254	28,956	2,881,055
1760-69	1,264,325		301,263		127,568		149,621	248,104	117,476	138,299	89,279	48,786	21,313	2,506,034
1770-79	2,199,446		485,329		224,061	69,651	135,807	214,250	162,295	109,191	88,623	72,684	51,667	3,813,004
1780-89	2,516,098	46,794	521,557	205	239,712	113,111	112,804	159,513	311,195	70,074	105,223	56,772	52,036	4,305,094
1790-99	2,231,592	44,210	591,342	2,068	264,962	193,811	99,695	211,211	359,165	81,160	48,782	60,225	99,930	4,288,153
1800-09	1,188,976	65,731	630,983	2,812	289,649	203,749	81,052	226,038	310,124	97,707	12,893	55,829	194,046	3,359,589

Table 5.2 Estimated Average Annual Income from Mining Taxes, Viceroyalty of New Spain, 1680–1809. (Source: Same as table 5.1)

Initially the treasury districts did not fully reflect the actual location of the mines. The central treasury of Mexico, which ranked fourth in mineral output, took the largest total of mine taxes. In this and in several other key tax categories, Mexico acted far more like a national treasury than a regional one, which was unusual for eighteenth century American treasuries. Even after new regional treasuries were established in the mining districts, there was often a long delay before many local taxes on mining and other activities were finally retained there. This was the case for those established after 1780. For most mining district treasuries, however, their relative ranking in recorded mine tax receipts reflects local mine production well, at least as portrayed in the very detailed 1780s listings reported by Humboldt.[15]

Strong regional variation was the norm in mine tax revenues, at least before the middle of the eighteenth century. Thus while the trend was one of steady growth for most of the eighteenth century (reflected for example in the mine tax receipts of the treasuries of Mexico and Guanajuato) the major production zone of Zacatecas experienced its own local boom and bust cycle at variance with viceregal trends. In turn Guanajuato suffered a crisis in production beginning in the 1750s, a decade earlier than most other treasuries. Among the smaller treasuries, the fluctuations were sui generis. Thus Pachuca experienced an unusual peak in taxes in the 1720s, only to go into a severe decline until the 1750s; while Guadalajara stagnated from 1700 to 1759. San Luis de Potosí, which had began, and would end, as a major producer of mine tax revenues, was a very small producer from 1710 to 1779. In each case these local treasuries were responding to the collapse of individual mines. As Humboldt and others noted, although there were several hundred mines working in each district, most of the production came from the largest half dozen or so enterprises. The collapse of any one of these larger units often had a dramatic effect on total revenues. Thus the tales of flooding and fires, which fill the history of mining in this period, tend to account for local fluctuations in given treasuries when these do not correspond to viceregal trends. What is worth noting is that the 1760s crisis was general throughout the major mining districts of the viceroyalty, although only Durango continued its decline into the next decade.

Until the 1780s income from mining taxes moved upward at a strong and rapid pace, but in the last twenty years of the century, the trend was toward stagnation and then decline. This was primarily due to the severe drop in revenues from the Mexican treasury, since those of the four leading producers (Guanajuato, Zacatecas, Durango, and San Luis Potosí) all continued to increase, with even formerly minor centers such as Sombrerete becoming a producer of mine tax revenues worth over 200,000 pesos. The decline of Mexico was sufficient to drop total mining revenues by 22 percent between the 1790s and the first decade of the nineteenth century.

As for the much debated question of the impact of royal fiscal and legal policies on mine production, the recent detailed local studies prove that this was not a major factor in influencing growth. Moreover, as Bakewell has shown, Mexico from the very beginning received the greatest tax concessions of any mining zone in America and probably never fully paid the quinto tax even in the seventeenth century.[16] In fact, along with tax abatements for the Mexican miners, the crown also provided extensive credit for mercury sales. If mining faltered, it was not the fault of government fiscal activity, but rather the dynamics of capital markets, international trade restrictions, and ore reserves that most affected local growth. The study of the Zacatecas mines, which showed that taxes and minting fees accounted for only 18 percent of total costs, indicated that extraction costs averaged from 40 to 50 percent of total expenditures. Constant local concessions or simple violations of local laws in turn meant that major changes in mining codes had little impact on local practice. In Zacatecas, for example, the move toward integration of mines for common drainage and production arrangements both violated standard laws on the size of holdings and also preceded the viceregal mining code of 1783, which would legitimate these developments. Thus royal fiscal reform tended to follow the changing structure of Mexican mining practice, rather than anticipating it. Only on the question of subsidized mercury prices and guaranteeing the free flow of exports was the role of the crown a major influence in mine production.[17]

In contrast to mine income, trade, agricultural, and commercial taxes tended to grow in quite close harmony with total revenues until 1800 (table 5.3). Regional variation in these trade taxes, however, was quite pronounced.[18] Here the key factor was the exogenous development of international warfare, which greatly affected international trade and in turn influenced the commercial and trade revenues that were generated by the key port of Veracruz. The trade tax income generated in the caja of Acapulco, however, tended to be relatively flat over most of the period and appeared little influenced by the dramatic trade crises caused by the European wars of the eighteenth and early nineteenth centuries. This was obviously due to its concentration in Pacific commerce, which was relatively immune to European-Atlantic events. Similarly neither international war nor the impact of the free trade decree of 1788 are very evident in the movement of trade taxes into Mexico's caja, whose income was generated largely from taxes on internal agriculture, commerce, and trade.

With regard to trade tax flows into the Veracruz treasury, however, Humboldt's hypothesis concerning the impact of both the free trade decree of 1788 and the European wars of the 1790s and early 1800s appear to hold. A long-term relative decline in this tax category, which began in the mid 1720s, finally began to reverse itself in the early 1770s, to rise dramatically after 1778. This growth was followed by a downturn during the French War of 1793–96 and an even greater decline during the disastrous English War of 1796–1802.[19] Without that warfare, it would appear from recent alternative figures taken from local port records in Veracruz and Spain, Mexican international trade was on the increase in the 1780s and 1790s. Taking Veracruz's exports to Spain in 1784 as a base (just after the end of the first English war), the value of these exports grew steadily, except during war years, and had almost doubled by 1796.[20] Though exports from Veracruz to Spain more than doubled in the interwar period from 1803 to 1805, much of this growth must have been based on pent-up

Table 5.3 Part I

Decade	México	Veracruz	Puebla	Chihuahua	Guanajuato	Rosario	Michoacán	Zacatecas	Saltillo	Oaxaca	Guadalaj.	Durango	S.L. Potosí	Acapulco	Arispe
1680-89	404,545	69,367			0			19,030			25,988	2,066	1,018	39,507	
1690-99	268,579	99,116			1,650			15,990			28,479	2,671	992	220,819	
1700-09	380,948	336,388			0			22,082			30,270	2,825	818	208,702	
1710-19	443,618	284,008			20,000			16,622			29,293	8,345	570	209,841	
1720-29	480,878	210,532			0			1,651			43,374	3,154	1,071	99,314	
1730-39	575,521	166,700			0			1,096			41,437	7,832	0	214,880	
1740-49	822,167	159,058			0			1,033			53,625	9,241	0	177,024	
1750-59	1,126,501	168,010			0			13,500			64,065	12,144	3,916	69,833	
1760-69	1,096,357	206,423			0			12,297			71,731	15,716	0	85,895	
1770-79	1,443,367	429,835			12,611	3,250		27,722			116,847	20,715	20,841	124,792	
1780-89	2,071,965	1,176,805	330,693	24,111	187,974	43,786	138,928	55,368			286,436	52,011	124,230	105,018	14,985
1790-99	3,052,035	918,354	312,385	43,480	175,840	66,084	169,638	78,309	28,006	99,501	238,606	62,136	98,953	137,753	13,411
1800-09	1,908,791	931,424	421,156	30,231	180,581	77,123	209,842	101,019	39,521	120,208	356,796	66,418	106,714	127,634	22,643

- II -

Decade	Pachuca	Bolaños	Mérida	Tabasco	Zimapán	Campeche	Sombrerete	Pr.Carmen	TOTAL
1680-89	0		5,828				12,665		580,014
1690-99	0		2,398				10,636		651,330
1700-09	0		2,617				8,274		992,924
1710-19	17,090		4,030			20,999	5,716		1,060,132
1720-29	0		3,428	1,746	0	21,016	4,104	0	870,268
1730-39	0		4,060	3,414	0	15,531	8,096	0	1,040,567
1740-49	0		5,012	2,618	0	15,809	9,711		1,255,298
1750-59	0	0	6,982	2,911	0	23,130	3,996		1,494,988
1760-69	0	11,746	7,258	4,725		23,660	0		1,535,808
1770-79	10,461	16,496	5,141	7,123	7,690	35,321	23,406	1,228	2,306,846
1780-89	23,411	21,534	9,157	6,252	13,511	61,724	20,308	7,489	4,775,696
1790-99	32,420	18,620	33,228	3,466	9,744	45,628	32,884	3,023	5,673,504
1800-09	21,943	2,200	61,835	9,863	6,295	54,775	44,015	5,387	4,906,414

Table 5.3 Estimated Average Annual Trade Tax Income in the Viceroyalty of New Spain, 1680–1809. (Source: Same as table 5.1)

demand, since the volume of exports from 1797 to 1801 were only around half of the 1796 figure. But by 1813 and 1814, again a relatively normal time for trade, the value of exports to Spain comfortably exceeded the 79 million peso level of 1796.[21] This fact would suggest that the royal government, despite all the exactions of the state in the previous two decades of the English War of 1805–8, did not destroy the Mexican economy or its ability to export large quantities of silver to Europe up until independence. Independence from Spain, however, was another issue, and after 1821 there was a severe decline in exports from Veracruz.[22]

Although some interior treasuries experienced severe declines in trade receipts in the 1790s, most interior treasuries and that of Mexico held firm, with the latter growing by almost a third, thus guaranteeing that total trade receipts actually increased in the decade of the 1790s. But the trend established by Veracruz in relationship to the impact of the English war soon showed itself in the receipts of Mexico and other treasuries. Despite the temporary reprieve in the period of the Peace of Amiens (1802–5), total receipts declined in the decade from 1800 to 1809, with Mexico alone dropping by 37 percent.

Another series of historical events analyzable through these trade tax records is the economic and fiscal impact of the Bourbon administrative reforms of the last quarter of the eighteenth century. These regional trade tax statistics show that with the reorganization of the royal treasury in the 1780s and 1790s, there was a notable growth in total trade revenues as well as a better regional distribution of these taxes. The fiscal reforms associated with the implementation of the intendant system of the 1780s were unqualifiedly of prime importance in expanding the collection of trade and commercial taxes in the older mining centers such as San Luis Potosí, Zacatecas, Durango, and Sombrerete, which had been negligible producers up until that time. New mining centers such as Rosario and Saltillo also contributed trade revenues on a significant scale. The creation of new treasury offices in such thriving agricultural, manufacturing, and commercial centers as Puebla, Michoacán, and Oaxaca increased total receipts considerably without diminishing the sums collected by the Mexico treasury. Finally some of the older centers, such as Guadalajara, grew at dramatic rates. Even the minor producers Mérida and Campeche experienced growth in this period, although the older agricultural and trade center of Tabasco continued to stagnate.

Before their early nineteenth century collapse, the growth in trade and commerce taxes had been so pronounced that this category finally became the single most important source of government income in the last two decades of the eighteenth century. In the decade of the 1780s, trade and commerce taxes already had passed mining taxes in total value. Then in the 1790s, as mining tax revenues stagnated, trade and commercial tax income grew by 24 percent, generating 1.4 million pesos more for the crown during this period than did mine income.[23]

Even more rapid in its growth in the late eighteenth century was the category of consumption taxes levied on royal monopoly products. To these were added such exotic estancos as the sale of snow from the mountains of the region. Finally the crown in the 1760s created a separate renta outside the framework of the royal exchequer to produce cigarettes and other tobacco products for monopoly sale to the colonial population.[24] By the last quarter of the century, this renta was producing approximately the same amount as the entire output of all other monopoly taxes, or on the order of 6 million pesos of gross income, a figure almost six times as large as the tobacco renta made in Peru.[25] But tobacco profits were never included in the general royal accounts and were sent separately to Spain by the administrator.

The movement of monopoly consumption income suffered more of a late seventeenth and early eighteenth century decline than did that of gross income (table 5.4). In the 1710s there was a turn in fortune as income again began to climb, passing the 1680s level in the next decade. This era of prosperity ended at midcentury, with income for the 1760s actually declining by 2 percent from that of the previous decade. The entire viceroyalty again witnessed growth of these revenues in the 1770s, which continued until a temporary decline occurred in the 1790s. While I have listed 6.9 million pesos as the total average income per annum for monopoly consumption receipts in the decade of the 1780s, this number should be treated with caution. Some 1.1 million pesos of the total is accounted for by two exceptional year listings for mercury receipts in the port of Veracruz, which in all its history only had such receipts for a total of five years, and in the other three years was of insignificant amounts. Excluding this mercury income from Veracruz would bring the total income for the 1780s more in line with the general growth pattern of the period for other major tax categories.

In terms of the treasuries that most influenced the total flow of monopoly income, it is obvious that Mexico here, as elsewhere, played an unusually important and transregional role. Although its relative importance varied considerably from decade to decade, it usually accounted for above half the total income. In the case of the other treasuries, there was a constant pattern of ebb and flow, and at various times such treasuries as Zacatecas, Rosario, Guanajuato, Puebla, and even San Luis Potosí, Chihuahua, and Guadalajara became vital producers of these funds.

Within each treasury the mix of incomes was quite different, with the importance of the traditional estancos differing from the liquor and mercury sales. Overall traditional estancos accounted for about half of all monopoly incomes, mercury for about 30 percent, and liquor sales for about 20 percent. These differences are explained by the nature of the local economy and population. Thus mercury accounted for over half of monopoly sales in the mining centers of Sombrerete, Bolanos, Pachuca, Durango, Guadalajara, Zacatecas, and Guanajuato. In turn traditional estancos accounted for over half of the revenues in such market and production towns as Mérida and Chihuahua, while liquor sales dominated in the Indian zones of Oaxaca, Campeche, and Puebla. What is most interesting, however, is the steady and almost universal nature of monopoly incomes. In all but four of the twenty-three treasuries, monopoly

Decade	México	Rosario	Saltillo	Veracruz	Puebla	Guanajuato	Zacatecas	Chihuahua	S.L. Potosí	Guadalaj.	Bolaños	Durango	Pachuca	Arispe	Oaxaca
1680-89	542,348			9,778		31,554	97,109		3,805	47,617		38,715	51,757		
1690-99	264,294			10,829		33,904	53,062		3,369	36,096		14,343	71,191		
1700-09	362,247			33,245		38,224	76,239		2,876	37,655		16,753	21,813		
1710-19	482,261			26,627		50,009	113,392		2,646	38,644		24,877	46,583		
1720-29	522,939			19,106		80,891	136,025		1,775	32,397		12,470	86,850		
1730-39	740,859			71,278		102,397	126,136		5,805	56,845		11,564	54,690		
1740-49	785,153			55,394		151,497	119,669		4,477	52,268		17,746	40,957		
1750-59	902,556			95,416		116,913	115,293		37,404	73,086	219,560	32,647	60,142		
1760-69	1,047,264			79,123		138,523	54,520		33,151	105,210	74,723	79,873	62,086		
1770-79	1,387,489	81,969		71,393		259,751	93,875		110,286	124,346	65,555	102,125	38,170		
1780-89	3,808,916	221,464		1,421,727	92,628	218,214	168,934	188,597	347,105	167,736	59,535	89,162	40,629	41,393	
1790-99	3,077,397	344,876	224,331	87,497	183,124	392,319	341,315	158,344	416,210	287,337	123,301	139,930	100,509	37,136	24,120
1800-09	2,463,694	340,340	239,551	73,162	181,332	647,369	371,801	163,431	284,838	217,862	31,503	174,020	47,727	55,360	54,914

-II-

Decade	Sombrerete	Michoacán	Campeche	Mérida	Acapulco	Zimapán	Tabasco	Pr.Carmen	TOTAL
1680-89	23,171			1,237	197				847,288
1690-99	14,710			591	206				502,595
1700-09	7,591			1,408	0				598,051
1710-19	5,141		14,857	1,746	0				806,783
1720-29	3,353		14,999	959	0	0	0		911,764
1730-39	18,557		24,026	471	1,520	0	0		1,214,148
1740-49	44,441		18,901	544	236,479	0	0		1,527,526
1750-59	17,635		14,418	1,130	171	124	0		1,686,495
1760-69	7,367		20,826	1,032	189	1,256	0		1,705,143
1770-79	11,549		16,960	1,134	22,495	14,964	0	0	2,402,061
1780-89	15,433	10,501	12,207	29,384	34,618	6,275	648	2,330	6,977,436
1790-99	95,577	19,416	12,612	33,045	34,849	22,985	1,616	4,620	6,162,466
1800-09	53,494	34,610	14,203	36,261	43,852	3,895	1,534	4,070	5,538,823

Table 5.4 Estimated Average Annual Monopoly Tax Incomes for the Viceroyalty of New Spain, 1680–1809. (Source: Same as table 5.1)

consumption taxes provided important and steady royal incomes. Thus along with commercial and trade taxes, monopoly consumption taxes were the most widely distributed in the viceroyalty. Moreover while many of the former taxes were concentrated in the central treasury of Mexico, despite their regional origin, monopoly taxes seem to have been collected almost everywhere.

Unlike the other major taxes so far examined, the tribute head tax on Indian males was much more highly concentrated regionally (table 5.5).[26] By the end of the seventeenth century, the tax regions in the northern part of the viceroyalty were rather complex in their social makeup, with mestizos and landless and noncommunity Indians making up the majority of the population. It was only the central and southern zones, the old core area of the Aztec empire, where the majority of the settled Indian peasant communities could be found, which provided the bulk of royal tribute monies. Until the creation of separate treasury offices, the income from Puebla and Oaxaca poured into Mexico, which until the 1730s accounted for over 90 percent of these revenues. Guadalajara, which was the second most important treasury in terms of this tax, accounted for an average of only 5 percent of total collections. Even with the creation of the cajas of Michoacán and Puebla in the 1780s, and of the crucial one of Oaxaca in the 1790s, the role of Mexico remained predominant, although it now accounted for less than half of total tribute receipts.

The surprising sensitivity of Indian population to general economic trends is well revealed in the high correlation between tribute income and total revenues. Until the 1780s Indian tribute monies averaged between 5 and 8 percent of total income. The tribute tax proved equally immune to crises in international trade and regional mine production and continued to grow until the Hidalgo rebellion of 1810.

Toward the end of the eighteenth century, a previously insignificant tax category rose to prominence in the viceroyalty of New Spain. This was the category of forced and voluntary loans and other special emergency taxes related to supporting the increasingly bankrupt imperial treasury. With the onset of the long series of protracted European wars, the first with England from 1779 to 1783, but especially those after 1790, first with France (1793–95) and then again with England (1796–1802, 1805–8), the hard-pressed Spanish crown sought to raise new revenues through a series of forced and voluntary loans. It even went to the extreme of nationalizing church properties in an attempt to pay for its increasing deficits. As I have shown elsewhere, the expenses of the Spanish crown in local and imperial activities, even during times of peace, left little margin for new activities and expenditures, especially the costs involved in protracted international conflict.[27] While the first imperial war with England and that with France could be fought with temporary loans, voluntary contributions, and special war taxes, all such sources had been exhausted by the late 1790s, and the crown was forced to undertake new measures to tax personal and institutional savings, first in the metropolis and then in the colonies. This led, for example, to the absorption of the private treasuries of benevolent and religious societies, which were forced to deposit their capital with the crown

Decade	México	Puebla	Oaxaca	Michoacán	Mérida	Guadalaj.	Tabasco	S.L. Potosí	Guanajuato	Pachuca	Acapulco	Campeche	Rosario
1680-89	275,451				2,643	7,296		57	0	0	5,230	0	0
1690-99	161,339				1,329	11,833		11	0	0	3,817	0	0
1700-09	292,530				1,405	15,046		0	0	0	699	0	0
1710-19	346,803				2,406	15,046		0	0	536	533	1,992	0
1720-29	385,564				4,219	19,053	2,184	0	0	410	1,173	8,807	0
1730-39	437,645				6,386	18,709	2,274	0	8,777	0	0	4,620	0
1740-49	607,757				12,738	9,538	2,218	0	0	0	694	2,254	0
1750-59	706,038				48,665	34,879	4,594	0	0	0	1,004	1,628	0
1760-69	659,171				33,728	38,827	4,130	15,473	9,120	0	5,482	2,210	0
1770-79	834,229				9,895	48,665	2,950	16,029	3,904	0	0	1,958	1,638
1780-89	771,610	79,326		46,822	70,948	60,547	3,852	18,199	3,346	0	2,836	7,696	5,655
1790-99	651,085	186,859	185,226	88,366	142,663	82,769	6,673	36,103	87,089	40,230	21,888	15,935	9,777
1800-09	737,885	254,418	264,638	96,175	157,514	100,577	8,242	53,189	120,594	52,293	16,231	20,129	12,014

-II-

Decade	Veracruz	Zimapán	Zacatecas	Pr.Carmen	TOTAL
1680-89	0	0	2,668		293,345
1690-99	9,283	0	1,809		189,421
1700-09	9,800	0	2,250		321,730
1710-19	8,358	0	6,388		382,062
1720-29	5,471	0	7,099	0	433,979
1730-39	6,844	0	7,388	0	492,643
1740-49	6,873	0	12,486		654,558
1750-59	1,572	0	8,290		806,670
1760-69	4,737	0	9,332		782,210
1770-79	7,365	0	11,213	798	938,644
1780-89	2,003	0	30,083	782	1,103,705
1790-99	60,084	12,390	9,968	1,268	1,638,373
1800-09	48,751	15,733	26,433	1,407	1,986,223

Table 5.5   Estimated Average Annual Tribute Income for the Viceroyalty of New Spain, 1680–1809. (Source: Same as table 5.1)

treasury, in return for receiving interest on their monies. By the first decade of the nineteenth century, this source alone (listed variously as "imposición y . . . rendición") yielded over 8 million pesos. Also many new loans, taxes, and sales of offices and honors were promoted by the crown in the next two decades, all of which swelled royal coffers enormously. Whereas loans and grants from private sources amounted to only some 900,000 pesos per annum in the 1780s (table 5.6), they jumped to 6.6 million per annum in the 1790s and 21.6 million by the first decade of the new century. A host of miscellaneous war and special taxes also became extremely important sources for royal revenues.[28] These other miscellaneous new taxes, which brought in an annual average of 400,000 pesos in the 1770s (table 5.7), climbed to 1.7 million pesos in the 1780s, 7.8 million in the 1790s, and 21.3 million in the decade from 1800 to 1809.

It should also be stressed that not all of these forced loans were fully collected, and one of the most complex analytical tasks is to detail the flow of these funds into the treasury offices. There is also evidence that the royal treasury found itself in the unenviable position of owing some 80 million pesos to Mexican institutions and citizens by 1816, as a result of these special loans and grants.[29] Adding to the investigative difficulties is that their movement to Europe and other American treasuries can only be traced through a more detailed examination of the expenditure side of royal treasury account books. These two tasks have been undertaken recently by a group of Mexican scholars, who show how the consulado and other semiprivate corporate groups were forcibly incorporated into the process and how these special funds were distributed to other American treasuries, as well as to Europe.[30] But all this activity was at the expense of the efficiency of the taxing authority and was designed to mortgage future revenues that the crown might hope to obtain. The whole system became so complex that by the early decades of the nineteenth century, the very administration of the royal treasuries was beginning to break down, and the keeping of accurate treasury accounts became ever more difficult.[31]

This uncertainty concerning the new revenue figures (principally the extraordinary sums for loans and miscellaneous taxes) makes it difficult to rely on total treasury income figures from the income side of the ledger after 1790 until more detailed local treasury office research is undertaken in both the income and expenditure accounts listed in the *libros manuales*.

However much was actually collected from these new and special taxes and loans, there is little question that their volume caused a fundamental shift in the basis of royal tax policy in the Viceroyalty of New Spain. Whereas production, trade, monopoly consumption, and tribute taxes had formed the basis of royal income prior to 1780, after that date loans and new miscellaneous special taxes became the new mainstay, accounting for 31 percent of total revenues in the 1790s and 65 percent of all income by the first decade of the nineteenth century. This change meant that the crown had shifted its tax base from production and consumption to taxing the private savings of individuals and institutions. The result of this policy was temporarily but dramatically to increase

Decade	México	Veracruz	Durango	Acapulco	Guadalaj.	Zacatecas	Arispe	Bolaños	Chihuahua	Campeche	Guanajuato	Michoacán	Mérida	Oaxaca	Puebla
1680-89	134,052	0	0	15,677	1,297	436					0		0		
1690-99	28,669	0	411	19,791	1,439	1,202					0		0		
1700-09	66,120	98,660	617	1,648	3,036	16,400					0		0		
1710-19	45,850	3,784	472	4,883	6,095	425				0	0		0		
1720-29	7,458	28,000	1,797	0	11,667	63,499				0	860		0		
1730-39	2,887	0	1,772	0	1,609	0				0	0		0		
1740-49	152,299	23,713	5,510	17,291	6,488	12,551				0	0		9,259		
1750-59	17,597	0	2,032	10,790	10,000	0		1,000		0	0		0		
1760-69	8,299	3,858	0	0	1,932	0		0		0	0		0		
1770-79	505		0	0	0	0	0	0		6,135	0		0		
1780-89	618,131	64,102	4,920	2,334	151,534	822	3,643		0	23,702	0	0	1,634		
1790-99	5,786,523	241,532	13,425	4,934	177,298	11,566	2,548	1,384	15,473	4,892	62,634	81,798	23,392	48,403	123,256
1800-09	21,337,680	65,704	3,582	44,454	55,832	8,861	882	20	7,901	5,310	22,847	5,612	15,352	3,929	22,930

-II-

Decade	Pachuca	Pr.Carmen	Rosario	S.L. Potosí	Sombrerete	Saltillo	Tabasco	Zimapán	TOTAL
1680-89	0			0	0	0			151,462
1690-99	0			1,233	0				52,745
1700-09	0			571	0				187,052
1710-19	0			6,000	0		0	0	67,509
1720-29	0			0	0		0	0	113,281
1730-39	0			0	0		0		6,268
1740-49	0			0	0		0	0	227,111
1750-59	0			0	0		0		41,419
1760-69	0			0	0		0		14,089
1770-79	0	0	0	0	20	0	0	0	6,660
1780-89	1,826	114	9,924	0	3,687	0	1,669	4,945	892,987
1790-99	3,574	15,607	2,643	2,497	16,502	5,220	995	1,278	6,647,374
1800-09	174	6,975	3,171	908	4,442	17,252	1,349	147	21,635,314

Table 5.6 Estimated Annual Average Loans and Situados Income for the Viceroyalty of New Spain, by Treasury Office, 1680–1809. Source: (Same as table 5.1)

Decade	México	Veracruz	Acapulco	Campeche	Durango	Guadalaj.	Guanajuato	Sombrerete	Zacatecas	S.L. Potosí	Puebla	Pt.Carmen	Pachuca	Chihuahua	Michoacán
1680-89	26,440	3,372	1,656		31	3,544	203	1,803	8,615	893			209		
1690-99	28,069	0	2,017		77	268	2,946	172	270	5,722			921		
1700-09	81,376	1,782	1,572		1,367	241	1,868	1,288	4,586	418			281		
1710-19	127,545	11010	9,489	246	2,856	4,410	4,607	915	10,391	1,077			182		
1720-29	149,058	7848	35,662	1,630	2,642	10,886	3,520	449	4,335	449		0	292		
1730-39	61,597	5,084	9,182		73	1,673	119	205	416	47		0	97		
1740-49	91,903	23,743	27,460	1,481	98	5,169	429	4,893	41	39			144		
1750-59	36,791	4,360	7,078	10,038	1,255	3,780	390	162	0	291			722		
1760-69	134,218	27,040	4,060	7,556	72	1,739	5,087	81	0	760			245		
1770-79	64,646	96,981	29,408	35,390	624	6,602	2,333	96	1,510	35,427		78,704	63		
1780-89	232,279	1,269,242	15,778	60,902	3,808	14,649	3,976	149	47,966		17,133	77,951	181	17,033	16,755
1790-99	1,288,467	6,275,460	13,476	42,828	3,572	17,688	10,674	2,105	6,709	12,892	10,202	61,007	342	8,867	24,025
1800-09	4,367,996	16,470,332	29,712	20,469	8,288	18,555	13,026	10,579	21,570	13,944	92,090	122,537	1,764	9,220	23,392

-II-

Decade	Mérida	Zimapán	Arispe	Bolaños	Tabasco	Saltillo	Rosario	Oaxaca	TOTAL
1680-89	324								47,090
1690-99	0								40,462
1700-09	0								94,779
1710-19	4,266								176,994
1720-29	4,407	0			102				221,280
1730-39	966	0							79,459
1740-49	2,017				0				157,417
1750-59	1,743	293		91	124				67,118
1760-69	1,862	20		59	1,373				184,172
1770-79	352	2,240		1,055	120		7,870		361,911
1780-89	5,133	10	1,879	140	556		1,127		1,788,157
1790-99	38,335	608	1,323	606	3,277	5,900	3,662	3,379	7,835,404
1800-09	52,456	986	1,968	480	1,273	40,517	7,636	2,565	21,331,355

Table 5.7   Estimated Average Annual Miscellaneous Income in the Viceroyalty of New Spain, by Treasury Office, 1680–1809. (Source: Same as table 5.1)

Decade	Mines	Trade	Tribute	Monopoly	Loans	Miscl.	TOTAL
1680-89	100	100	100	100	100	100	100
1690-99	84	112	65	59	35	89	98
1700-09	121	171	110	71	123	201	119
1710-19	163	188	131	96	45	378	151
1720-29	209	155	148	108	75	472	169
1730-39	286	179	168	143	4	169	211
1740-49	300	216	223	180	150	334	278
1750-59	383	258	275	199	27	143	328
1760-69	333	265	267	201	9	391	328
1770-79	506	398	320	283	4	769	458
1780-89	572	823	376	824	590	3797	833
1790-99	569	978	559	727	4389	16639	1261
1800-09	446	846	677	654	14284	45299	1784

Table 5.8   Relative Growth of Major Income Categories and Total Income for the Viceroyalty of New Spain, 1680–1809 (Base=1680–89). (Source: Same as table 5.1.) Notes: "Total" figure used here comes from table 5.2 and includes loans and new taxes.

royal revenues, at the cost of long-term capital savings and ultimately of the economic well-being of the colony.

The volume of these new taxes also seriously eroded the relative importance of the older production taxes, which grew at far different rates from the special war-related taxes and loans (table 5.8). From all indices of growth of the major production and commerce tax categories, it is evident that the Mexican economy was slowing, if not stagnating, at the end of the eighteenth century, just as these new tax revenues began to increase drastically. This reflects increasing distancing of royal revenues from their economic underpinnings and a rising fiscal pressure on the local economy. Such a policy could not go on indefinitely, however, and the collapse of the royal exchequer in a series of bankruptcies, the invasion of Spain by France, and the effective protest of the local elite finally forced the crown to abandon most of these special taxes, as well as its attempt to nationalize the properties and capital of the American church.[32] Given the poor quality of royal tax records after 1810, it is difficult to estimate fully the effects of this reversal of post-1780 royal fiscal policy.[33] Actual production of silver, a major indicator of the export capacity of the economy, clearly did decline markedly from the peak output figures of the 1790s. By the 1820s output was less than half that of the previous maximum, a level not achieved again until late in the 1870s.[34]

Excluding special incomes of the period from 1780 to 1809, what can the changing pattern evident in total revenue flows and the movement of revenues in various categories of taxes tell us about general trends within the viceregal economy of New Spain by the end of the eighteenth century? There was obviously a late eighteenth century pause in colonial growth, with several historians suggesting that the agricultural crisis of 1784–86 marks the slow-down of an economy that had been in rapid expansion since the 1760s. All the major production, trade, and consumption tax incomes tended to stagnate or decline in the 1790s and to decline more rapidly in the first decade of the new century. Only tribute income, based directly on the continued growth of the Indian communal landowning population, continued, like total incomes, to increase at an uninterrupted pace to the end of the period. All evidence to date suggests that these taxes reflected real growth in the economy and the population and kept pace with both. This was also the opinion of Humboldt and al-most all later commentators. This dominant perspective has been challenged for Mexico by Claude Morin. He argues that the 1760s reforms of Gálvez gen-erated new growth in viceregal tax revenues before that growth actually took place in the economy itself. But in fact he offers little supporting evidence to establish this contrary case.[35] A more sophisticated restatement of this posi-tion is offered by Pérez Herrero, who though accepting growth in population and production in the late eighteenth century, still feels that fiscal pressure and severe inflation wiped out real growth. Here again, however, systematic supporting evidence of prices, production, and population figures is missing.[36]

But a variation of the argument that taxes increased faster than production or population and led to increasing fiscal oppression by the late eighteenth century Spanish state has recently been made on the basis of these royal tax revenues. In an early controversial essay, Juan Carlos Garavaglia and Juan Car-los Grosso argued that revenues from alcabalas in the last quarter of the eigh-teenth century grew faster than the growth in the local economy.[37] Recently this same theme has been taken up by Carlos Marichal on the basis of the post-1780 rise in importance of loans and other special exactions and the relative stagnation by the 1790s of the income generated from traditional trade and mining sources of tax revenues.[38] He also suggests in a more recent work that the remittances to Castile and the sending of silver to the Caribbean and other regions as subsidies constantly increased in the eighteenth century, but at a pace considerably faster than the total silver minted in New Spain. These ex-ports of royal silver outside the viceroyalty increased in a steady manner from an annual average 17 percent of minted silver in the decade of the 1720s to over 40 percent in the decade of the 1780s and 1790s.[39]

It is possible that the crown could not extract as much tax income in the early half of the century as in the latter half. But the fact that total volume of tax income increased by over a third in each of the last three decades being studied obviously cannot be explained by a corresponding growth in population and economy. Thus the period after 1790 would seem to offer a special case where the fiscal oppression thesis might hold. It still remains to be seen, however, whether these new funds were generated through "excessive" taxation of the population as a whole or only exploited the local wealth that had been idled by the war, temporarily diverting these funds into the special war loans. As has been pointed out by Carlos Marichal, the wars did cause a closing of interna-tional commerce and a general stagnation in the local economy, which undoubtedly freed large sums for loans. The fact that the crown repaid the first patriotic loan of 1783 in only two to three years, at the standard rates of interest, encouraged merchants and corporations to invest heavily in the loans of the 1790s, which only began to go bad in the first decades of the new century.[40]

But it has also been suggested that the crown extracted resources from the classes that could least afford them. One indication is the rather cavalier way in which royal officials stripped funds from the local Indian community treasuries (*cajas de comunidad*), which were a major source of savings for these communities, and used them to purchase government bonds or to provide patriotic donations. It is also seen in the long list of poor artisans and workers who provided patriotic "loans" to the government throughout the 1790s.[41] Was there then an economic crisis created by crown loan revenues in the 1790s and early 1800s, or were all these exceptional tax revenues just absorbing large quantities of excess and available capital in the colony? Would it have been possible to pay off the loans if the metropolitan government had not collapsed in 1808? Or were some of these new revenues paper funds that were never fully collected by the crown? At this stage in the analysis of royal treasury accounts, it is not possible to provide definite answers to these crucial questions. Nevertheless the vitality of post-1808 trade exports from Veracruz, discussed above, suggests that the Mexican economy was still producing at the peak levels of the late eighteenth century in the second decade of the nineteenth century. This would imply that royal exactions in the local capital market and the crisis of state finances were not as overwhelmingly devastating as some have suggested.

Available figures do, however, make it possible to answer the question of whether the inhabitants of New Spain were excessively taxed. In order to do so, it is necessary to include in this study two other sources of tax revenues not included in the treasury accounts. The first is the church tithes, or diezmos, collected on the harvest of Spanish- and mestizo-owned farm products and paid directly to the church. This came to approximately 1.8 million pesos per annum in the 1780s.[42] The second is the previously discussed monopoly on the manufacture and sale of tobacco products by the crown. In the decade of the 1780s, the tobacco renta averaged an annual 6.2 million pesos of gross income, of which 3.1 million was clear profit for the crown. A significant share of this 50 percent profit should be considered as a tax on consumption, since normal profits in this period from such an enterprise would probably not have exceeded 10 percent.[43] Thus the renta was one of the crown's most remunerative taxing activities and was worth at least 2.8 million pesos of taxable income, all of which went directly to Spain without passing through the royal treasury in the viceroyalty.

Adding these new funds to the treasury totals (and accepting Humboldt's previously cited estimates on the total value of output in mining, agriculture, trade, and commerce), it would appear that at a rough estimate royal taxes took between 15 and 20 percent of the total value in any one year in each of these categories. This figure compares quite favorably with estimates of mining tax ratios found in the works of Humboldt and contemporary scholars.[44] It would also appear to be a rate that Humboldt, at least, found to be a reasonable one by the standards of his time. As far as Humboldt could determine, the only really negative effects of tax policies arose from arbitrary minting fees and the problems of international trade and discriminatory taxes against English manufactures; the latter encouraged contraband trade. While estimates of such trade are always hazardous, Humboldt probably was quite close with his guess of illegal trade of 4 to 5 million pesos during times of peace and possibly 6 to 7 million pesos during times of war. This would represent roughly one-fourth of the total value of exports at the end of the eighteenth century.[45]

Expenditures

If the new tax burden could be reasonably born by the local economy, what profit in fact did the crown make from its Mexican taxation and what costs did it incur in extracting these monies? To begin with, were the crown's expenditures tied to its income in Mexico as in the rest of the empire? All calculations comparing income and expenditures over time, in fact, show a consistently high correlation between the two categories.[46] Moreover among the cajas, the major producers of income were at the same time the major disbursers of these funds. Here as well the central treasury of Mexico, located in the City of Mexico, on average accounted for over half of total viceregal expenses, with Veracruz absorbing about 27 percent (table 5.9).

The crown expended these funds locally for the same activities as it did in the two other colonies under examination here. Administrative expenses absorbed a surprisingly small percentage of total expenditures (on the order of 3 percent of total revenues), a figure low even compared to Peru and Charcas (table 5.10). Average expenditures in individual cajas were also relatively low. In the central treasury of Mexico, the rate was but 4 percent. The exceptional case is Veracruz, where administration costs accounted for an astonishingly low 1 percent of total expenditures. Finally expenditures of collections within individual ramos also tended to be quite reduced and very steady throughout the late eighteenth and early nineteenth centuries.[47]

Expenditures associated with collecting individual taxes in the viceroyalty as a whole, however, did show some variation. Overall a survey carried out by royal officials for the quinquennium of 1795–99 found that the crown expended 10 percent of gross receipts on salaries and another 10 percent for administrative costs, leaving 80 percent of rents available for use by the crown as it deemed fit. But mining and minting taxes took a higher than average percentage of funds for salaries and administrative costs, while trade and tribute taxes were generally obtained with less than the average expenditures, the latter amounting to just 7 percent. The famous tobacco rents, which involved the crown in actual production expenditures, still cost only some 29 percent of total gross income to run.

Given that total costs were at most 20 percent of collections (including salary, administrative, building, and maintenance costs), it is not surprising

Table 5.9 — Part 1

Decade	México	Veracruz	Acapulco	Arispe	Bolaños	Chihuahua	Campeche	Durango	Guadalaj.	Guanajuato	Michoacán	Mérida	Zacatecas	Oaxaca	Puebla
1680-89	2,674,638	1,023,248	224,420					129,579	218,813	95,158		18,922	430,442		
1690-99	1,805,868	785,660	223,834					90,303	162,232	121,853		7,848	183,687		
1700-09	2,195,937	1,838,904	251,768					115,774	187,711	154,596		11,014	296,170		
1710-19	2,643,842	1,807,888	300,451				61,615	244,000	195,193	177,749		25,543	451,747		
1720-29	3,042,802	1,998,144	224,430				64,030	218,432	246,524	269,853		25,496	515,375		
1730-39	4,169,738	3,272,794	226,965				67,283	246,885	326,938	444,299		19,815	414,644		
1740-49	5,023,747	4,291,155	241,919				55,374	325,260	223,074	586,320		39,022	354,327		
1750-59	5,751,526	4,424,561	221,542		620,366		21,559	297,554	331,828	462,202		108,338	324,266		
1760-69	6,329,928	4,491,133	251,924		236,898		177,584	400,122	394,997	578,952		72,328	205,529		
1770-79	8,490,901	6,019,351	352,396		215,713		166,235	588,088	505,966	907,581		106,202	349,697		
1780-89	13,280,287	12,320,640	434,413	260,794	225,927	600,213	399,952	610,637	825,227	1,012,171	423,292	200,803	495,310		1,027,578
1790-99	23,443,257	13,656,738	688,914	243,718	250,712	993,163	364,149	800,677	1,178,999	1,246,242	552,191	411,022	1,478,390	423,140	1,042,499
1800-09	45,025,367	10,481,693	734,949	335,639	74,010	1,019,334	479,065	709,425	1,117,828	1,499,559	562,307	415,864	2,103,555	434,253	1,573,962

-II-

Table 5.9 — Part 2

Decade	Pachuca	Rosario	S.L. Potosí	Sombrerete	Zimapán	Saltillo	Tabasco	Pr.Carmen	TOTAL
1680-89	102,781		93,122						5,011,123
1690-99	147,538		96,933	81,973					3,707,728
1700-09	87,233		78,571	47,621					5,265,298
1710-19	135,251		82,852	43,703					6,169,834
1720-29	252,808		79,696	25,820	33,023		3,492		7,047,728
1730-39	237,142		93,040	84,622	41,947		3,732	47,802	9,697,646
1740-49	87,027		62,972	140,764	45,728		1,212	47,802	11,477,901
1750-59	275,569		274,709	49,544	56,908		1,844		13,222,316
1760-69	272,144		163,779	32,088	51,584		5,813		13,664,803
1770-79	201,184	238,468	336,273	82,024	103,988		5,149	167,677	18,836,893
1780-89	155,868	440,972	868,767	90,361	92,678		11,374	118,865	33,896,129
1790-99	751,557	1,125,935	946,502	425,858	118,615	380,752	19,602	167,677	50,710,309
1800-09	857,269	854,758	822,604	619,562	86,675	530,389	20,168	204,440	70,562,675

Table 5.9 Estimated Average Annual Total Expenditures for the Viceroyalty of New Spain, by Treasury Office, 1680–1809 (in pesos a 8). (Source: Same as table 5.1)

Decade	México	Veracruz	Zacatecas	Acapulco	Durango	Guadalaj.	Guanajuato	Pachuca	S.L. Potosí	Sombrerete	Mérida	Campeche	Bolaños	Arispe	Chihuahua
1680-89	159,202	7,266	37,509	6,343	15,541	60,536	3,259	2,999	2,115	5,585	10,329				
1690-99	166,177	6,851	31,932	7,325	23,032	53,848	3,266	3,088	3,260	3,571	5,260				
1700-09	170,123	7,339	29,012	8,401	11,462	111,573	4,017	2,286	2,940	5,019	5,984				
1710-19	175,244	9,614	45,070	5,775	12,503	111,304	2,743	4,370	1,078	1,954	5,555	0			
1720-29	126,590	9,745	17,925	6,846	10,497	78,411	3,946	3,386	0	1,613	5,646	0			
1730-39	138,323	9,748	6,970	7,133	4,438	31,842	3,191	2,590	0	2,347	5,124	0			
1740-49	199,888	16,114	6,528	11,541	5,936	31,513	2,993	2,605	3,768	3,063	7,770	0			
1750-59	218,329	14,303	6,110	7,188	5,505	33,340	4,216	3,171	0	4,687	10,149	115	6,630		
1760-69	238,764	21,106	9,551	8,756	6,412	24,640	4,664	3,897	4,037	3,827	14,241	1,061	8,872		
1770-79	276,777	48,419	8,254	7,144	11,377	32,914	6,941	6,532	5,339	3,029	12,609	2,174	10,192		
1780-89	288,829	82,774	14,783	8,952	17,078	39,651	9,957	5,229	8,638	3,866	19,083	7,401	8,284	18,402	6,784
1790-99	555,174	118,037	18,393	137,228	24,589	50,050	18,694	6,571	18,447	5,552	19,178	9,993	8,189	22,833	16,358
1800-09	2,434,556	76,097	19,287	164,244	15,939	49,802	18,787	5,059	14,375	6,752	20,521	10,127	5,575	12,066	22,230

Decade	Michoacán	Puebla	Oaxaca	Zimapán	Tabasco	Pr.Carmen	Rosario	Saltillo	TOTAL
1680-89									310,682
1690-99									307,610
1700-09									358,156
1710-19									375,210
1720-29				1,587	464	0			266,656
1730-39				1,598	465	0			213,769
1740-49				1,701	913				294,333
1750-59				4,197	465				318,405
1760-69				3,248	569				353,645
1770-79				3,582	983	70,101	8,044		514,411
1780-89	16,158	16,716		4,253	1,739	66,074	15,477		660,128
1790-99	14,581	18,340	19,975	5,127	11,035	22,068	9,940	4,393	1,134,745
1800-09	12,822	19,250	20,009	3,905	14,200	3,367	8,138	11,485	2,968,593

Table 5.10 Estimated Average Annual Administrative Costs for the Viceroyalty of New Spain, 1680–1809. (Source: Same as table 5.1)

that of the average annual 20 million pesos the crown was collecting in this second half of the 1790s, it was able to ship to Spain 6.4 million pesos per annum and spend another 5 million on situados to the Caribbean and Pacific outposts. Of these the four largest recipients were Cuba (at 2.5 million pesos per annum), the Philippines (734,000 pesos), Santo Domingo (620,000 pesos), and Louisiana (525,000 pesos).[48]

In contrast to its relatively low administrative expenses, Mexico spent far more on "war" expenditures—some 31 percent of its total expenditures. The bulk of these funds were spent on situados for maintaining forts in mainland America and in the Caribbean islands and even the Philippines. These expenses were concentrated as to treasury office, with the cajas of Mexico and Veracruz accounting for 89 percent of all such expenses (table 5.11). In fact the port of Veracruz here played an extraordinary role, spending almost as much as the central treasury of Mexico on such needs in absolute terms, and a much higher relative share of its local costs (50 percent for Veracruz vs. just 29 percent overall for the central treasury of Mexico). This was after all the treasury that provided most of the situados for maintaining the frontier forts. In addition to these steady basic costs, there was also a close correlation between military expenditures and international conflicts, as the sharp rise of such payments in the last quarter of the nineteenth century shows. In the 1780s particularly, there was a very steep rise in situado expenses for the Caribbean, as the crown undertook a major military initiative during the wars of the American Revolution to retake lost colonies from the English.[49] In the late 1790s, for example, the crown spent 3.4 million pesos per annum on military salaries alone and another 1 million for armaments; these 4.4 million pesos per annum accounted for 22 percent of total gross incomes, in addition to the 5 million per annum being paid as situados.[50]

But in one fundamental way, the Viceroyalty of New Spain in the eighteenth century differed from the other regions. Not only did it maintain regional military outposts and missionary frontiers along with deficitory but geographically important treasuries, it was also the largest exporter of surplus revenues to the metropolis, including large silver payments to the Philippines (see table 2.1). These latter funds were used to help pay for the deficitory trade Spain maintained with Asian exporters of textiles and porcelains. In short the crown took great profit out of this extraordinary mining and agricultural colony.

Given the very heavy costs of maintaining a defensive fortified frontier in the north and the Caribbean, of subsidizing most of the economies of the Spanish islands,[51] and of maintaining a major bureaucracy and military presence within the viceregal provinces themselves, it is amazing just how much the crown was able to ship home.[52] Humboldt estimated that in the period from 1796 to 1801, the government shipped an average of 8 to 9 million pesos per annum in its own name to Spain.[53] While this sum was only a minority of total royal revenues from all sources, it is still impressive. These government silver exports represented well over a third of the value of all silver and gold exports from the viceroyalty and made up more than three-quarters of Indies income

Table I

Decade	México	Veracruz	Acapulco	Arispe	Bolaños	Chihuahua	Durango	Guadalaj.	Guanajuato	Zacatecas	Campeche	Michoacán	Mérida	Oaxaca	Puebla
1680-89	360,022	199,169	19,952				43,631	0	0	49,556			0		
1690-99	281,061	399,369	21,799				44,873	77,297	0	102,352			0		
1700-09	696,725	654,293	26,584				41,020	0	35,816	113,879					
1710-19	600,362	602,140	13,581				67,356	77,297	24,374	113,818	61,615		11,898		
1720-29	1,375,540	824,117	22,579				65,635	0	89,124	206,829	62,920		4,600		
1730-39	1,857,751	1,043,565	15,164				0	0	0	0	67,283		6,997		
1740-49	3,337,192	2,514,591	21,255				0	2,935	0	0	51,228		10,805		
1750-59	3,848,991	2,284,067	14,442		0		0	0	0	0	2,527		11,506		
1760-69	4,172,429	3,020,237	13,691		0		0	6,387	5,358	0	133,372		9,868		
1770-79	5,817,519	4,026,151	29,165		0		201,351	14,717	1,789	0	142,164		32,316		
1780-89	7,527,074	6,981,007	91,016	204,582	601	381,644	185,776	191,401	2,655	0	217,567	405	74,959		90,629
1790-99	3,345,986	5,936,763	57,742	204,490	4,443	452,108	181,554	285,240	12,494	3,210	152,562	9,733	110,974	5,596	160,649
1800-09	2,840,801	4,574,365	56,472	225,639	1,789	470,219	2,115	342,347	36,135	3,665	230,982	22,708	121,372	10,901	142,025

-II-

Decade	Pachuca	Rosario	S.L. Potosí	Sombrerete	Pr.Carmen	Saltillo	Tabasco	Zimapán	TOTAL
1680-89	0	0	574	52,186					725,090
1690-99	0	0	2,409	73,839					1,002,997
1700-09	0	0	9278	32,428					1,610,025
1710-19	0	0	0	16,893					1,589,334
1720-29	0	0	0	16,400	42,460		0		2,710,204
1730-39	0	0	0	0	42,460		0		3,033,220
1740-49	0	0	0	0			0		5,938,006
1750-59	0	0	0	0			0		6,161,533
1760-69	1,376	0	8,808	0			0		7,371,526
1770-79	7,662	86,166	94,722	0	5,614		0		10,459,336
1780-89	8,696	109,999	300,155	0	14,059		7,985		16,390,210
1790-99	0	31,606	181,000	0	51,693	362,726	9,228		11,559,797
1800-09	0	24,648	31,885	0	91,717	45,822	0		9,275,607

Table 5.11 Estimated Average Annual War Expenditures in the Viceroyalty of New Spain, 1680–1809. (Source: Same as table 5.1)

bound for Spain during the period; they were clearly the largest single source of royal revenues from the New World.

Even at the level of gross revenues, the 48.2 million pesos generated by the royal treasury of New Spain in the 1790s was impressive by the crown's own standards. From a population of 6 million persons, it represented a per capita tax of approximately 8 pesos, using extraordinary totals. Taking an estimated 20 million pesos for ordinary rents would yield a tax of 3 pesos 3 reales per person. In the same period the crown grossed almost 50.2 million pesos from a metropolitan population of 10.5 million Spaniards, or a tax rate of almost 4 pesos 7 reales per person. This means that the richest colonials, those of the viceroyalty of New Spain, were paying over 40 percent more in per capita rates than the inhabitants of the metropolis (when extraordinary rents were included), and just over a peso less if ordinary revenues are used as the denominator.[54]

Finally this survey of the history of tax revenues in the Viceroyalty of New Spain offers some data that can be used to determine the importance and effectiveness of the late eighteenth century Bourbon reforms and administration.[55] Clearly the creation of new treasury districts that better reflected local economies had an impact on expanding tax revenues in all categories. Bourbon policies, especially as they related to international affairs and imperial pretensions, were another matter. International warfare ultimately had a disastrous effect on local mining production and on trade, especially for the products of the metropolis in American markets. Moreover the bankrupting of the government treasury in these wars (which stopped New World silver shipments and closed local ports) explains the rather extraordinary decision of the crown to generate new taxes from personal income, properties, and church mortgages in its American empire, a policy which would severely disrupt the colonial capital market. In the short term this policy of special forced loans and taxes may have been effective in generating income; in the long run it would be devastating for the local economies.

6

Conclusion

Results of This Study

Obtaining an overview of the structure and relative importance of different groups of taxes through space and time is merely a preliminary step in using these Spanish American royal treasury accounts. The ultimate objective of this new scholarship is to exploit these numbers to determine the long-term trends in both the colonial economy and royal finances from the late sixteenth to the early nineteenth centuries. Was the seventeenth century an era of crisis and depression, as traditional historiography asserts? If the crisis occurred, was it the same in all regions, or were there important variations? Was there an eighteenth century economic renaissance, and if so, how long did it last? Was it experienced in the same way in all regions, and what impact did local economic factors play in these regional variations? Did Bourbon imperial policy in itself create the seeds of independence and/or economic stagnation in the nineteenth century? Did the large post-1780 specie transfers out of New Spain in fact represent a factor in nineteenth century stagnation, or could the local economy have sustained these transfers had the metropolitan state not collapsed?

From this analysis of the royal treasury records, some very preliminary statements can be made about some of these issues, all of which have generated such debate among historians. The first issue these numbers help to resolve is that of the so-called seventeenth century crisis. From the view of America, the crisis in Potosí production was clearly not matched by a generalized crisis throughout the Americas. Examining just the growth in bullion production shows a trend of moderate growth for Mexico, alongside a severe decline for Peru and Charcas, leading to an overall moderate decline in total American output (see table 2.1).

Clearly the three decades from the 1640s to the 1660s were the most severe for Mexican production, and they marked the beginning of a long secular decline for Peru and Charcas. But this overall downturn in production at mid-century was not as profound as the old figures of bullion importation to Spain would lead one to assume (graph 6.1). This finding confirms recent work in other areas. The research of Earl Hamilton on American bullion imports into

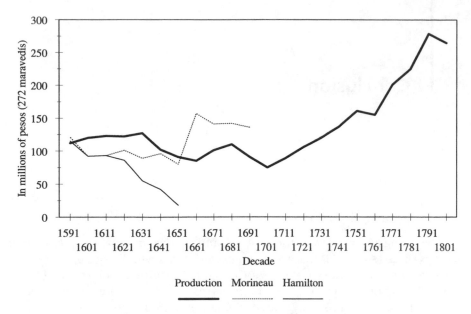

Graph 6.1   Spanish American Bullion Production and Estimates of Bullion Imports into Europe by Hamilton and Morineau. (Source: Graph 2.2; E. J. Hamilton, *American Treasure and the Price Revolution in Spain* (Cambridge, MA: Harvard University Press, 1934), table 1; M. Morineau, *Gazettes et Fabuleux Metaux* (Paris: Cambridge University Press, 1985) table 42)

Spain, which had stood since the 1930s as a major guidepost, has been challenged by data from the American royal treasury records as well as other sources, in terms of the numbers he does not include.[1] Michel Morineau, in his study of Dutch importation figures, has even questioned the validity of the Hamilton importation numbers for the period after 1620, suggesting, in fact, a late seventeenth century boom in Spanish American bullion imports into Europe.[2] Though less controversial than the still untested figures generated by Morineau, the work of TePaske and others in recreating Spanish American production figures for silver and gold has also suggested a moderate century-long crisis and a far more complex evolution, in which moderate growth was the norm for mineral production in the crucial Mexican region, even as Charcas experienced a severe secular decline.

Reconstruction of the Mexican production figures is based on the accounts of the Viceroyalty of New Spain, which indicate a quite unexpected divergence from the orthodox picture. This was a startling result, since it was the Mexican experience that was first used to posit the existence of a seventeenth century crisis in the Americas.[3] The local treasury records, however, showed that several new fiscal districts were created in recently opened mining centers of the

north in this period. These new cajas absorbed funds previously collected by
the central treasury of Mexico City, which caused a decline in mining taxes reported in the capital but did not mean that colonywide revenues or production had actually decreased.[4]

Once these new regional caja accounts were added to the old Mexico City
ones, it became clear that Mexican silver production expanded much earlier
than previously supposed. Far from experiencing a century-long crisis, New
Spain was in fact undergoing steady economic growth in this period (with only
modest declines at midcentury), led by the expanding mining industries of the
northern provinces. Thus the reliance of previous studies on Hamilton's figures
and on the accounts of the Mexico City Mint has proved to be profoundly
misleading.[5] Historians have incorrectly assumed that there was a decline in
production, when in fact the apparent decrease in revenues was merely a reflection of administrative change.[6]

But if these higher output figures are correct (and all recalculations show
the same results[7]), then where did the tax and bullion funds go? Here there are
two answers. The detailed analysis of royal government spending has shown a
major increase in royal expenditures in the New World for public works, mostly
for defense, in the seventeenth century.[8] In fact, by the middle of the century,
most American treasure was spent in the Indies. Growing challenges to Spain's
hegemony in the New World during the seventeenth and eighteenth centuries forced colonial authorities to order major increases in expenditures for local defense. The relative decline of Spanish sea power led to a massive program
of port fortifications and local shipbuilding for regional armadas in the Pacific and the Caribbean, all paid for by a revitalized silver-mining industry. It
also spawned a retrenchment of internal colonial frontiers and motivated the
subsequent construction of interior fortifications against unpacified Indians
throughout North and South America. Although the crown still extracted a
profit in "surplus" funds from the colonies, an ever higher ratio of these net
revenues was used in the colonies themselves.

The work of TePaske has also revealed the increasing diversion of Peruvian
and Mexican silver in the seventeenth century into the Philippine trade and
thus into the Asian market, through the port of Acapulco.[9] Indeed vast quantities of treasure were shipped to the Philippines to pay for American importation
of Asian luxury goods and for the defense of the Iberian Far East. The decline
of royal authority in America meant that illegal Asian imports were booming.
Colonial consumption of such goods rose dramatically, both in New Spain and
in distant Peru. In addition the Spanish Indies became directly involved in Europe's balance-of-payments problems. European trade with Asia showed a deficit until the nineteenth century, due to a fundamental inability to supply the
Oriental market with desirable goods. The only way to pay for imports was with
New World silver. Much of the debt was cleared through the normal channels
of trade, but a fair proportion appears to have been paid for through shipments
made directly from America to Asia. It is these two major diversions that ex-

plain why American production was not matched by a steady or only moderately declining level of crucial bullion imports into Spain in the seventeenth century.

If the seventeenth century crisis was not as universal a phenomenon as previous scholars have argued, and was definitely not a factor in Mexican development during that century, then the entire "feudal" model elaborated by Chevalier and Borah is thrown into question by this analysis of the royal treasury records, just as it has previously been challenged by historians studying alternative records.[10] Their argument that economic decline and demographic decline in the seventeenth century in Mexico caused a return to subsistence agriculture and the emergence of a "feudal" hacienda system has itself come under wide-ranging scrutiny. That there was a severe decline in the Indian population is not questioned, but fiscal statistics lead one to believe that its long-term negative impact on the market economy, particularly in zones that were not predominantly Indian by population, has been exaggerated. Equally scholars have challenged the validity of the "feudal" model by showing the vigorous survival of Indian communities throughout the colonial period, the growth of local markets in the sixteenth and seventeenth centuries, the vitality of a land market, and finally the market orientation of the landed elite.[11]

But at the same time it must be admitted that parts of the seventeenth century crisis model are still valid. The metropolitan government did in fact go into a severe fiscal crisis in the seventeenth century, and that decline may have had an impact on the colonial American situation.[12] Recent theorists have suggested that the decline of the Spanish center might well have led to a renaissance in the peripheral economies of America.[13] The mechanisms suggested by this hypothesis are closely related to the internal life of the treasury administration. Thus one might argue that the seventeenth century crisis in Spain led to the sale of American fiscal offices to individuals who were deeply implicated in the local power structure and/or were far less trained than nonpurchasing candidates, producing a consequent decline in taxing efficiency.[14] This in turn would have allowed the retention of more funds in the colonies, as political pressure eased and enforcement ability declined. This model, growing out of the work of Gunder Frank and Immanuel Wallerstein, and receiving support in recent theories of dependency, has clearly been important in offering one interpretation of the seventeenth century as a period of "benevolent neglect" for the colonies. Recent studies have also suggested that such a decline in administrative efficiency, along with the decrease in Spanish trade to America, was a major factor in the growth of contraband trade. This latter argument, however, may not be consistent with a model of local growth due to lesser exploitation from the metropolitan center, since it might be argued that such growth in contraband trade with France, England, and the Netherlands would simply have redirected the external dependency to a new source, without changing internal relations. Also while European goods may have been cheaper, they were primarily directed toward the upper classes, rather than for mass consumption.

It is true, however, that the decline of taxation would have granted a higher return to exporters.

Although colonial tax materials cannot resolve all of these questions, they can help determine the validity of competing interpretations. The first studies undertaken in the past decade showed that economic evolution was not uniform across the face of America. Thus the Viceroyalty of Peru experienced major growth in the late sixteenth century, a boom which lasted until the early decades of the seventeenth century. There then came a sharp decline in silver production, in Potosí and elsewhere, which was immediately reflected in a major drop in royal mining and minting taxes. This depression soon affected all public revenues and lasted through the 1600s, with recovery delayed until the middle decades of the eighteenth century.[15]

This general picture also seems to be applicable to the Audiencia of Charcas. Indeed an examination of caja receipts in the nonmining zones of Charcas also reveals a general tendency for their treasuries to experience declines in tax revenues during the years of crisis. These findings support the theories of regional integration proposed by Carlos Sempat Assadourian, who argued that semi-autonomous regional markets existed within colonial Spanish America.[16] Thus the satellite economies of the northern Río de la Plata provinces and the Upper Peruvian agricultural valleys experienced sharp downturns reflected in their local caja receipts, as they began to lose important segments of their Potosí market. This led to local retrenchment of haciendas, the rise of minifundias, a general retreat toward local subsistence economies, and declines in long-distance trading. Even in Chile changes in economic structure in these years point to the pervasive nature of the crisis, though the local Indian wars of that distant colony guaranteed the continued flow of outside funds.

All of these findings suggest that the downturn of the local economies based on Potosí, along with the corresponding decline of the metropolitan center, did not lead to any major growth. Imperial neglect may have occurred, but if the local productive forces were themselves in decline, growth could not take place, despite suggestions to the contrary in the recent theoretical literature. Tax pressure may have eased, but the decline in all major tax revenues suggest that it was the dynamics of the local economy that drove the local market and not any change in bureaucratic pressure and/or efficiency.

Judging from the available figures for Peru and Charcas, then, the dependency model does not seem to hold. Rather, fiscal records apparently confirm the more traditional theories. The thesis that "peripheral" growth occurs when central control is weakened appears to be partially supported by the Mexican case. But here too it can be argued that the dynamism of new mining discoveries and the growth of major industrial activity in the seventeenth century were more related to internal forces of population growth and local capital development than to any relief from fiscal burdens that may have occurred because of a decline in efficiency of the royal government. Obviously the fiscal reconstruction that has taken place now allows us to see that local conditions determine how a colony reacted when European crises forced a relaxation of metropolitan control. The Peruvian example shows that declines in local production and the consequent crises in regional markets did not allow colonial regions to respond positively to such an opportunity. In contrast the Mexican case indicates that when a local economy was in a period of expansion, such a relaxation would probably lead to further local growth, as formerly exported surpluses were diverted to colonial markets.

This macroanalysis of the annual cartas cuentas has also refined our information concerning the well-known shift in relative power among the viceroyalties of the New World. Despite the profound impact of the seventeenth century crisis in Peru, even as late as the 1690s, the Andean treasuries were still producing more income per annum than the Mexican cajas. While both the Andean and Mexican regions experienced a major crisis at the end of the seventeenth century and the first decade of the eighteenth century, the crisis for New Spain was far milder than for the two Andean treasuries. This meant that by the first decade of the 1700s, Mexican income figures passed those of Peru and Alto Peru combined. By the 1710s they had surpassed the peak 1680s figures, and they never turned back. In contrast the Viceroyalty of Peru did not surpass its 1680s figure until the 1780s, and Charcas took a decade longer. By then both Andean regions were producing under half of the tax income of the New Spain cajas, even when the special post-1780 loans and miscellaneous incomes are excluded.

These trends also reveal important shifts in local economies within each region. Although Potosí still dominated Charcas at the end of the colonial period, the rapid growth of Oruro and La Paz in the eighteenth century meant that its relative importance had seriously declined. Similarly, though Lima and the central highland and sierra zones were still of major importance in the late eighteenth century, the southern sierra had seen a surprising rate of growth, which was beginning to affect total receipts more than ever before. Finally the emergence of new treasury offices directly reflected the rise of western and north-central New Spain as major sources of treasury income and economic growth, though the extraordinary expansion of loans and miscellaneous taxes in the two treasuries of Mexico City and Veracruz masked their increasing importance.

Along with these shifts within the regions, the changing relative weights of the Andean zone and New Spain meant a new role for Mexican treasuries within the imperial framework. By the early eighteenth century, Mexico was the only major region producing enough surplus income to consistently supply funds directly to the metropolitan treasury.[17] Thus Mexican income became an ever more important part of total imperial revenues, so that the dramatically increasing trends of secular growth in the Mexican treasuries profoundly influenced the trends in total American revenues generated by these three surplus-producing regions. Even excluding the unusual influence of forced loans, New Spain's revenues show the same long-term trends of growth and its dominant influence in total American returns, despite the modest recovery of the Peruvian and Charcas cajas in the late eighteenth century.

Finally there exists the real question of what happened in Mexico in the period after 1780. Data from the various categories of taxes show a slowing of taxes related to mining, trade, and monopolies in the 1790s, if not before, and a seeming stagnation or the beginnings of a decline at the end of the eighteenth century and the first decade of the nineteenth century.[18] Yet the New Spain treasuries were shipping out ever larger volumes of specie and claiming ever expanding treasury receipts. There is a question here of the increasing breakdown of normal treasury procedures, which suggests a rise in double counting some of these funds. But even rejecting the higher figures, the amounts that other scholars and I have registered as leaving the viceroyalty for Caribbean subsidies or Spanish metropolitan coffers still indicate very high rates of wealth extraction. I have already dealt with this topic at great length in the preceding chapter, but it is worth repeating here that such extraction has been seen by some to have been the cause of Mexico's collapse in the first half of the nineteenth century. There is no question that failure to repay the war loans of the 1790s and 1800s, along with the royal decision in 1803–5 to absorb the wealth tied up in church properties and used for local credit in New Spain (the "consolidación" of vales reales), did create a crisis in capital in the colony. Had Spain not collapsed in 1808 with a bankrupt royal treasury, and had it repaid the loans of the last English wars as it had those of the 1780s, there is some question as to how negative all of this capital export would have been. Even with the failure to repay colonial loans, the Veracruz export data from the period after 1800 suggest that the colony could have recovered quickly and might have been expanding in the 1810s, when revolutionary movements brought growth to a halt. Whatever the outcome of this debate, it is clear that far more work will be needed at the level of the account books to fully determine what happened in this crucial period.

Finally these reconstructed treasury records have proved useful in resolving an old debate about the respective costs and benefits of colonialism. The problem, of course, is relevant for the entire colonial period, particularly regarding the shipment of crown revenues from the Americas to Europe.[19] The issue is currently most important in eighteenth century historiography, however. Did the colonials pay more than the metropolitan population, and were they overtaxed by the standards of the day?

This question is not quite as easy to answer as one might suppose. There are in fact several ways to estimate such a per capita tax, and the base population figures themselves are in some doubt. The best data come from the Viceroyalty of New Spain. Using a level of gross revenues of approximately 20 million pesos per annum in the 1790s (the annual average estimate given by crown officials for the quinquennium of 1795–99)[20] for a population of 6 million persons yields a per capita rate of almost 3 pesos 3 reales. Using the figure of 48.2 million pesos, which includes the special loans and new war taxes, however, yields a per capita tax of approximately 8 pesos. Finally there is the contemporary estimate made by Alexander von Humboldt of a rate of 2 pesos 4 reales per capita.[21]

In the same period the crown grossed almost 50.2 million pesos from a metropolitan population of 10.5 million Spaniards. Thus depending on the number used, the colonials were paying either a third (or more) less, or one and a half times more, than the 4 pesos and 6 reales per capita paid by the inhabitants of the metropolis.[22] But Humboldt himself, who determined the lowest per capital tax rate for late eighteenth century Mexico, thought that the Mexican colonials were heavily taxed compared to the inhabitants of most other European colonies and argued that the English extracted half as much per capita from the East Indians, the model of exploitative colonial taxation at the time. On the other hand, a recent estimate of French and English per capita tax rates in the 1790s would suggest (using Humboldt's rate of 2 pesos 4 reales, or even the contemporary royal officers' quinquennium rate of 3 pesos 3 reales) that the Mexicans were paying less than the metropolitan French and somewhat more than the metropolitan English.[23]

While the study of the issue of comparative contemporary levels of taxation is just beginning, the question of the impact of the more efficient eighteenth century tax administration and the use of extraordinary loans and new taxes after 1780 has created an intense debate. As a result an entirely new area of discussion has opened up, concerning what some historians have seen as an increasing level of "tax oppression" supposedly characterizing late eighteenth century Bourbon government. This thesis of the "reconquest of America" has been proposed as a fundamental background cause of the independence movement.[24] That is, the increasing tax efficiency brought about by the Bourbon reforms of the eighteenth century are interpreted as having extracted too much wealth from the colonies, so much so that their economies suffered. In this context it might be argued that the post-1780 pattern of massive exploitation of colonial wealth by the crown (both for increased colonial situados and quite dramatic increases in capital transfers to Spain itself, through voluntary and forced loans) suggests that royal fiscal policies after 1780 were one of the more important factors affecting the economic collapse of Mexico even before the period of its Wars of Independence.

While the evidence from tax records would seem to imply that long-term reform did not lead to fiscal oppression and consequent economic decline, the second theme of a rapine policy after 1790, at least for Mexico, is still an open question. If Mexico did not stagnate in the early nineteenth century, but in fact grew at reasonable rates until 1820, despite royal failure to repay all war loans, then it would appear that the period of the wars of independence produced a far more severe economic collapse than previously assumed. One might also argue, however, that the pause of the Mexican economy in the 1790s was a response to fiscal oppression rather than part of the normal business cycle. As can be seen, no easy answers can be assumed from the study of these records.

Whatever the conclusion of these debates, they all contribute to the ongoing discussion begun by John Coatsworth concerning the growth of the Mexican economy in the nineteenth century.[25] One conclusion is that while nineteenth century growth was rather good, it started from a far lower base than suggested in the traditional literature, thus explaining the relative backwardness of Mexico at the end of the nineteenth century, despite a century of growth. But it is still hotly debated whether the decline occurred in the late eighteenth or early nineteenth century and whether it was due to Bourbon reforms, to the special war taxes and loans only, to the collapse of state finances in 1808, or to the wars of independence themselves. These records offer intriguing suggestions, if only partial answers.

In evaluating the debates over reform, taxes, and growth, it should also be remembered that most of the new tax monies, even for New Spain, were not destined for the exclusive use of metropolitan authorities in Europe. Treasury accounts show that the crown actually spent more of its tax income in the colonies than it shipped to the metropolis. In addition expenditures on such agencies as the navy, which served the entire empire, often outstripped remissions to Spain. While heavy taxes generated major surpluses, over three-quarters of the excess was spent in America, defending the interior peace and tranquillity of what was at the time one of the world's largest customs unions. By the eighteenth century, in fact, only the Viceroyalty of New Spain consistently sent a major part of its income as surplus funds to the mother country. Moreover more than half of the Mexican surpluses were spent in America.[26]

Thus royal revenues collected in the colonies were used to guarantee three centuries of peace and order to Spanish Americans. Maintaining order may have meant oppressing Indians and keeping Blacks enslaved, but the crown's functions in both regards were clear enough. Its policy was carried out with a notable economy of violence and singleness of purpose. Despite aggressive imperial raids by all the expanding northern European powers and repeated Indian attacks on its frontiers, the Spanish American empire remained intact. And all the Indian, peasant, and popular rebellions within this empire, from the uprisings of the Tzeltal in Chiapas and the Quechua in Cuzco under Tupac Amaru to the mass movements of Hidalgo in central Mexico, were put down with the aid of royal funds. The colonists' high taxes paid for both internal and external security and guaranteed an era of peace and stability unmatched in modern times. That cycles of growth and decline occurred in all regions is obvious from the data. Nonetheless imperial tax revenues and their redistribution over the face of the empire guaranteed that such factors as war and rebellion would not be the primary cause for alterations in the social and economic conditions of the colonists or in the well-being of the elites.

While recent research has revealed the benefits as well as the costs of royal taxation for the colonials, it should also be remembered that the crown also did rather well. Total tax revenues generated in America were greater than those obtained by Madrid from its metropolitan treasuries (on the order of 38 million pesos from America compared to some 35 million pesos from Spain in the early 1780s). Of these gross revenues, the crown averaged between 8 and 9 million pesos of net revenues per annum by the last decades of the century, or approximately 20 percent of gross receipts. These funds in turn represent 20 percent of total royal revenues, when net receipts from America are added to total peninsular income.[27]

There was also a host of indirect benefits and incomes that ultimately derived from the crown's possession of its American empire. These, of course, are not directly reflected in the American treasury records. To begin with, local tax receipts supported a substantial body of colonial offices that were filled by the Spanish-born, some of whom eventually returned to serve in Madrid or elsewhere on the peninsula after training in the colonial service. Equally the security of the Spanish American market guaranteed a handsome profit to resident peninsular merchants. The profits from their operations were often shipped to metropolitan Spain, where they were invested by their owners and eventually taxed by the crown.

More importantly still, despite significant foreign penetration, the merchants of Spain itself were dominant in Indies commerce, one of the largest contemporary international trades. Spanish America imported close to 60 million pesos worth of European goods per annum at the end of the eighteenth century. This was almost equal in value to all British overseas exports during the same period. Although the seventeenth century crisis of the metropolitan economy led to vibrant illegal trade and a smaller role for Spanish-produced goods, the Sevilla and Cadiz merchant houses never lost dominant control. Moreover once the Spanish economy recovered in the eighteenth century, all sectors of Spain benefited from American commerce.[28]

It should be remembered that Spanish America was the major unexploited market for European manufactured goods, especially for textiles in the eighteenth century. England, in particular, hungered after this market, which paid for its imports with precious metals and thereby facilitated European trade with the East. Despite the ambitions of the English, French, and other interlopers, however, the recovery of Spanish manufacturing in the eighteenth century was largely based on the American market. With this industrial renewal, economic benefits tended to remain in peninsular hands. American-induced prosperity was subject to royal taxation and was thus reflected in increased royal revenues on the peninsula.

Spain derived another indirect benefit from colonialism. Since all imports and exports from America were, by law, shipped in Spanish-owned vessels, control of the American trade guaranteed the maintenance of a major merchant fleet. This was important militarily. Given Spain's imperial pretensions in the eighteenth century and its attempt to maintain one of the world's largest naval forces, the existence of a merchant marine provided the crown with a supply of trained personnel for its armadas. By the time of the Napoleonic wars in Europe, Madrid commanded Europe's third largest fleet, thanks in large part to sailors and timbers coming from America.[29]

Thus in terms of both direct and indirect taxes and benefits, the crown gained an enormous amount from controlling its American colonies. Equally, although the colonials often paid taxes as high as the Spaniards themselves and unquestionably more than most other European colonials, they obtained major benefits. The bulk of surplus American revenues was spent in the colonies. The portion that was shipped, along with indirect tax benefits in the peninsula, was sufficient to guarantee Spain's role as a major world power. That the Crown would eventually waste these resources in a series of ill-conceived and poorly executed wars should not be blamed on the colonial system per se. Nor should the exploitative nature of the colonial system be judged solely on the basis of the last years of fantastic efforts to repatriate colonial savings to the mother country.[30] Dynastic considerations always dominated in questions of war and peace, to the detriment of both the metropole and its overseas dominions. It was these noncolonial and antieconomic considerations that finally led to the international wars that brought ruin to the Indies-Spain connection and initiated a major depression in the colonial economy. It was these wars and their economic consequences that in turn planted the seeds of imperial destruction.

Further Research Possibilities

Since this is the first book-length study based on reconstructed treasury records from 1680 to 1809, both the limitations and potentials inherent in these materials are worth discussing. A number of the problems related to these numbers have already been discussed; here I would like to look at positive aspects of their potential, beyond this study of macrotrends.

Many of the records created by the royal treasury in America can be used to elucidate other basic issues of social and economic conditions in the colonial world. For example the tribute tax was based on actual censuses taken of the taxed population and can be found in many of the archives of Latin America. In the sixteenth and seventeenth centuries, such a census was usually just a simple listing of the male tributarios, along with those men who were about to enter the category and those who had retired from it. Then in the eighteenth century, these *padrones de indios*, or *revisitas*, became full-scale censuses that listed each person in the tributary family, which part of the communal organization they belonged to, and their relative economic worth in terms of the differing head tax they paid. These censuses are the best ones we have for any colonial population and provide a wealth of demographic, economic, and even social information that can be used to reconstruct the evolution of the Indian population of colonial Spanish America. Since these censuses persisted in some states until the end of the nineteenth century, they can even be used in rare cases to reconstruct the peasant populations of the republican era.[31]

In much the same way, the trade taxes used here in the examination of macrotrends can also provide a major set of data on the nature of local commerce and markets in America. While a significant literature exists on international commerce, taken from the records of the almorifazgo (taxes on overseas and maritime trade), only recently has local trade become a major concern. In every customs house (aduana) in Spanish America, detailed books were kept of the *guías* issued to every passing merchant who registered the value and quantity of merchandise being transported, the taxes paid, and the origin of the goods. These guías are the prime source for analyzing commerce in the colonial period, especially of the local and regional variety. Under the impact of recent concerns about reconstructing microhistory and the study of regional markets, colonial scholars have again stressed the need to examine the sources and movements of local commerce and the structure of regional economies. Model studies have begun to appear based on these alcabala records, including topics as diverse as the provisioning of the urban market of late eighteenth century Potosí and numerous detailed studies of regional markets in many parts of Mexico.[32]

The field of international trade studies, in contrast to the American commerce examples, is a more developed one, based for the most part on Spanish and Spanish American treasury records. Such research has been devoted to estimating the volume and value of trade: firstly between America and Spain; and secondly among the colonies.[33] Several studies have also been made (using tariff figures, ship registrations, and consulado papers) of the interprovincial trade among the various American and Asian colonies.[34] There are also studies of individual tariffs, special taxes, and other royal treasury materials related to American trade.[35] But much of this work needs to be integrated into larger series and tied into local economic and international market systems.

There exists a fair amount of research on the various monopolies that the crown maintained in America.[36] But these studies concentrate more on the institutional arrangements than on the economics of these special taxes and administrations. Combined with the treasury accounts, an examination of the monopolies could yield important information on American manufactures as well as patterns of monopoly product sales and consumption.

The untangling of colonial accounts and individual ramos also promises to provide nineteenth century historians with a crucial base from which to analyze republican state finances, a theme now coming much into vogue. It is quite evident that until well into the late nineteenth century, most Latin American republican societies maintained the colonial tax structure intact. This was especially the case with alcabalas, almorifazgos, and estancos. Papel sellado, for example, was especially important in the late nineteenth century Mexican economy. In the special case of Bolivia, the tribute tax survived until the 1870s as a major tax item in the national budget and never really ended until the 1950s. Capitation taxes in all the republics were most likely based on the tribute formula of the colonial period; thus increasing knowledge and understanding of the colonial fiscal structure is fundamental to an understanding of nineteenth century republican fiscal systems.

In using these summary accounts, finally, there are a number of technical problems that can only be revealed by a complete examination of the lower-level accounting books. This effort will obviously bring changes to the final accounting figures, but even the best reconstruction so far undertaken has in fact resulted in little serious change of the basic trends.[37] That such reconstruction will require enormous individual research efforts will probably mean that the work will only be undertaken in conjunction with other concerns. But such research is now beginning, largely on the part of those working from an interest in the local economies of colonial Spanish America.

Providing a systematic set of the total aggregated amounts generated by a local treasury is only a first, though vital, step in recreating the economic experience of any given area. For those interested in short-term fluctuations and local economic patterns, a further set of reconstructions will be required, one that will involve intensive archival research. Seasonal variations in accounts, for example, and the extremely difficult problem of income transfers among accounts during the course of a given year, can only be addressed by examining the libros manuales of each treasury office. Future research on Spanish colonial fiscal history will obviously move in this direction, as it attempts to correct the first approximations based on annual reports. In any event this is a natural progression. As more informed questions are asked, more sophisticated use will be made of the available accounts.

Appendix 1
Origins of the Estimated Numbers

Justification for Using Decade Averages

From the beginning I was faced with the problem of the accidents of historical preservation and their impact on the analysis of royal accounts. Though a majority of the accounts have been preserved, there are still large gaps in either missing years or missing ramos.[1] These gaps must be accounted for if the bias of accidental preservation is not to distort the final figures. How to fill those gaps will lead different scholars to attempt different ways of summing the figures. In many cases the way one calculates the missing figures (via regression equations, for example, or through the use of averages) will affect final estimated figures. But these different approaches to estimating the missing data will have more of an impact on shaping the trends—either smoothing the secular trends or making them more abrupt—than in changing their direction.

In this book I have used the averaging method to construct my estimated income and expenditure figures because of missing data and problems of lag between changes in the economy and changes in tax receipts. I have adopted this average figure to construct an annual average estimate for each decade, using information for one or more extant years in that decade to arrive at the estimated figure. I have then summed the averages of the individual ramos or cajas to arrive at a total figure Thus my figures for total income or expenditure in any decade are not the sums that would be obtained by simply adding up the available individual treasury account numbers. In fact, given the gaps in the data, such sums would be impossible to obtain for all treasuries for all years.

Generating Annual Estimates from Multiyear Accounts

A special problem also exists for accounts in the late seventeenth century, especially in its last quarter. In the late Hapsburg era, there occurred a temporary decline in efficiency among some of the local royal treasuries. Against all the rules, some local treasury officials provided their results only in varying multiyear accounts or, conversely, in accounts valid only for a few months. Therefore it has been necessary to generate the annual figures for these treasuries by first calculating average monthly incomes. It was necessary to use this procedure for the majority of the treasuries of New Spain as well as for a few in the Andean area.[2] An especially chaotic treasury was that of Lima, which did not return to annual accounts until after the year 1700.[3]

In only one area did I not make any changes, and this was the unusual fiscal year used for the accounts of both some Peruvian cajas and most of those of the Audiencia of Charcas for the seventeenth century and the first half of the eighteenth century. Instead of using the calendar year as the fiscal one, as occurred with all other treasuries by 1700, if not before, those of Peru and Charcas moved in the late sixteenth century to a fiscal year stretching from May to April. This lasted in all local offices until 1770. Given that these were very consistently twelve month accounts, I have not felt it necessary to correct for the overlap of decades.

Justification of Tax Categories

To deal with these accounts effectively, it has been essential to regroup the almost 6,000 individual taxes (3,458 income ramos and 2,456 expenditure ramos; see Appendix 3) into a reduced series of categories of taxes, in order to keep the analysis within coherent bounds and to relate these complex taxes to modern economic categories. In the colonial period the monarchy established a three-tiered system of accounts, in which a clear distinction was made as to where the income from the taxes could be spent. There were those taxes that produced funds meant to be sent directly to Spain to meet any and all metropolitan expenses (that is, which entered what might be called the Castillian "general fund"). A second category of taxes was composed of those designed to pay for predetermined costs on the peninsula and elsewhere (that is, dedicated funds, such as azogues or *bulas de cruzada*). A third group was made up of those taxes generating monies that could be disbursed freely at the local level or anywhere the crown chose. Lastly the monarchy also distinguished between the genuine royal revenues mentioned above and private trust funds (*ramos agenos*), also administered by treasury officials.

In the early 1970s, studies began to suggest possible ways to redefine these ramos for both quantitative and comparative analysis on a modern basis.[4] Fortunately these problems of definition of accounts also concerned colonial officials. Consequently there existed a fairly extensive body of literature upon which a modern recategorization could be built. Among the earliest of these studies of individual ramos and their changing fiscal nature was the survey by Gaspar de Escalona Agüero (*Gazofilacio Real del Peru*), which analyzed seventeenth century accounts in the Lima viceroyalty. Even more impressive was the late eighteenth century *Historia general de Real Hacienda*, a survey of the Mexican ramos by two royal officials, Fabián de Fonseca and Carlos de Urrutia. Since the 1970s much of this basic work has been reexamined, as various scholars turn toward treasury records to examine specific taxes in more detail.[5]

In this work I have adapted the grouping of taxes that John TePaske and I developed in the early 1980s.[6] This system is an attempt to relate taxes directly to their economic source as coherently as possible. Thus for example, taxes have been regrouped into those levied on mining and minting (the most important industry for export and taxes in America); trade, commerce, and manufactures; sales of products from state monopolies; special tribute taxes on Indians; and all the specialized taxes on officeholders of clerical and civil appointments. More occasional taxes were also collected, such as special forced loans, mostly from corporations such as the consulados and the church, as well as from the periodic sales of public lands (*composición de tierras*) and even sales of annuities (*censos*). At times these special taxes, especially the forced loans used during periods of imperial war, could reach enormous proportions. But on the whole they were relatively low producers of funds. Aside from regular taxes, municipalities levied local taxes (*sisas*) in their own name, and the crown itself created a separate Renta de Tabaco to manufacture and sell tobacco products. Profits from these sales were never handled by the Royal Treasury, but were dealt with by a separate administration.

Even after taxes were grouped in these rough divisions, it is obvious that some represented direct indices of production and trade, while others were more indirect. Some reflected demographic developments in only one subgroup of the society (for example the tribute tax on Indians); while another set only reflected the size and salaries of a small segment of the population, in this case the government and church officials. As for expenditures, they have been grouped by major governmental activity, most specifically those dealing with the costs of administration and the military.

Meaning of Annual Estimated "Total Income" Figures

Having grouped taxes as to their sources and the various ramos and their functions, it was necessary to separate annual income figures from carryover incomes and various deposits of funds held in the treasuries. This is essential if an annual total income figure is to be generated. Throughout this book I have used my own definition of "total" revenue, which excludes what other scholars and I consider to be obviously double-counted sums. Total revenue in all tables and graphs in the present work is defined as "gross income" or "expenditure," less a series of uncollected incomes, double-counted accounts, and cash deposits of one kind or another. Thus "total incomes" are gross income figures less Existencia del año anterior, Depositos, Deudas para cobrar, and the Real Hacienda en común categories; while "total expenditure" figures exclude Depositos, Deudas para cobrar, specie or other government valued paper (papel sellado, *bulas*, etc.), as well as *reales labrados de barras*.

Even with these subtractions, however, total income and expenditure figures may still mask considerable levels of double-counted revenues. Only detailed breakdowns of individual treasury accounts at the libros manuales level can resolve this problem. Nevertheless, and recognizing the possibility of considerable future revisions of the numbers presented here, I am convinced that the general trends indicated in this work will stand up under the more detailed scrutiny of future studies.

Appendix 2
Using Current Prices

Almost all economists looking at these tax data have wanted to have them deflated for changes in prices over this long period. But for reasons I discuss below, all funds reported in this work have been listed in current prices. There have been a few attempts to convert these into real prices, but they have not met with much success. The problem is that the requisite price indices have not been reconstructed for the colonial period.[1] There exist a number of partial price series of quite local markets, the best being for Mexico and Charcas, as well as those prepared by Hamilton for Spain. I have run regressions on seven major series, those offered by Garner for eighteenth century maize and wheat prices, Rabell's estimated change of prices of a basket of consumer goods for San Luis de la Paz, Florescano's maize prices for the City of Mexico, and Tandeter and Wachtel's price data for Potosí.[2] To these were added Hamilton's composite agricultural and nonagricultural price series for Spain during the same seventeenth and eighteenth century period.[3] But these series do not agree with each other, and there is no particular reason for choosing one over the other to deflate the current price information. I would also stress, as Garner does, that "a convincing case for severe long-term price inflation has not yet been made for eighteenth century Mexico."[4] Nor for that matter, for any other colony.

Given the relatively stable prices which most series show until the last quarter of the 18th century, and the lack of consistency among the series, I have opted for using current prices. This is not a severe problem, since once complete and coherent price data exist, these treasury numbers and estimates can be inflated or deflated with the proper indices.

Appendix 3

Income-Producing Taxes by Type of Activity

Mining and Minting

.5% barras de plata
.5% de plata
1% de oro y plata
1% de perlas
1% de plata
1% de plata de azogue y fuego
1% del oro
1% diezmos de plata labrada
1% diezmos plata az paga azogue
1% diezmos plata azogue pabellón
1% diezmos plata de bolanos
1% diezmos plata fu paga azoguc
1% diezmos plata fuego pabellón
1% diezmos plata inc con oro
1% diezmos señ de plata labrada
1% diezmos señ plata comisada
1% deizmos señ plata de azogue
1% diezmos señ plata de bolanos
1% diezmos señ plata de fuego
1% diezmos señ plata inc con oro
1% diezmos y señorage de plata
1% diezmos y señorage del oro
1% quinto señ plata comisada
1% quinto señ plata de rescate
1% quinto y diezmos de plata
1% y diezmos de perlas
1% y diezmos de plata

1% y diszmos de plata de azogue
1% y diezmos de plata de fuego
1% y diezmos de plata inc con oro
1% y diezmos de plata paga azogue
1% y diezmos plata fuego y azogue
1% y diezmos plata paga de extra
1% y diezmos plata paga de sal
1% y quinto de plata
1% y quinto de plata de rescate
1% y quinto de plata labrada
1% y quinto de plata S L Potosí
1% y quinto del oro
1% y quinto plata de Chuquisaca
1% y real quinto
1.2% y diezmos de plata
1.2% y quintos de plata
1.5% cobos y duezmos
1.5% de cobos
1.5% de plata
1.5% de plata labrada de indulto
1.5% del oro
1.5% diez señ oro y oro inc plat
1.5% diezmo señ oro labrado
1.5% diezmos plata fuego azogue
1.5% diezmos señ oro de azogue
1.5% diezmos señ oro de fuego
1.5% diezmos señ oro inc plata
1.5% diezmos señ oro labrado
1.5% diezmos señ plata labrada
1.5% diezmos y quinto del oro
1.5% diezmos y señ del oro

1.5% oro y plata de Casa Moneda
1.5% y diezmos de plata
1.5% y diezmos de plata y oro
1.5% y diezmos del oro
1.5% y diezmos del oro inc plata
1.5% y diezmos del oro labrado
1.5% y diezmos oro de azogue
1.5% y diezmos oro de fuego
1.5% y diezmos plata lab indulto
1.5% y quinto de perlas
1.5% y quinto de plata
1.5% y quinto de plata Chuquisaca
1.5% y quinto de plata labrada
1.5% y quinto de reales
1.5% y quinto del oro
1.5% y quintos de plata y oro
1.5% y veintavo del oro
10% de señoreage
2/3 de 1.5% y quinto del oro
3 granos cada marco de minería
3% avería y diezmo plata labrada
3% de señoreage
3% del oro
3% del oro de azogue
3% del oro de fuego
3% del oro inc con plata
3% del oro labrado
3% del oro puro
Afinación
Alhaja preciosa
Amonedación
Arrendamiento de casa de moneda
Arrendamiento de minas
Aumento de barras
Aumento de fundición de plata
Aumento de señoreage de minería
Barras de plata
Bocados de plata rescate
Bocados para ensaye Casa Moneda
Cambio de platas
Casa de fundición
Casa de moneda
Casa de moneda provisional
Cobos
Cobos y diezmos

Cobos y diezmos de plata
Cobos y quintos
Cobre
Composición de minas
Consumido de plata
Contribución temp real en marco
Crecimiento de barras
Der de plata casa de moneda
Der plata labrada y oro labrado
Der y diezmos del oro filipinas
Der y quinto del oro filipinas
Derecho de 1% de plata
Derecho de barajas
Derecho de barras
Derecho de fondados
Derecho del 3% del oro puro
Derecho del más a más
Derecho y quinto de oro
Derechos de ensaye y fundición
Derechos de oro de azogue
Derechos de oro de fuego
Derechos de oro y plata
Derechos de plata
Derechos de plata de escobillas
Derechos de plata labrada indulto
Derechos de plata pura
Derechos del oro
Derechos y diezmos de plata
Derechos y diezmos plata N León
Derechos y quinto de plata
Diez por ciento
Diezmos al quinto n ben del oro
Diezmos de barras
Diezmos de Chuquisaca
Diezmos de cobre
Diezmos de especies
Diezmos de estaño
Diezmos de oro
Diezmos de oro y plata labrada
Diezmos de plata
Diezmos de plata labrada
Diezmos de plata quintada
Diezmos de vajilla
Diezmos de vajilla de oro y plata
Diezmos reales

Diezmos y cobos
Diezmos y quintos de plata
Ensayadores casa de moneda
Ensaye
Estaño
Extracción de 3%
Extracción de plata
Extracción del oro
Extravíos de piñas
Fábricas
Fletes Acapulco México Zacatecas
Fletes de Acapulco a México
Fletes de Guadiana a Zacatecas
Fletes de México a Guadiana
Fletes de México a Zacatecas
Fletes de plata
Fletes de Veracruz a Guadiana
Fletes de Veracruz a México
Fletes de Veracruz a Zacatecas
Fomento de minería
Fondo de rescates
guardia de a pie
Indultos de oro y plata
Indultos de plata labrada
Ingenios de Tarapaya
Mermas de plata
Minas
Minas de su majestad
Minería
Minería por enteros
Minería por rescates
Mitad der plata az quebradilla
Mitad der plata azogue pabellón
Mitad der plata azogue veta negra
Mitad der plata fu quebradilla
Mitad der plata fuego pabellón
Mitad der plata fuego veta negra
Mitad derechos plata quebradilla
Moneda columnaria antigua
Moneda macuquina
Oro de azogue
Oro de Carabaya
Oro de fuego
Oro de San Luis Potosí
Oro de vajilla

Oro incorporado con plata
Oro labrado
Oro pasta
Oro puro
Oro y plata
Pagado por los mineros
Perlas
Perlas de California
Pesos en quinto
Picos de quintos de plata
Piñas del extravío
Plata con oro
Plata de azogue
Plata de inventario
Plata de piña
Plata de rescate
Plata descaminada
Plata ensayada proc de plata corr
Plata estaño
Plata hallada
Plata labrada
Plata labrada quintada
Plata para vajilla
Plata pasta
Plata por moneda
Plata prestada
Plata rescatada
Plata vuelta a la caja
Plata y oro labrado
Premio del oro cambiado
Premio y cambio de doblones
Productos de ensaye depositos
Quinto al veintavo oro labrado
Quintos a diezmos
Quintos a diezmos de plata labr
Quintos al veintavo del oro
Quintos de 9.1%
Quintos de azogues
Quintos de barras
Quintos de esmeraldas
Quintos de estaño
Quintos de joyas de oro
Quintos de joyas de oro almojar
Quintos de oro y plata
Quintos de oro y plata lab a dzo

Quintos de oro y plata labrada
Qintos de perlas
Quintos de plata
Quintos de plata al diezmo
Quintos de plata corriente
Quintos de plata ensayada
Quintos de plata labrada
Quintos del oro
Quintos del oro en oro
Quintos del oro ensayado
Quintos del oro labrado
Quintos diezmos y 1.5% de plata
Quintos reales
Quintos reales de estaño
Quintos sobre la tasa
Quintos y cobos
Quintos y derechos de plata
Qiuntos y derechos del oro
Quintos y diezmos plata de azogue
Quintos y diezmos plata de fuego
Quinzeno de mineros de plata
Real de señoreage
Real del ducado
Real en marco de minería
Real en marco para socabón
Real en marco por nuevo arbitrio
Real marco de nuevo
Real oro de quintos
Reales labrados de barras
Receptores de quinzenos y sal
Reensaye
Reensaye de plata
Rescate de reales
Rescates del oro
Restos de oficiales de fundición
Resultas de plata
Señoreage
Señoreage de la casa de moneda
Señoreage de minería
Señoreage de plata
Señoreage de plata de azogue
Señoreage de plata de fuego
Señoreage de plata de rescate
Señoreage de plata labrada
Señoreage de plata y oro

Señoreage del oro labrado
Señoreage del oro
Señoreage del oro de azogue
Señoreage del oro de fuego
Señoreage del oro inc con plata
Señoreage del oro puro
Señoreage para los doctrineros
Tarifa de quinto a quintar
Tercias partes plata descaminada
Tercio de extravío de piñas
Vajilla de oro y plata
Vales para oro
Vasijas de azogues
Veintavo del cobre
Veintavo del oro
Veintavo o quinto de cobre
Veintavo o quinto del oro
Veintiuno y derechos de plata
Venta de casa de moneda
Venta de minas y tierras
Ventas y composiciones de tierras

Trade, Commerce, and Agriculture

.5% Acrecentado a la alcabala
.5% de armada
1 cuartillo quintal palo tinta
1 peso un barril
1 rl cada quintal palo de tinta
1% a de bar en lugar 2 rls naipes
1% de Armada de barlovento
1% de avería
1% de avería aplicada a Rl Hac
1% del dinero venido del Perú
1% para la Fuerza Real
1% para reparo de Fuerzas Reales
1% y impuesto para Armada de bar
1.5% del consulado
1.5% efectos del comercio
1.5% sobre efectos de comercio
16.67% mercad permiso de fil
18.75% de conducción a España
19% de merc de fil sin registro
2% arm de bar 4% de alcabalas
2% de alcabalas

2% de alcabalas de 4 cabezón

2% de alcabalas de 5 cabezón

2% de alcabalas encabezadas

2% de armada de bar 5 cabazón

2% de la Rl Armada de barlovento

2% de mercaderías de los permisos

2% del consulado para Armada barl

2.5% de 3.5% de merc de Filipinas

2.5% de entrada cacao Guayaquil

2.5% de plata reg para Filipinas

21.5% de merc fil sin registro

22.5p pipa vino agte 11.25p vinag

25 pesos cada pipa del vino

25p pipa vino agte 12.5p vinagre

3% salida de Manila sin registro

3.5% de frutas tierra a sosonante

3.5% de frutas tierra embarcada

3.5% de mercaderías renunciadas

3.5% frutas tierra a Filipinas

3.5% géneros nao de China

3.5% salida a mercaderías a Fil

4 pesos un barril de harina

4% de alcabalas

4% de alcabalas cobr de consulado

4% plata registrada a Filipinas

4p un barril de harina extranjera

5% de entrada barcos ven del Perú

5% de plata reg para Filipinas

5% del nao a China

5% dcl pescado entra en Acapulco

5% plata 3.5% frutas de tierra a Fil

5% y 10% de Filipinas

6 pesos un barril de harina

6% de salida nao China para Fil

6% que ha rendido las alcabalas

6.5 pesos cada pipa del vino

6.5 pesos un barril de aguardiente

8% del cacao de Guayaquil

8% del cargo

9 pesos cada negro

9% consignaciones nao de China

9.5% de ciudades

Admin de rentas unidas Huamanga

Administración de rentas unidas

Aduana

Aduana de Buenos Aires

Aduana de Montevideo

Alcabalas 3 cabezón Armada de bar

Alcabalas 5 cabezón Armada de bar

Alcabalas 6% adm cabildo Veracruz

Alcabalas almos villas fronteras

Alcabalas almos y pulperías

Alcabalas antiguas

Alcabalas conmutación de especie

Alcabalas corrientes

Alcabalas de 1.5% Armada de barl

Alcabalas de 2%

Alcabalas de 2% y 4%

Alcabalas de 2.5%

Alcabalas de 3%

Alcabalas de 4%

Alcabalas de 4% doblada

Alcabalas de 4% y 6%

Alcabalas de 5%

Alcabalas de 6%

Alcabalas de 6% agregadas Rl Hac

Alcabalas de 6% de Tlacotalpam

Alcabalas de 6% de venta

Alcabalas de 8%

Alcabalas de aduana

Alcabalas de aguardiente de caña

Alcabalas de arrendamiento

Alcabalas de asiento

Alcabalas de Buenos Aires

Alcabalas de cabezón y viento

Alcabalas de cabezones

Alcabalas de Campeche

Alcabalas de carnicerías de 6%

Alcabalas de Castilla

Alcabalas de Castilla y Corregid

Alcabalas de Castilla y de tierra

Alcabalas de Chilapán

Alcabalas de Chile

Alcabalas de Chuquito

Alcabalas de comestibles

Alcabalas de comisos

Alcabalas de composición de hac

Alcabalas de contratos públicos

Alcabalas de cortas extracciones

Alcabalas de cuentas

Alcabalas de Culiacán
Alcabalas de diezmo
Alcabalas de efectos de Castilla
Alcabalas de encomenderos
Alcabalas de entra registros a 3%
Alcabalas de entrada com interior
Alcabalas de entrada de 4%
Alcabalas de entrada de nebros 4%
Alcabalas de esta ciudad
Alcabalas de hac y pulperías
Alcabalas de internación de 6%
Alcabalas de Jalapa
Alcabalas de la provincia a 4%
Alcabalas de la tierra de 3%
Alcabalas de la tierra de 5%
Alcabalas de la tierra dn arrend
Alcabalas de la visita
Alcabalas de las recept de juris
Alcabalas de mercad de Filipinas
Alcabalas de minas de Charcas
Alcabalas de mulas
Alcabalas de Oruro
Alcabalas de otras tesorerías
Alcabalas de Paucarcolla y Puno
Alcabalas de primera venta a 3%
Alcabalas de pulperías
Alcabalas de receptores de 4%
Alcabalas de repartimientos
Alcabalas de responsivas
Alcabalas de reventas
Alcabalas de salida frutos país
Alcabalas de sana
Alcabalas de Tachal y Valle Fert
Alcabalas de tarifa
Alcabalas de tarifa corregidores
Alcabalas de temporalidades
Alcabalas de tiendas
Alcabalas de tierra
Alcabalas de tierra carnecería
Alcabalas de tierra comercio int
Alcabalas de tierra de 6%
Alcabalas de tierra ventas púb
Alcabalas de vecinos
Alcabalas de ventas y contratos
Alcabalas de viento

Alcabalas de viento y tierra
Alcabalas debido de cobrar
Alcabalas del campo
Alcabalas del comercio libre
Alcabalas del consulado
Alcabalas del mar
Alcabalas del mar de 3%
Alcabalas del mar de 4%
Alcabalas del mar de 5%
Alcabalas del mar de 6%
Alcabalas del mar de 6% y 8%
Alcabalas del mar de 8%
Alcabalas del quinto cabezón
Alcabalas del todo el reino
Alcabalas del viento y a tierra
Alcabalas del virreinato
Alcabalas dobladas sal a 2%
Alcabalas duplicadas
Alcabalas en administración
Alcabalas en arrendamiento
Alcabalas en común
Alcabalas en recaudación
Alcabalas encabezadas
Alcabalas encabezadas Antequera
Alcabalas encabezadas de México
Alcabalas encabezadas de Puebla
Alcabalas encabezadas Tepoztlán
Alcabalas encabezadas V Carrión
Alcabalas encabezadas Veracruz
Alcabalas entrada 7% efectos ext
Alcabalas foraneas
Alcabalas fuera de México
Alcabalas maritimas
Alcabalas naipes tabaco de Parral
Alcabalas no encabezadas
Alcabalas para Buenos Aires
Alcabalas para la Armada de barlo
Alcabalas reales
Alcabalas reales y generales
Alcabalas rezagos
Alcabalas salida de cueros a 4%
Alcabalas sit Valdivia y Panamá
Alcabalas u de armas Armada barlo
Alcabalas y almojarifazgos
Alcabalas y almos de comisos

Alcabalas y almos de sana
Alcabalas y Armada de barlovento
Alcabalas y azogues
Alcabalas y cabezón
Alcabalas y deudas minas Charcas
Alcabalas y media anata Charcas
Alcabalas y nuevo impuesto
Alcabalas y pulques
Alcabalas y sisa del vino
Alcabalas y unión de armas
Alcance de novenos
Almacenaje
Almirantazgo
Almo 10% 1% fletes av merc de Fil
Almo 10% avería merc fil sin reg
Almo 10% mercaderías de Filipinas
Almo 16.67% salida filipinas
Almo 2.5% avería y armada 2% sal
Almo 2.5% salida de la flota
Almo 2.5% salida navios sueltos
Almo 3% entrada géneros España
Almo 33.33% entrada de Filipinas
Almo 5% avería y armada 2% entrada
Almo Armada de bar avería fletes
Almo avería armada de 12%
Almo avería armada de 17%
Almo avería armada de 22%
Almo avería armada de 4.5%
Almo avería armada de 6%
Almo avería armada de 9.5%
Almo de 10% de entrada de flota
Almo de 10% entr navíos sueltos
Almo de 10% navíos sin registros
Almo de 10% permiso para Filipinas
Almo de 14% efectos extr sin reg
Almo de 15% de mavíos al través
Almo de 15% y 17.5% de avisos
Almo de 15% y 17.5% doblado
Almo de 16.67% de salida
Almo de 18% entrada de Filipinas
Almo de 2.5% entrada del Perú
Almo de 2.5% salida a Filipinas
Almo de 2.5% salida plata a Fil
Almo de 2.5% y 3.5% navíos a Perú
Almo de 25% y 30% de mercaderías

Almo de 3.5% salida a Filipinas
Almo de 33.33% de entrada
Almo de 5% entr cacao Guayaquil
Almo de 5% entrada del Perú
Almo de 5% entrada navíos sueltos
Almo de 5% y 7.5% de entrada
Almo de 5% y 7.5% descamino naos
Almo de 5% y 7.5% doblado
Almo de 6% plata reg a Filipinas
Almo de 6% salida a Filipinas
Almo de 7.5% de descaminos
Almo de 7.5% entr navíos sueltos
Almo de 7.5% mercaderías descam
Almo de entr y salida ropas tierr
Almo de entrada 3% efectos esp
Almo de entrada 5% 7.5% y 15%
Almo de entrada 7% efectos extra
Almo de entrada de negros a 6%
Almo de entrada efectos ext a 4%
Almo de entrada registros 3% 6 7%
Almo de entrada ropas de tierra
Almo de salida 2.5% navíos Perú
Almo de salida 3% y 7% B Aires
Almo de salida de efectos a 3%
Almo de salida de plata a 4%
Almo de salida efectos España
Almo de salida efectos extranj
Almo de salida frutos del país
Almo de salida géneros Esp y ext
Almo de salida plata frutos a 4%
Almo de salida plata frutos a 6%
Almo de salida ropas de tierra
Almo entr y salida Río Alvarado
Almo entrada ropas americanos
Almo fletes del mar y avería fil
Almo nuevo de 5% de Filipinas
Almo y der comercio Filipinas
Almo y exportación de moneda
Almojarifazgo de 10% y 15%
Almojarifazgo de 17.5
Almojarifazgo 21% salida Havana
Almojarifazgo 5% salida a Perú
Almojarifazgo Armada b de salida
Almojarifazgo Castilla y México
Almojarifazgo de .625% entrada

Almojarifazgo de .625% salida

Almojarifazgo de 1%

Almojarifazgo de 1.25% entrada

Almojarifazgo de 1.5%

Almojarifazgo de 10%

Almojarifazgo de 10% descaminos

Almojarifazgo de 12.5%

Almojarifazgo de 15%

Almojarifazgo de 15% doblado

Almojarifazgo de 16%

Almojarifazgo de 16.67% entrada

Almojarifazgo de 17%

Almojarifazgo de 18% de entrada

Almojarifazgo de 2%

Almojarifazgo de 2.5%

Almojarifazgo de 2.5% de entrada

Almojarifazgo de 2.5% de salida

Almojarifazgo de 20%

Almojarifazgo de 20% doblado

Almojarifazgo de 21%

Almojarifazgo de 29%

Almojarifazgo de 3%

Almojarifazgo de 3% de entrada

Almojarifazgo de 3% de salida

Almojarifazgo de 3.5% de salida

Almojarifazgo de 30%

Almojarifazgo de 4%

Almojarifazgo de 4.5% de salida

Almojarifazgo de 5%

Almojarifazgo de 5% de entrada

Almojarifazgo de 5% de salida

Almojarifazgo de 5% doblado

Almojarifazgo de 5% y 10% entrada

Almojarifazgo de 5% y 15% salida

Almojarifazgo de 6%

Almojarifazgo de 6% de salida

Almojarifazgo de 7%

Almojarifazgo de 7% de entrada

Almojarifazgo de 7% de salida

Almojarifazgo de 7.5%

Almojarifazgo de 8% de salida

Almojarifazgo de años anteriores

Almojarifazgo de entrada

Almojarifazgo de entrada 5%

Almojarifazgo de entrada de 1.25%

Almojarifazgo de entrada de 1.75%

Almojarifazgo de esta año

Almojarifazgo de Guayaquil

Almojarifazgo de Islas Filpinas

Almojarifazgo de llegada

Almojarifazgo de manifestaciones

Almojarifazgo de México

Almojarifazgo de Puerto Callao

Almojarifazgo de ropas Castilla

Almojarifazgo de ropas de tierra

Almojarifazgo de salida

Almojarifazgo de salida 2.5%

Almojarifazgo de Tampico

Almojarifazgo de unión de armas

Almojarifazgo del consulado

Almojarifazgo entrada negros 4%

Almojarifazgo no cobrado

Almojarifazgo nuevo

Almojarifazgo recargado

Almojarifazgo viejo

Almojarifazgos

Almojarifazgos de administración

Almojarifazgos de comisos

Almojarifazgos de plata labrada

Almojarifazgos y averías

Almojarifazgos y comisos

Anclaje y buques

Ancoraje

Ancoraje y toneladas

Aplicado a Armada de barlovento

Aprovechamientos de armas y almac

Arb de grana tinta vainillas

Arbitrio de 1%

Arbitrio de cacao para milicias

Arbitrio de esta ciudad

Arbitrio temporal

Arbitrios de 4 rls fanega cacao

Arbitrios de milicias

Arbitrios de Santa Fe

Arbitrios extraord y temporal

Arbitrios para el hospital

Arbitrios y sisa

Armada de bar medio anata novenos

Armada de barlo apl alcaldes may

Armada de barlo y seno mexicano

Armada de barlovento
Armada de barlovento esta cuenta
Armada de barlovento u de armas
Armada de barlovento y avería
Armada y avería
Arrend venta composición tierras
Arrendamiento de haciendas
Arrendamiento de puente
Arrendamiento de puertos
Arrendamiento de pulperías
Arrendamiento de trapiches
Arrendamiento del Puerto Iquique
Arrendamiento reales pulperías
Arrendamientos y censos
Aumento anual especies y vinos
Aumento de 2% de alcabalas
Aumento de tributos
Auxilio de buques
Avería
Avería de armada
Avería de imposición
Avería de negros bozales
Avería de San Juan de Ullua
Avería y armada 2% de entrada
Avería y armada 2% de salida
Avería y armada de 1%
Avería y armada de 2% doblada
Azúcar y cacao
Barcos de Antigua
Barras de lienzo
Buques
Buques de entrada
Buques de salida
Cajas del permiso de Filipinas
Canchas de bolas
Cascarilla de Calisaya
Caudal de los navíos
Cebada
Cinco sesmos de 2% plata a Fil
Comercio de negros de 6%
Composición de caminos
Composición de cosecheros
Composición de ingenio
Composición de molinos de pólv
Composición de pulperías

Composición del cacao
Compras de cecina
Compromisarios de Fil servicio an
Consulado
Consulado de Lima a .5%
Consulado de México
Consulado de Sevilla
Contr Almirantazgo com Filipinas
Contribución de flota Santillan
Contribución de tiendas
Contribución por arbitrios
Convoy
Cosecheros de la ciudad
Cuatro novenos beneficiales
Cuerdas de arbabuzes
Cueros
Der comercio libre de Filipinas
Der de 1.5% Canal de Guadarrama
Der de 2.5% salida barcos a Perú
Der de 3.5% de géneros del Perú
Der de 5% efectos China a sosnte
Der de barco retornado a C Rica
Der de barcos salida a California
Der de barcos salida a Costa Rica
Der de entrada a barcos Perú a 2.5%
Der de entrada bracos Perú a 5%
Der de entrada mercaderías de Fil
Der de entrada vc rebajados 4%
Der de mercad emb a Guatemala
Der de naos de Filipinas
Der de salida mercad para Fil
Derecho 5 mvds hospitales Madrid
Derecho de 1.5%
Derecho de 10%
Derecho de 11.5%
Derecho de 12%
Derecho de 16%
Derecho de 17%
Derecho de 20%
Derecho de 22%
Derecho de 3%
Derecho de 32% de fragatas
Derecho de 4%
Derecho de 6%
Derecho de 8%

Derecho de 9%
Derecho de 9.5%
Derecho de apartado
Derecho de de bacalao de 21%
Derecho de buques
Derecho de cera
Derecho de cuarta parte
Derecho de entrada de 20%
Derecho de entrada de 21%
Derecho de entrada de 6%
Derecho de entrada de 8%
Derecho de entrada y salida
Derecho de de esclavos de 33.5%
Derecho de seda
Derecho de toneladas
Derecho de cacao
Derecho de consumo
Derecho del vino
Derechos de 10%
Derechos de 5%
Derechos de 5% y 10%
Derechos de consumo y apartado
Derechos de entrada de 2.5%
Derechos de entrada de 3%
Derechos de entrada de 7%
Derechos de Guatulco
Derechos de Huacas
Derechos de los géneros del Perú
Derechos de mar y tierra
Derechos de navíos de permiso
Derechos de salida de Campeche
Derechos de salida de España
Derechos de salida de Guaranao
Derechos de salida de Havana
Derechos de salida de Puertobelo
Derechos de salida de Trinidad
Derechos de salida flota y aviso
Derechos del 1.25%
Derechos dobles
Derechos mercaderías filipinas
Diezmos de brea
Efectos de Castilla
Enterado para la carena de un nao
Entrada de macaderías
Entrada de negros

Entrada y salida de navíos
Entradas del ramo de propios
Entregado por comercio Filipinas
Escrituras comercio de Filipinas
Escuderage
Especies de trigo maíz aves
Estancias
Extracción de efectos de tierra
Extravíos de negros
Fábrica
Fincas
Fletes
Fletes de carros de Nuevo México
Fletes de dinero sin licencia
Fletes de Filipinas
Fletes de mercaderías descaminadas
Fletes de navíos de Filipinas
Fletes de navíos venidos de Perú
Fletes del mar ropa ven de Fil
Fragata Venus
Fragata Victoria
Géneros entregados Armada del sur
Guacas
Guarda costa
Guias
Hacienda el Pochitocal
Impuesto de ganados
Impuesto del cacao
Impuesto provincial de Tabasco
Impuestos generales
Indulto del comercio de Filipinas
Islas de Filipinas
Jornada de Filipinas
Lana de vicuña
Lana de vicuña en especie
Lic fierros para herrar ganados
Licencias y aduanilla de negros
Manifestaciones
Manifestaciones de brebaje
Manifestaciones de esclavos
Manifestaciones de negros
Marchamo
Mercadería de Filipinas sin lic
Mercaderías de almojarifazgos
Mercedes

Miel de purga
Ministros de fábricas
Molinos
Mulas pert a su majestad
Noveno al Real Seminario
Noveno mayor
Noveno y medio
Noveno y medio de diezmos
Noveno y medio de esta cuenta
Noveno y medio de fábrica
Noveno y medi del hospital
Noveno y medio hospital Chillán
Noveno y medio hospital La Plata
Novenos atrasados
Novenos correduría restituciones
Novenos de este año
Novenos de la Villa de León
Novenos de Tlascala
Novenos integr para consolidación
Novenos nacionales
Novenos para el capellán mayor
Novenos por suplemento
Novenos reales
Novenos reales de amortización
Novenos reales de diezmos
Novenos reales de la catedral
Novenos y mesadas eclesiasticas
Novenos y oficios vendibles
Novenos y vacantes de obispados
Novenos y vacantes
Nuevo arbitrio aum contingente
Nuevo arbitrio de varios ramos
Nuevo arbitrio por alcabalas
Nuevo impuesto de 1% de avería
Nuevo impuesto de 2% de avería
Nuevo impuesto de caldos
Nuevo impuesto del cacao
Nuevo impuesto del vino
Nuevo impuesto del vino de Rl H
Nuevo impuesto por arbitrios
Nuevo impuesto temporal de guerra
Nuevo noveno decimal
Nuevo servicio de entrada
Nuevo servicio de salida
Nuevos arbitrios

Obrajes
Pagado de dueños de requas
Panadería y bayuca del Castillo
Peaje
Peaje y barcas
Pontazgo de Aconcagua
Producto de guias
Productos de Villa Rica
Propios
Propios de ciudades y villas
Propios y arbitrios de Campeche
Proventos
Provisión de almacenes
Puentes
Pulperías
Pulperías foraneas
Pulperías por administración
Quinto de corambres
Quinto de vacas
Real derecho de piso
Reintegros de alcabalas
Remate de mercaderías
Renta de aguardiente y vinagre
Rentas unidas
Resultas de alcabalas
Resultas del tercero cabezón
Rezagos de alcabalas
Salida de mercaderías
Salida del sal y palo
Seguros de alcabalas
Sementera de San Lázaro
Servicio de entrada
Servicio de entrada y salida
Servicio de salida
Sisa
Sisa de carne
Sisa de carne de Camaná
Sisa de carne de Castilla
Sisa de de este año
Sisa de mulas
Sisa de agua
Sisa de vino
Sisa o nuevo impuesto
Sisa y cuartilla del vino
Subtracción de alcabalas

Sumarios de carne
Tablas de alerce
Tercero cabezón del consulado
Tercero y cuarto cabezón alcab
Tercio encabezamiento alcabalas
Tercios de yerba
Tiendas mestizas
Unión de armas
Unión de armas para Valparaiso
Valor de arroz
Venta de tribo
Venta de bien raíz de obras pias
Venta de caravinas
Venta de cuatro escopetas
Venta de esclavos negros
Venta de libros
Venta de ropa abasca
Venta de trapiches
Venta de vino por la Corona
Venta de víveres
Venta del viscocho
Ventas
Vino y aguardiente y vinagre
Víveres
Víveres de Valdivia
Víveres del Castillo

Taxes on Government and Church Officials

10% de sueldos
10% de sueldos de caciques
10% De sueldos y encomiendas
18% mesada eclesiástica
2.5% media anata para conducción
3% de sinodos
4% de sueldos para la guerra
5% de oficios
5% de sínodos
5% de sueldos
6% del subsidio eclesiástico
Alcance para media anata
Anata de corregidores
Anualidades
Anualidades eclesiasticas

Arrendamiento de oficios
Arrendamiento del escribano
Arrendamiento oficios y tierras
Bara alguacil mayor de Quenoxingo
Bara del alguacil mayor
Beneficios de oficios
Bienes del arzo alonso de cuevas
Bienes del obispo
Bienes del obispo de Oaxaca
Bienes del obispo de Yucatán
Bienes mostrencos
Bienes vacantes
Bienes vacantes y mostrencos
Caballerias de órdenes militares
Canónigo supreso
Canónigos suprimidos
Cinco porciento de sueldos
Cinco y diez porciento sueldos
Cobrado del síndico S Francisco
Composición capillas y oratorios
Composición de capillas
Condenaciones eclesiásticas
Conquistadores hijos nietos mujer
Consignaciones eclesiásticas
Cuarta arzobispal
Cuarta episcopal
Cuarta episcopal del Cuzco
Cuarta vacante de curatos
Curia
Der de contaduría de media anata
Der de regulación de media anata
Derecho de oficinas
Derechos de sucesión
Descuento de oficiales
Descuento de sueldos
Descuento de sueldos cons y secr
Descuento de sueldos de alemanes
Descuento para consejo y secr
Descuento para presente guerra
Descuentos por contribución
Diez porciento de sueldos
Diezmos de Pánuco
Diezmos eclesiásticos
Dispensa de edad menor de oficio
Dos meses de los corregidores

Emolumentos cont de media anata
Emolumentos de oficiales contrata
Emolumentos de oficialia R Hac
Emolumentos de oficinas
Emolumentos escr mayor de R H
Enterado del alguacil mayor
Escribanías vacantes
Espolios
Ferreterías y Rl rden Carlos III
Fondo para premios de militares
Inválidos
Lanzas de títulos
Lanzas de títulos por reintegro
Lanzas y medias anatas
Media anata
Media anata añadida
Media anata antigua
Media anata de buques
Media anata de corregidores
Media anata de fuera
Media anata de oficios conseguibles
Media anata de tierras
Media anata de Tucumán
Media anata debida
Media anata der contaduría gen
Media anata eclesiástica
Media anata mesadas eclesiástica
Media anata nueva
Media anata oficios del cabildo
Media anata oficios proveidos sm
Media anata para Buenos Aires
Media anata secular
Media anata suspendida
Media anata y Armada barlovento
Media anata y lanzas
Media anata y mesada ecles
Media anata y oficios vendibles
Mesada del obispo
Mesadas de curatos
Mesadas de oficios
Mesadas ecles oficios salinas
Mesadas ecles y herencias trans
Mesadas eclesiásticas
Mesadas eclesiásticas
Mesadas eclesiásticas

Mesadas para la Real Capilla
Mesadas particulares
Mesadas seculares
Mesadas y donativos
Mesadas y media anata ecles
Mesadas y media anatas
Mitad de sobras sueldos justicia
Mitad de sueldos
Mitad de sueldos de caciques
Mitad de sueldos de corregidores
Mitad de sueldos de preceptores
Mitad y sobras sueldos justicia
Mojonazgo
Monte de piedad
Monte pío
Monte pío batallones de marina
Monte pío cirujanos del ejército
Monte pío de brigada
Monte pío de cirugía general
Monte pío de cirugía militar
Monte pío de cirujanos
Monte pío de cirujanos de armada
Monte pío de ingenieros
Monte pío de maestranza
Monte pío de ministros
Monte pío de oficiales del mar
Monte pío de oficinas
Monte pío de pilotos
Monte pío militar
Monte pío militar y inválidos
Monte pío militar y ministros
Nuevos diezmos
Oficio de chancillería
Oficio de escribano
Oficio de registros
Oficio del alguacil mayor
Oficio del ensayador Casa Moneda
Oficio del factor
Oficio del tesorero Casa Moneda
Oficios antiguos
Oficios arrendados
Oficios de ens y fund Casa Moneda
Oficios de la Santa Cruzada
Oficios del cabildo
Oficios suspendidos

Oficios vendibles y renunciables
Pensión de cabildo
Quintas de oficios suprimidos
Quitas de salarios mayores
Quitas vac corregidores a mayores
Real rden de Carlos III
Renunciaciones de oficios
Residuos sueldos de justicia
Sínodos vacios y mesadas
Sobras de sueldos de preceptores
Sueldo del agente fiscal
Sueldo del preceptor
Sueldos de caciques
Sueldos de justicia
Sueldos de preceptores
Sueldos embargados
Tanto porciento de sueldos
Tercios de sueldos
Tercios ventas renun de oficios
Titulos de Castilla
Vacante de barbero
Vacante de escribano
Vacante de este arzobispado
Vacante de médico
Vacante de médico en Cajamarca
Vacante de México
Vacante de preceptores
Vacante del obispado de Tucumán
Vacantes
Vacantes de caciques
Vacantes de canónigos
Vacantes de curatos
Vacantes de doctrinas
Vacantes de justicia
Vacantes de justicia residuos
Vacantes de obispados
Vacantes de obispados Filipinas
Vacantes de oficios
Vacantes de prebendas
Vacantes de sínodos
Vacantes de sueldos
Vacantes de sueldos de caciques
Vacantes de sueldos de justicia
Vacantes ecles y espoleos
Vacantes eclesiásticas

Vacantes embargadas
Vacantes mayores
Vacantes mayores y menores
Vacantes menores
Vacantes menores atrasados
Vacantes remitidas
Vacantes y sobras sal justicia
Valimientos de 10% de sueldos
Valimientos de 10% de sueldos
Valimientos de 4% de sueldos
Valimientos de 5% de sueldos
Valimientos de 5% y 10% sueldos
Valimientos de caciques
Valimientos de rentas de oficios
Valimientos de sueldos
Valimientos de tercios de sueldos
Venta de oficios
Venta y arrendamiento de oficios

Taxes on Indians

1.5 reales del hospital
10% de servicio pecuniario
3% para seminario de La Paz
4% y 2% arbit bienes comu
5% de sínodos mojos y chuquito
5% de sinodos para mojos
Agasejos de indios
Almonedas extra cuenta anterior
Almonedas extraordinarias
Almonedas ordinarias
Almonedas reales
Arrendamientos de indios
Aumento de tributos
Bienes comunes de los indios
Bienes de comunidades de indios
Buenas leyes
Cajas de comunidad
Capellanías
Colegio Carolino
Composición de indios
Composición de indios 2 y 3 vida
Composición de tributos
Comunidad de lanzas
Comunidades

Comunidades de indios
Contrapartidas almonedas ordinari
Contrapartidas cargadas y no cobr
Contribución de indios
Contribución
Contribución al hospital
Contribución general
Contribución voluntaria de indios
Cuartilla de real para defensor
Derecho de mitas
Derecho del montado
Diezmos de encomiendas
Diezmos de Huexutla y Yahualica
Diezmos de tributos
Emolumentos
Encom Colegio San Carlos de Lima
Encomienda de vino y aceite
Encomiendas
Encomiendas embargadas
Encomiendas incorporadas
Encomiendas vacas
Enteros de corregidores
Escuderage y real de manta
Fondo general de tributos
Géneros de tributos rematados
Guias de forasteros
Holpatán o medio rl de ministros
Hospital de los indios de México
Hospital de San Andrés
Hospital de San Lázaro
Hospital del Cuzco
Hospital Real
Imposición de tomín
Imposiciones y rendiciones princ
Impuesto en cada manta
Impuestos de tajamares
Indio del campo
Indios acabaleros y forasteros
Indios de encomienda
Indios foraneos
Indios yanaconas forasteros
Indultos de tributos
Lanzas
Lanzas y arcabuzes
Maíz de Acaponeta

Maíz del repartimiento
Mayor servicio
Media tasa de indios
Medio peso n servicio de Culiacán
Medio peso n servicio pueblos enc
Medio peso n servicio pueblos rls
Medio real de hospital
Medio real de ministros
Medio rl hospital indios de Méx
Mercedes de indios
Misiones de mojos y chuquito
Mitas de particulares
Mitas para la mina Huancavelica
Nuevo servicio indios de su maj
Nuevo servicio y unión de armas
Pagado a los indios tlapisques
Pensión de indios
Pensión en encomienda de indios
Pensiones de encomiendas
Principales de censos de indios
Producto de guias de forasteros
Productos de Curuguati
Pueblos nuevos
Quarta parte del num de indios
Quillacas y aconaques
Quintos de indios
Quintos de la guerra chichimeca
Quintos de tributos
Ramos de dos reales
Real de manta
Reditos de censos de indios
Remate de almonedas
Repartimientos
Retazas en prorrata
Rezago de mitad de encomiendas
Rezagos de tributos
Servicio de indios años anterior
Servicio de medio peso
Servicio nuevo de Culiacán
Servicio nuevo indios enc rezagos
Servicio nuevo indios v Qualtiche
Servicio nuevo pueblos de indios
Servicio pecuniario
Servicio real de indios
Servicio real de indios rezagos

Servicio real indios chichimecas

Servicio rl pueblos encomendados

Servicios a su majestad

Situación hospital de Santa Ana

Situaciones de encomiendas

Sobras de tomín

Sobras de tributos

Sobras de tributos de provincias

Sobras tributos de forasteros

Tercio encom y tribs vacios

Tierras de comunidad de indios

Tomín del hospital

Tomín y encomienda San Andrés

Tostón del nuevo servicio indios

Trib en din maíz gallinas sv rl

Trib en maiz y gallinas Culiacán

Trib indios laborios de Culiacán

Trib indios negros mul ind lab

Trib indios negros mulatos libres

Trib lnz Chuquicota Sabaya Sacaba

Trib negros mulatos y indios lab

Trib nuevas leyes y conquistad

Trib rls lipes, Condes de Arabate

Trib rls quillacas y asanaques

Trib sv rl pueblos encomendados

Trib Yanaconas Cochabamba Misque

Tribs Orurillo para Univ de Lima

Tribs Ana Antonia de la Garda

Tribs ayllu Culaira Narasaca Sai

Tribs Callachaca San Sebastián

Tribs capilla Lima en Orurillo

Tribs capilla Univ de Lima

Tribs de parroq de hospital

Tribs de Paucarapa y Sallaypata

Tribs de Sallaypata y Paucarpata

Tribs del valle de Ñeque Ñeque

Tribs emb de Alejo de Salas y Valdez

Tribs forasteros mulatos negros

Tribs indios mostrencos foraster

Tribs lanzas Aullagas Uruquillas

Tribs lanzas Caquina y Picachuri

Tribs lanzas Caracosa o Arechaca

Tribs lanzas Chuquicota y Sabaya

Tribs lanzas Colque y Andamarca

Tribs lanzas quillacas asanaques

Tribs lanzas Sabaya y Sacabaya

Tribs lanzas Santiago de Curí

Tribs lanzas Tacobomba Potobamba

Tribs lanzas Totora y Curaguera

Tribs María Montes de Heredia

Tribs Pumamarca y Sanoc San Seb

Tribs reales Santiago de Curí

Tribs rls Aullagas y Uruquillas

Tribs rls Caquina y Picachuri

Tribs rls Caracosa o Arechacha

Tribs rls Carangas y Chuquicota

Tribs rls Chichas y Tarija

Tribs rls Chuchoa y Marcapata

Tribs rls Collhguas de la Chimba

Tribs rls de Arones Yandaray

Tribs rls de Caira Urua y Camaná

Tribs rls de Cosus de los Mages

Tribs rls de Guanca Guanca

Tribs rls de indios mostrencos

Tribs rls de la guardia de a pie

Tribs rls de Larapa y Antamachay

Tribs rls de Murca y Pairiaca

Tribs rls de parroquia Santiago

Tribs rls de Presto y Tarabuco

Tribs rls de repart de padres

Tribs rls de San Pedro de B Vista

Tribs rls de Universidad de Lima

Tribs rls de Vilque y Manazo

Tribs rls de Viraco y Machaguay

Tribs rls de Yancoayllochungara

Tribs rls de Yanqui Collaquas

Tribs rls de Yauriyatimcana

Tribs rls Macha Aymora Copoata

Tribs rls Moromoro y Yamparaes

Tribs rls parroquia San Gerónimo

Tribs rls Santiago de Moscari

Tribs rls Soconcha y Manogasta

Tribs rls Tacobamba y Potabamba

Tribs rls y tostón de indios

Tribs Sto Tomás y Colquemarca

Tribs yanaconas cuzcos de ciudad

Tribs yanaconas de totora vacios

Tribs yanaconas la Plata y distr

Tribs yanaconas Misque y Pocona

Tributos 1/3 parte de Chayanta

Tributos 2/3 parte de Chayanta
Tributos atrasados
Tributos consignaciones de lanzas
Tributos Cristobal de Cartagena
Tributos de almonedas
Tributos de Andamarcas y Lucanas
Tributos de Charcas
Tributos de Culiacán
Tributos de Diego de Silva
Tributos de encomiendas
Tributos de indios chichimecas
Tributos de indios en cacao
Tributos de indios en grana
Tributos de indios en ropa
Tributos de indios en sal
Tributos de indios en trigo
Tributos de indios esta cuenta
Tributos de indios laborios
Tributos de indios rezagos
Tributos de indios y yanaconas
Tributos de la Real Corona
Tributos de las 12 provincias
Tributos de Nueva España
Tributos de Nueva Galicia
Tributos de nuevas leyes
Tributos de Titla y Chilapa
Tributos de vacantes
Tributos de yanaconas
Tributos de Zumpango de la Laguna
Tributos debido de cobrar
Tributos del marqués del Carpio
Tributos dinero años anteriores
Tributos embargados
Tributos en dinero
Tributos en gallinas
Tributos en gallinas años ante
Tributos en gallinas v Qualtiche
Tributos en géneros
Tributos en géneros rematados
Tributos en géneros vac encom
Tributos en géneros vac encom esp
Tributos en maíz
Tributos en maíz años anteriores
Tributos en maíz v de Laltenango
Tributos en maíz v de Qualtiche

Tributos en maíz y gallinas
Tributos foraneos
Tributos géneros años anteriores
Tributos indio lab sirv españoles
Tributos indios din este año
Tributos indios géneros rezagos
Tributos indios neg mul serv rl
Tributos indios y año de hueco
Tributos Juan de Layseca Alvarado
Tributos lanzas
Tributos lanzas de Aullagas
Tributos lanzas de Aymaya
Tributos lanzas de Caracara
Tributos lanzas de Chaqui
Tributos lanzas de Chuquicota
Tributos lanzas de Chuquito
Tributos lanzas de Copoata
Tributos lanzas de Macha
Tributos lanzas de Sacaca
Tributos lanzas de Tinguipaya
Tributos lanzas de Totora
Tributos lanzas de Visisa
Tributos lanzas Santiago de Curí
Tributos marquesa de los Veles
Tributos n servicio v Laltenango
Tributos n servicios años anter
Tributos para gastos de guerra
Tributos pueblos de Adel Montejo
Tributos reales Antigua Veracruz
Tributos reales de Acopia
Tributos reales de Acos
Tributos reales de Andamarcas
Tributos reales de Andaray
Tributos reales de Atacama
Tributos reales de Aymaya
Tributos reales de Ayquile
Tributos reales de Azaviri
Tributos reales de Belén
Tributos reales de Cachona
Tributos reales de Cajapucara
Tributos reales de Canta
Tributos reales de Capamarca
Tributos reales de Caracara
Tributos reales de Carangas
Tributos reales de Caratopa

Tributos reales de Catca
Tributos reales de Chaqui
Tributos reales de Chayanta
Tributos reales de Chichas
Tributos reales de Chillques
Tributos reales de Chiriguanes
Tributos reales de Chunguara
Tributos reales de Chupa
Tributos reales de Chuquicota
Tributos reales de Chuquito
Tributos reales de Cochabamba
Tributos reales de Cochas
Tributos reales de Collaguas
Tributos reales de Colquemarca
Tributos reales de Comacha
Tributos reales de Copabilque
Tributos reales de Copoata
Tributos reales de Coporaque
Tributos reales de Corca
Tributos reales de Coroma
Tributos reales de Cosoxa
Tributos reales de Cotaguasi
Tributos reales de Cupe
Tributos reales de duque de Alba
Tributos reales de esta ciudad
Tributos reales de forasteros
Tributos reales de Gualparoca
Tributos reales de Guancane
Tributos reales de Guancarama
Tributos reales de Guanuquite
Tributos reales de Hatuncamaina
Tributos reales de Huarochiri
Tributos reales de indios
Tributos reales de Jalapa
Tributos reales de Jauja
Tributos reales de Lipes
Tributos reales de Lipes y Conde
Tributos reales de Livitaca
Tributos reales de Lucanas
Tributos reales de Macha
Tributos reales de Machaguay
Tributos reales de Misque
Tributos reales de Mohina
Tributos reales de Moromoro
Tributos reales de Moyos

Tributos reales de Nloyna
Tributos reales de Nlunapata
Tributos reales de Ocona
Tributos reales de Omacha
Tributos reales de Omachamua
Tributos reales de Orurillo
Tributos reales de Oruro
Tributos reales de Pacajes
Tributos reales de Panacache
Tributos reales de Parcas
Tributos reales de Paria
Tributos reales de Paucarapa
Tributos reales de Paucarcolla
Tributos reales de Pichigua
Tributos reales de Pilaya
Tributos reales de Pocona
Tributos reales de Pomachapi
Tributos reales de Porco
Tributos reales de Potosí
Tributos reales de Puna
Tributos reales de Puquices
Tributos reales de Quataoma
Tributos reales de Quichuas
Tributos reales de Quiguares
Tributos reales de Quintillalta
Tributos reales de Quispicanche
Tributos reales de Sacaca
Tributos reales de Sallauparco
Tributos reales de Sallaypata
Tributos reales de Sangara
Tributos reales de Sansaban
Tributos reales de Santo Tomás
Tributos reales de Sipesipe
Tributos reales de Sondor
Tributos reales de Tambobamba
Tributos reales de Tancarcalla
Tributos reales de Tapacari
Tributos reales de Tarija
Tributos reales de Tarromas
Tributos reales de Tayacaxas
Tributos reales de Tingsupaya
Tributos reales de Tinguipaya
Tributos reales de Tinta
Tributos reales de Tomina
Tributos reales de Totora

Tributos reales de Ubinas
Tributos reales de Uminacanches
Tributos reales de Visisa
Tributos reales de Yamparaes
Tributos reales de Yanaconas
Tributos reales de Yanaguaras
Tributos reales de Yauyos
Tributos reales de Yucay
Tributos reales embargados
Tributos reales Macha y Chaqui
Tributos reales Paria y Capinota
Tributos reales Pomabamba Grande
Tributos reales y vacos
Tributos recargados
Tributos rls condes de Arabate
Tributos rls Cualparocas de Guata
Tributos rls de indios de Jauja
Tributos rls Totora y Curaguara
Tributos rls Yotala y Quilaquila
Tributos vacos
Tributos vacos de Orurillo
Tributos vacos en deposito
Tributos vacos Juan Julio Ojeda
Tributos vacos Presto y Tarabuco
Tributos vacos y tercias partes
Tributos y alcabalas
Tributos y almonedas rls indios
Tributos y nuevo servicio indios
Tributos y servicio real indios
Tributos y sv real no aplicado
Tributos yanaconas de Arequipa
Tributos yanaconas de Charcas
Tributos yanaconas de Cochabamba
Tributos yanaconas de la Plata
Tributos yanaconas de Paria
Tributos yanaconas de Pitantora
Tributos yanaconas de Porco
Tributos yanaconas de Potosí
Tributos yanaconas sin reducciones
Tucuiachi
Única contribución de indios
Vacantes de encomiendas
Vacantes de indios
Villas nuevas
Yanaconas

Yanaconas de San Blas
Yanaconas de San Cristoval
Yanaconas de San Sebastián
Yanaconas de Santa Ana
Yanaconas parroquia de Santiago

Royal Monopolies, Including Liquors and Bulas de Cruzada

2 reales cada fanega de sal
4 reales cada fanega de sal
Administración de bulas de sc
Administración del sal
Alcance papel sellado vino nieve
Alumbres
Aumento de bulas de Santa Crzda
Aumento de tasas bulas de cruzada
Aumento un real cada libra tabaco
Barajas
Bidimus e instrucciones de sc
Breas
Bulas cuadragesimales
Bulas cuadragesimales b corrte
Bulas cuadragesimales b futuro
Bulas cuadragesimales b pasado
Bulas de s cruzada de Filipinas
Bulas de s cruzada de Oaxaca
Bulas de Santa Cruzada
Bulas de sc bienio corriente
Bulas de sc bienio futuro
Bulas de sc bienio pasado
Bulas de sc de Geronimo de Soto
Bulas de sc de Guatemala
Bulas de sc de Núñez Pérez
Bulas de sc de otras tesorerías
Bulas de sc de Yucatán
Bulas de sc y cuadragesimales
Bulas sc y licencias decir misas
Cajas y arpilleras de naipes
Casa de gallos
Cobre de labor
Coliseo de gallos
Comisos y nieve
Cordobanes
Cruzada

Depositos de la renta del tabaco
Derechos del tabaco
Espec reconoc en bulas y boletos
Espec reconoc en papel sellado
Extraordinario y papel sellado
Indulto quadragesimal
Indultos quadr en especie b pas
Indultos quadragesimales b corrte
Juego de gallos
Lastre
Licencia para andar a cavallo
Limosnas de bulas de santa crzda
Lotería
Lotería auxiliar
Lotería forzosa
Minas de cobre
Naipes
Naipes de arrendamiento
Naipes de su majestad
Naipes y juego de gallos
Naipes y papel sellado
Nieve
Nieve y aguardiente
Nieve y aloja
Nieve y vinos mescales
Papel habilitado
Papel rubricado
Papel sellado
Papel sellado bienio corriente
Papel sellado bienio futuro
Papel sellado bienio pasado
Papel sellado de las Filipinas
Papel sellado remitido
Papel sellado sobrante
Papel sellado y común gastado
Permiso para una mesa de truecos
Plaza de toros
Plomo
Pólvora
Pólvora y naipes
Pólvora y naipes de Parral
Producto de tabaco en polvo
Producto indulto cuadragesimal
Rentas estancadas
Sal

Sal blanca
Sal chanpurada
Sal de lamar
Sal fiada
Sal fiada de Penol Blanco
Sal fiada de Santa María
Salinas
Salinas apl Armada de barlovento
Salinas de Acaponeta
Salinas de Campeche
Salinas de Centitapac
Salinas de Chametla
Salinas de Culiacán
Salinas de Jerez y Lagos
Salinas de la Purificación
Salinas de Penol Blanco
Salinas de Santa María
Salinas y quinto de perlas
Saltierra
Saltierra debido de cobrar
Santa bula
Sellos bienio corriente
Sellos bienio pasado
Tabaco de Parral
Tabaco pólvora naipes
Tabaco y naipes
Tabacos
Tributos de naipes

Miscellaneous Income

25% de comisos remisibles
1% de conducción
2% conducción a Buenos Aires
2% de administración
2% de amortización nov y vacante
2% de los ramos de Real Hacienda
2% de ventas de solares y casas
2% del valor de tierras realengas
2% redito de capitales
3% de sínodos para seminario
3% para el colegio de Monterrey
3% para el seminario
5 y 10%
5% redito de capitales

6% de creditos
10% de arrendamiento de casas
10% de comisos
10% de encomiendas
10% de fincas
10% de mercedes y juros
10% del servicio pecuniario
100 quintales de Jalpa
15% amortización de principales
15% aplicado a manos muertas
15% de amortización
15% de amortización de vales rls
15% de capellanías
16% de censos de indios
18% conducción a España
18% de conducción
25% de comisos remisibles
25% derechos del estado
65% de mercedes y juros
70% de encomiendas
70% de mercedes y juros
75% de mercedes y juros
A la universidad
Acrecentamiento salarios del r c
Administraciones subalternas
Agente fiscal
Aguas
Ajustamiento de la cuenta
Almacenes de artillería
Alquiler de la casa de la misión
Amortización de vales
Amparo de una aguada
Anclajee
Anticipaciones hechas en España
Apl a defensores veedores protect
Aplicado a bolsillo
Aplicado a los chasquis
Aplicado al tribunal
Aplicado para el fuerte
Aprovechamientos
Aprovechamientos de escribano
Arbitrio para mantener tropas sud
Arbitrios
Arbitrios extraordinarios
Arbitrios extraordinarios guerra

Arcabuzes
Armamento
Armas
Arrend de cajones fierro viejo
Arrend de mina Villa Rica Cerro
Arrendamiento cajones antiguos
Arrendamiento cajones de palacio
Arrendamiento cajones nuevos
Arrendamiento de casas
Arrendamiento de casas reales
Arrendamiento de casas y tiendas
Arrendamiento de indios
Arrendamiento de la mina de Porco
Arrendamiento de suertes
Arrendamiento de tiendas
Arrendamiento Plaza del Corredor
Arrendamiento puerto de Iquique
Arrendamiento Rl Hacienda Charcas
Arrendamiento y venta de minas
Arrendamiento y venta de tierras
Arrendamientos
Arrendamientos de haciendas
Artillería
Asignaciones
Asignaciones para España
Asignaciones y reint para España
Atenciones de California
Aumento en la reducción de reales
Aumento en la remesa a México
Azogues papel sellado media an
Baja del ley
Bajas
Balanza
Banco de rescate
Banco nacional de San Carlos
Banco real
Banco vitalicio
Bandanas
Bara de la Santa Hermandad
Bara de Sta Hermandad de Minas
Barco del Río Maule
Barras vendidas
Bastimentos armas municiones
Bastimentos de Valdivia
Bastimentos de Valparaiso

Beaterio de Jesús María y Joseph
Bienes confiscados
Bienes confiscados de insurgentes
Bienes de contrabando
Bienes de extranjeros
Bienes del arzobispo
Bienes embargados
Bocas de fuego
Bolsillo de Su Majestad
Bolsillo del Rl Consejo de Indias
Bosques y plantios
Brevarios
Buenas cuentas
Buenos efectos y residuos
Caballería
Caballos vendidos
Cabezones de haciendas
Caja
Cajones de rivera
Cajonsillos de regalo de Fil
Camara del Real Consejo de Indias
Canal del Río Maipo
Canoneras
Capellán mayor del ejército
Capilla real
Capilla real de Granada
Capilla real de Lima
Capitales impuestos a censo de 4%
Cargado demás
Cargas de particulares
Cargas generales
Cargo a presidio
Cargo de Buenos Aires
Carros matos
Casa de contratación
Casa de recojidas
Casa escusada
Casas de aposentos
Casas de esclavos vendidos
Castillo de San Juan de Ullua
Catedral de Lima
Caudal inv en buenas cuentas
Caudal inv en dobl de cordoncillo
Caudal inv en moneda sencilla
Caudal inventariado en oro

Cédulas contra diferentes personas
Censos
Censos de bienes mostrencos
Censos de casas
Censos de indios
Censos de indios y 16%
Censos de tierras realengas
Censos en la caja
Censos por temporalidades
Censos sobre renta de tabaco
Censos y arrendamientos
Cien dozenas de bandanas
Ciudad de Ancón
Cobrado de la minería
Cobrado de personas diversas
Cobrado de resultas por tribunal
Cobrado de una residencia
Cobrado para el titulo de ciudad
Cobrado para Real Caja Veracruz
Cobrado por el factor
Cobrado por la caja de Lima
Cobrado por órden del tribunal
Cobranza
Colegio de San Antonio de Abad
Colegio de San Felipe de Lima
Colegio de San Francisco de Borja
Colegio seminario
Colegio seminario de la Plata
Colegio seminario del Cuzco
Colegio seminario Yslas Mariannas
Com del cont Bart de Estrada
Comisión alcabala Alonso de Tapia
Comisión oidor Alonso de Salvador
Comision secreta de Havana
Comisos
Comisos de fragata Warren
Comisos de galeones del marqués
Comisos de ministros
Comisos de plata aplicada a S M
Comisos de Su Magestad
Comisos del corregidor de México
Comisos del excmo sup gen de R H
Comisos del ministro de Indias
Comisos del Rl Consejo de Indias
Comisos para España

Comisos y descaminos
Comp de tierras y extranjeros
Comp de trapiches y obrajes
Composición de caminos
Composición de extranjeros
Composición de indios de Tucumán
Composición de obrajes
Composición de tierras
Composición de tierras Armada bar
Composición de tierras realengas
Composición de tierras y aguas
Composición del alguacil mayor
Composición del camino Mextitlán
Composición del consulado
Composición gachupines Sacatula
Composición pasar 3 vida encom
Composición y venta de tierras
Composiciones de encomiendas
Composiciones de los portugueses
Concursos
Cond apl al fuerte de Acapulco
Cond criadas marq Villa Manrique
Cond de bulas de Santa Cruzada
Cond del hijo de Gómez Machuca
Cond del oidor J Miguel Agosto
Cond para pobres del cárcel
Condenación de estrados
Condenación para fábrica cárcel
Condenaciones
Condenaciones apl a Rl Cámara
Condenaciones de Antonio Bolinas
Condenaciones de cámara
Condenaciones de corregidores
Condenaciones de Diego de Orejón
Condenaciones de guerra
Condenaciones de J Sáenz Moreno
Condenaciones de la audiencia
Condenaciones de la visita
Condenaciones de negros
Condenaciones de Pedro de Quiroga
Condenaciones de residencia
Condenaciones de tribunal cuentas
Condenaciones del consulado
Condenaciones del contrabando
Condenaciones del fuerte Callao

Condenaciones del oro S L Potosí
Condenaciones del Real Bolsillo
Condenaciones del Real Consejo
Condenaciones en Guatulco
Condenaciones en Manila
Condenaciones en Veracruz
Condenaciones gastos de justicia
Condenaciones para capilla real
Condenaciones para casa real
Condenaciones para el fuerte
Condenaciones para real fisco
Condenaciones visita Juan Palafox
Condenaciones y gastos de visita
Conducción de reos
Conducción de tejos de oro
Conducción terrestre
Confirmación de tierras
Confirmaciones de encomiendas
Confiscaciones
Consejo Real de Indias
Consignaciones
Consignaciones para España
Consolidación de Guatemala
Consolidación de vales reales
Consolidaciones
Construcción de aduana
Construcción de bajeles
Construcción de cigarrillos
Consumo del corregidor de México
Contaduría de tributos y otras
Contrabando
Contribución de 4%
Contribución de coches
Contribuciones herencias trans
Correduría de lonja
Corregidores al mayores y ten
Correos
Corveta
Cosas remitidas al rey de China
Cosas vendidas de rl almacenes
Costos de retazas
Creditos activos
Creditos antiguos
Creditos pasivos
Cuenta con Havana

Cuenta con Laguna
Cuenta con Mérida
Cuenta con pres San Fel Bacalar
Cuenta con presidio del Carmen
Cuenta con Veracruz
Debido de cobrar der de esclavos
Debido de cobrar ramos de Rl Hac
Demarcación
Der de desfalcos de soldados
Der de encomenderos de indios
Der extr de España para rnos estr
Derecho de conducción
Derecho de guerra temporal
Derecho de internación en España
Derecho de los cuatro granos
Derecho de subvención
Derecho del estado
Derecho del realtor del Rl Con
Derecho del seleníssimo almirante
Derechos arreglados al proyecto
Derechos de contaduría
Derechos de esclavos
Derechos de esclavos de Angola
Derechos de internación
Derechos de salida de Tabasco
Derechos de Tomás de Razón
Derechos extraordinarios
Descaminos
Descaminos de esclavos sin lic
Descaminos de mercaderías
Descaminos de negros
Descaminos del cargo Filipinas
Descaminos y comisos
Descontado
Descontado del situado
Descubierto de la caja
Descubierto de Pablo Agudo
Descubierto ministros suspensos
Descuento de libranzas
Descuento de mrs a ind pres mil
Descuento de suplementos
Descuento de tropa
Descuento en favor de Luisiana
Descuento para reintegro
Descuentos de mercedes y ventas

Descuentos de oficiales militares
Descuentos para España
Detenido en Rl Caja para minería
Deudas de los suspensos
Deudas debidas a Su Majestad
Deudas tes Bernardo Albornoz
Devoluciones
Diezmos de conmutaciones del maíz
Diezmos ecles de California
Diezmos eclesiásticos
Diferencia de ensayado
Diferentes efectos de R Hacienda
Dinero metido en caja div persona
Dispensación de un casamiento
Divisoria de límites
Doctrina forastera
Dos milliones de ducados
Dos sellos de plata
Dos sellos del real acuerdo
Dos tercias partes
Dotación de Isla Juan Fernández
Dotación de la plaza y castillo
Duenos de requa
Efectos beneficiados
Efectos de camara de Indias
Efectos de hacienda
Efectos de la visita Rl Hac
Efectos de los oficiales reales
Efectos de los soldados
Efectos de nuevo reino de León
Efectos de residencia
Efectos de Villalua
Efectos del consulado de Sevilla
Efectos del Rl Consejo de Indias
Efectos diferentes
Efectos remisibles a España
Ejecutorias del R Con de Indias
Emb de vexaciones de guerra
Embargo de encomiendas
Embargos
Embargos de Real Hacienda
Emolumentos de balanzario
En cuenta general
En favor de su majestad
En la caja

Encom colegio San Carlos de Lima
Encomiendas
Encomiendas de particulares
Encomiendas del marqués de Lara
Encomiendas fábrica de catedral
Enterado en esta caja
Enterado en la caja
Enterado por admin de Paita
Enterado por el cabildo
Enterado por Gaspar de Solís
Entero de correspondido
Entregado a ten de cav castellano
Entregado en la caja proprietario
Envaces
Errores en los papeles de cuenta
Escalfe
Esclavos asiento de J B Robalasca
Esclavos chinos venido de Manila
Esclavos vendidos
Escopetas
Escribanías publicas
Escribano del Real Consejo
Escrituras
Escrituras de bastimentos
Escrituras de Buenos Aires
Escrituras de papel
Especie vendida
Especies reconocidas en azero
Establecimientos fixos de marina
Estado mayor
Estancia de Lluillui
Estrados reales
Examen del ensayador enterado
Exequias de la reina Isabel
Exlingaje
Expedición
Expedición a Islas Malvinas
Expedición a Matagroso
Expedición a misiones
Expedición a Uruguay
Expedición de historia natural
Expedición de la vacuna
Expedición de mojos
Extincción de vales reales de 15%
Extra del libro nuevo de memoria

Extra del libro viejo de memoria
Extranjería
Extravíos
Fábrica artillería de Ximena
Fábrica de bajeles
Fábrica de casas reales
Fábrica de cuarteles
Fábrica de galera
Fábrica de iglesias
Fábrica de la capilla
Fábrica de la casa de moneda
Fábrica de la catedral
Fábrica de receptores
Fábrica del fuerte del Callao
Fábrica del real palacio
Factoría
Falta de azogues
Falta de fragineros
Falta de ley en barras
Falta de plata remitido a México
Falta de soldados
Falta del tesoro
Ferreterías
Fiadores de los reales oficiales
Fierro
Fierro viejo
Fincas enagenadas manos muertas
Fisco real
Fletes de avería
Fletes de azogues años anteriores
Fletes de bulas de Santa Cruzada
Fletes de buques
Fletes de jalpa
Fletes de media anata
Fletes de mesadas
Fletes de navíos
Fletes de papel sellado
Fletes de pasajeros a Filipinas
Fletes de sal
Fletes del mar y tierra
Fletes del oro
Fletes y aprovechamientos
Flores americanas
Fondeado
Fondo de beneficios

Fondo de California y depositos
Fondo de construcción de aduana
Fondo de lacordada
Fondo de los forzados
Fondo de policia
Fondo del banco vitalicio
Fondo del ejército
Fondo piadoso de California
Fondos del soberano congreso
Formación de provisión de retasa
Fortificación
Fortificación antigua
Fortificación de Acapulco
Fortificación de Valdivia
Fortificación nueva
Fortificación para Valparaiso
Fortificaciones de Portobelo
Forzados
Fragatas
Frascos de azogues
Frascos de fierro
Fuelles
Fuerte de Santa Teresa
Fuerte San Felipe Bacalar
Fuerzas marítimas
Fundación piadosa de Zúñiga
Futuras sucesiones
Gastos comunes
Gastos de chichimecas
Gastos de contratación
Gastos de embarcaciones del río
Gastos de estrados
Gastos de guerra
Gastos de iglesia
Gastos de justicia
Gastos de navidad
Gastos de navíos
Gastos de oficinas
Gastos de Real Hacienda
Gastos del ejército acantonado
Gastos del ejército de operación
Gastos extra de operaciones
Gastos extraordinarios de guerra
Gastos extraoroinarios
Gastos generales

Gastos justicia y penas estrados
Gastos y penas de cámara
Generos dados a mineros
Gobierno de Francisco Amusquíbar
Gracias al sacar
Gran cruz
Gran masa
Gran masa de artillería
Gran masa de dragones
Granalla y barredera de la caja
Gratificación de hombres
Gratificaciones de la mesa
Guardia del resguardo
Guerra
Guerra con indios infieles
Guerra extraordinaria
Hacienda de Guisp y Loaiyas
Hacienda de Guispihuanca
Hacienda de Loaiyas
Herario del órden de S Domingo
Herencias transversales
Hierros
Hospital
Hospital de Belén
Hospital de Mendoza
Hospital de Santa Ana de Lima
Hospital general de Madrid
Hospital militar
Hospital rl Santa Veracruz
Hospitalidades de la tropa
Iglesia
Imposición a censo
Imposición de barras
Imposiciones
Impuesto patriótico
Incorporado de ramos particulares
Indulto de comerciantes
Indulto de minería y comercio
Indulto del comercio
Indultos
Indultos de hacienda
Indultos de la visita
Indultos y composición de tierras
Ingenieros de mojos
Interesados en retasas

Intereses
Intereses de barras
Internacion de efectos de Castilla
Internaciones
Inventario de la caja
Isla de Lobos
Jornales de indios cotabambas
Juros
Juros y censos
Lanchas cañoneras
Lasto resultado
Legados herencias transversales
Legitimaciones
Legitimaciones de mestizos
Leva de soldados
Librado para pagar Rl Caja México
Libranzas
Libranzas contra banco de Potosí
Libranzas en favor J Enr de Otero
Libranzas en favor J M de Hervas
Libros de nueva recopilación
Libros del concilio mexicano
Libros del nuevo rezado
Lic de duenos canoas buceo perlas
Lim canonización del Rey Fernando
Limosnas
Limosnas a Gregorio López
Limosnas a guerra contra infieles
Limosnas a San Isidro de Madrid
Limosnas canonización de S Teresa
Limosnas convento Calpa Castilla
Limosnas convento Sra del Carmen
Limosnas de cera y aceite
Limosnas de cera y vino
Limosnas de Lima
Limosnas de vino y aceite 6% enco
Limosnas hospital Santiago de Gal
Limosnas Nra Sra de Guadalupe
Limosnas para las monjas de Chile
Limosnas para monjas descalzas
Limosnas San Gerónimo de Espeja
Limosnas San Ginés de Madrid
Limosnas San Luis de Burgos
Lo que metido en la caja
Lo que metido pero no aplicado

Lo que se falta en tes remitido
Lutos
Lutos y otras cosas del tumulto
Luzes de la tropa
Maestranza de artillería
Maiz de los reales oficiales
Malvinas
Manda forzosa de Gregorio López
Mandas de cruz conmut votos disp
Mandas forzosas
Manufactura de apartado
Marcos fundidos en barras
Marina
Marina de Havana
Masillas
Mayorazgos
Media anata A de barl nuevo sv rl
Media anata y Armada de barlo
Media anata y papel sellado
Medio porciento libranzas de Méx
Mercaderías descaminadas
Merced del oficio
Mercedes de tierras
Mesadas ecles novenos vacantes ob
Mesadas ecles y vinos mescales
Milicias
Misas y brevarios
Misiones
Mitad de encomiendas
Mitad de rentas
Mitad de tercios de sínodos
Mitades de mercedes
Muebles de oficina
Mulatos de buenazo y bozales
Multas
Multas de la visita
Multas del conde de Baños
Multas del Real Consejo de Indias
Multas eclesiásticas
Multas militares
Multas seculares
Multas y condenaciones
Multas y condenaciones del R Con
Multas y penas de cámara
Municipal de guerra

Muralla de Lima
Navío del Carmen
Navíos de transporte
Negros por cuenta de Su Majestad
Novenos y mesadas eclesiásticas
Nueva fundición de la villa
Nuevo expuestos
Obrajeros de Tlascala
Obras de carnicerías
Obras de la Calapa
Obras de murallas
Obras del cárcel
Obras del castillo
Obras pias
Obras pias y capellanías
Obras públicas
Obras reales en esta ciudad
Obras y reparos de casas reales
Obras y reparos de esta ciudad
Obras y reparos de plazas
Ofertas para restablemto milicias
Oficios salinas novenos
Oficios vendibles salinas extra
Orden de su magestad
Ornamentos de iglesia de B Aires
Pagado al adelantado
Pagado el tostón de los mineros
Pagado para una residencia
Pagado Rl Fuerza soldados Acapulc
Pagado su órden
Pagamento de soldados
Palios exc entrada del virrey
Palo de tinta
Partidas almonedas órd cuenta ant
Pasages del Río de Itata
Pavellones pert a Su Majestad
Penas de cámara
Penas de cámara de fuera
Penas de cámara de Lima
Penas de cámara rezagos
Penas de estrados
Penas de estrados gastos justicia
Penas de estrados rezagos
Penas eclesiásticas
Pensión alguacil mayor

Pensión capellán mayor de Su Maj
Pensión carolina
Pensión de capellanes de Almadén
Pensión de coches
Pensión de la biblioteca
Pensión de lic para cavallos
Pensión de mitras y catedrales
Pensión de Universidad Salamanca
Pensión del obispo de Luisiana
Pensión del prin Clemente Saxonia
Pensión del seminario de nobles
Pensión embargada
Pensión en favor de Juan Muñóz
Pensión en favor de Rafael Muñóz
Pensión sobre mitras arcedianato
Pensión vitalicia
Pensiones
Pensiones y obras pias
Pensionistas
Pesquisa de los quintos
Piso
Pistolas
Plata cobrada de caja de México
Plata labrada socorro B Albornoz
Pleitos contra los culpados
Pólvora env a presidio Acaponeta
Pontazgo
Por la sexta
Por satisfacer de mercaderías
Posadas del Rl Consejo
Posesión y amparo de un herido
Predios urbanos
Premio de guerra
Premio por libranzas
Premios militares
Presas
Prin rec por subrog a menos redit
Principal ramo de consolidación
Principales a redito
Procedido de Nueva México
Producto de cárcel
Producto de encomiendas
Producto de la inquisición
Producto de un legado
Propios y arbitrios

Prorrata
Prorrata por visita
Provincia de Chilques
Provisiones audiencia Guadalajara
Provisiones y mandamientos
Provistos por Su Magestad
Quarta comiso de Su Magestad
Quarta comiso ministro de Indias
Quarta comiso para sup Rl Hac
Quarta comiso Real Con de Indias
Qunice porciento de amortización
Ramos agenos
Ramos particulares
Ramos particulares y agenos
Real botica
Real cámara
Real cuerpo de brigada
Real del ducado
Real fisco
Real palacio
Real piso
Real provisión de Lima
Real sexta
Real y Sup Consejo de Indias
Realtor y escribano Rl Con Ind
Rebaja de Ocopa
Rebajas de plazas vac de presidios
Recaudado pert rl caja Durango
Receptorias de la audiencia
Recibido de marineros gente mar
Redencion de cautivos
Reditos
Reditos de principales a censos
Reditos prin de obras pias y cap
Reedificación de esta plaza
Reformación de rentas
Refuerzo de navíos Mar del Sur
Reintegro a la caja de Lima
Reintegro a tesorería de B Aires
Reintegro a tesorería de Madrid
Reintegro de correos
Reintegros
Reintegros a la caja de Lima
Reintegros a la Real Hacienda
Reja de fierro

Rem al mayores para Fuerza Real
Remate de un indio
Remisible a Campeche
Remisible a Havana
Remisible a otras tesorerías
Remisible al banco nac San Marcos
Remisible general
Remision a España azogues Almadén
Remitido a aduana de B Aires
Remitido a la rl caja de México
Remitido a Manila a sup gobierno
Remitido a Nuevo México
Remitido a otras tesorerías
Remitido a Valdivia
Remitido al presidio del Carmen
Remitido de Rosario
Remitido de Sonora
Remitido para los gastos de Texas
Renta de correos
Renta del conde de Torr Alba
Renta del estado
Renta encom defensa monarquía
Rentas de encomenderos
Reparo de la laguna
Repartimientos
Repoblación de Osorno
Represalia
Represalia de los franceses
Represalia de los ingleses
Represalia de los portugueses
Represalia de negros
Represalia rl cia de Inglaterra
Resguardo
Residencia de Díaz Fajardo
Residencia de gob y reg Durango
Residencia de Guadalajara
Residencia del gobierno
Residuos de sueldos
Responsivas
Restituciones
Resultas de avería de armada
Retención de sínodos
Retención de sueldos
Revisiones de cuentas de 2% y 4%
Ropa comisada

Ropa manifiesta puerto Acapulco
Sala de armas
Salitre
San Cosme y San Damián
San Lorenzo del Escorial
Santa Brígida
Santa iglesia catedral
Santissmima Trinidad
Santos lugares de Jerusalem
Sec y asesoría del virreinato
Secretaría de la audiencia
Secuestro bienes duq de Monte León
Secuestros
Segunda composición del consulado
Sello real
Sementeras vacas
Seminario
Seminario conciliar
Seminario de nobles
Sereníssimo Infante
Servicio conf titulos de tierras
Servicio gracioso
Servicio mulatos negros lib rezag
Servicio negros y mulatos libres
Servicios
Sexta parte de comisos
Sínodos
Sínodos suspendidos
Sit pres Sta Rosa punta Sigüenza
Situación de Ant Ovando a la univ
Situación de María de Vargas
Situación de Rl Consejo de Indias
Situación Lorenzo Vaca de Silva
Situación M de Castro y a Ovando
Situaciones
Situaciones de la cuenta
Situaciones de lanzas
Situaciones y mercedes
Situado de Cartagena
Situado de Chile
Situado de Chiloe
Situado de condenaciones
Situado de Filipinas
Situado de Guatemala
Situado de Havana

Situado de la Florida
Situado de la marina de Havana
Situado de Laguna
Situado de Luisiana
Situado de marina de Havana
Situado de Panamá
Situado de Pensacola
Situado de presidios internos
Situado de Puerto Rico
Situado de San Blas
Situado de tierra de Havana
Situado de Valdivia
Situado de Ysla del Carmen
Situado de Yucatán
Situado del ejército
Situado para Vizcocho
Situado y leva de soldados
Situados
Situados ultramarinos
Sobrante administración Cajamarc
Sobrante de caja de caña
Sobras de cajas foraneas
Sobras de limpias de azogues
Sobras de sueldos
Sobras sueldos justicia Orurillo
Socorro de Antonio Dávalos
Socorro de Chile
Socorro de viudas
Solares
Su Excelentísimo Infante
Subscripción remisible
Substraido de caudal rem a México
Subvención remisible
Sueldo del agente fiscal
Sueldo del protector
Sueldos atrasados
Sueldos de caciques
Sueldos de caciques y preceptores
Sueldos de corregidores
Sueldos de escribanos
Sueldos de justicia
Sueldos de Real Hacienda
Sueldos militares
Sueldos militares
Sueldos varios

Sueldos vueltos
Superintendente gen de Rl Hac
Superintendente y su secretaría
Suplemento a la Real Hacienda
Suplemento a la Rl Hacienda cuart
Suplemento a la Rl Hacienda prime
Suplemento a la Rl Hacienda quint
Suplemento a la Rl Hacienda segun
Suplemento a la Rl Hacienda terce
Suplemento de la casa de moneda
Suplemento del gobierno superior
Suplementos
Suplido de ramos particulares
Suplido del banco
Suplidos
Taller de armería
Tasa de negros y mulatos libres
Tercias de encom por valimientos
Tercias partes
Tercio de aprovechamientos
Tercio de comisos
Tercios de bienes confiscados
Tercios de encomiendas
Tercios de fuera
Tercios de Lima
Tercios de reducciones de indios
Tierras realengas
Tierras vacas y sementeras
Tomín de remisión a Lima
Traslación de Purén
Tres tanto
Trib de negros mulatos zambaigos
Trib negro mulato y comp tierras
Trib negros mulatos lib Culiacán
Tributos de mulatos
Tributos mulatos negros lib rezag
Tributos negros y mulatos libres
Tributos y servicio negros mulatos
Trigéssimo conciliar
Tropa arreglada
Tropa suelta
Utensilios
Vacantes de encomiendas filipinas
Vacantes por reintegro
Valeria

Valimiento de encomiendas
Valimiento y embargo encomiendas
Valimientos
Valimientos de ventas y mercedes
Vasijas de fierro
Vendido de reales almacenes
Vendido menaje caja marca Guadalc.
Venta de fierro
Venta de ingenio
Venta de minas
Venta de minas de Conchucos
Venta de tablas
Venta de tierras
Venta y arrendamiento de casas
Vestuario
Vestuario de forzados
Vestuario de inválidos
Vestuario de milicias
Villas de este obispado
Villas fronteras reparos y obras
Vino y aceite de encomiendas
Visita de Cristóbal de Calancha
Visita de Francisco Valles
Visita de Gonzalo Suárez
Visita de Juan de Cáceres
Visita de Juan Sáenz Moreno
Visita de la Real Hacienda
Visita de la rl caja de Campeche
Visita de la Santa Cruzada
Visita de las cajas reales
Visita de las Filipinas
Visita de Pedro de Gálvez

Income Remitted
from Other Treasuries

Caja de comunidad de arica
Caja de la prov de Culiacán
Caja real de Rrica
Caja real de Buenos Aires
Caja real de Coquimbo
Caja real de Córdoba de Tucumán
Caja real de Cuzco
Caja real de Huancavelica
Caja real de Jujui

Caja real de la Paz   Rem de caja de Méx para Veracruz
Caja real de Lima   Rem de Lima para comprar cobre
Caja real de Mendoza   Rem de Lima para comprar jarcia
Caja real de Nueva Granada   Rem de México para Rosario
Caja real de Oruro   Rem Lima comprar cuerdas arcabuz
Caja real de Panamá   Rem Lima para comprar caballos
Caja real de Paraguay   Remisible cuarta parte de comisos
Caja real de San Juan   Remisible de particulares
Caja real de Serena   Remisión de ciudad de la Serena
Caja real de Tucumán   Remisiones
Caudal de Cochabamba   Remitido a Castilla
Caudal para la tropa   Remitido a Chuquito
Caudal remitido de otras tesorer   Remitido a Córdoba de Tucumán
Caudal remitido por el virrey   Remitido a Huancavelica
Caudales remitido en moneda   Remitido de admin alcab Moquegua
Compras de jarcia   Remitido de admin alcab Tacna
Cuenta con Campeche   Remitido de admin de alcabalas
Cuenta con México   Remitido de administraciones
Cuenta con Tabasco   Remitido de aduana de B Aires
Cuenta de real caja de Arica   Remitido de Arica
Cuenta de rl caja de Potosí   Remitido de Arispe
Cuerdas de arcabuzes   Remitido de Buenos Aires
Env de México fuerza Acapulco   Remitido de bulas de sc Caracas
Enviado a rls oficiales de Manila   Remitido de bulas de sc Guatemala
Enviado de Méx gente guerra mar   Remitido de Cailloma
Enviado de México navios de China   Remitido de Cajamarca
Enviado de México r of de Manila   Remitido de cajas arribas
Enviado de México ret en Filipina   Remitido de Camarquillo
Ingeniero para Valdivia   Remitido de Carabaya
Oro de Valdivia   Remitido de Carangas para Potosí
Otras tesorerías   Remitido de Catamarca
Plata de Durango   Remitido de Chachapoyas
Plata de fuego   Remitido de Chihuahua
Plata de Guadalajara   Remitido de Chillaos
Plata de Guanajuato   Remitido de Chuquito
Plata de Nueva Galicia   Remitido de Cochabamba
Plata de Nueva Viscaya   Remitido de Comaygua
Plata de Pachuca   Remitido de Cumaná
Plata de Potosí Oruro y la Paz   Remitido de depositos
Plata de Zacatecas   Remitido de Havana
Plata oro y reales S L Potosí   Remitido de Huamanga
Poblaciones de villas fronteras   Remitido de la caja rl de Potosí
Préstamos y pagas al ejército   Remitido de la Paz
Reales y géneros de Guatemala   Remitido de Lima
Recibido caudales rescate plata   Remitido de Loja
Registrado subsistencia tropa rno   Remitido de los lamos

Remitido de Maracaibo
Remitido de México y Puebla
Remitido de Oaxaca bulas de sc
Remitido de Orizaba
Remitido de Oruro
Remitido de otras cajas
Remitido de particulares
Remitido de Potosí
Remitido de Puebla
Remitido de Real Hacienda
Remitido de rl caja de Acapulco
Remitido de rl caja de Campeche
Remitido de rl caja de Caracas
Remitido de rl caja de Durango
Remitido de rl caja de Guanajuato
Remitido de rl caja de Guatemala
Remitido de rl caja de México
Remitido de rl caja de Tabasco
Remitido de rl caja de Veracruz
Remitido de rl caja de Yucatán
Remitido de rl caja de Zacatecas
Remitido de rl caja Guadalajara
Remitido de Sana
Remitido de Santa Fe de Veracruz
Remitido de Santiago de Chile
Remitido de Santo Domingo
Remitido de Serena
Remitido de Soconusco
Remitido de Veracruz y Mérida
Remitido del Cuzco
Remitido del obispo de Puebla
Remitido gobernador de Soconusco
Situado de Buenos Aires
Situado de Chiloe
Situado de la Concepción
Situado de Santiago de Chile
Situado de Valdivia
Socorro del Río Maule
Tesoreria general Buenos Aires
Tesorerias de otros virreinatos
Venido de Arequipa
Venido de Arica
Venido de Bolanos
Venido de Durango
Venido de fuera
Venido de fuera para B Aires

Venido de fuera y extraordinario
Venido de Guadalajara
Venido de Guanajuato
Venido de la Paz
Venido de los lamos
Venido de Pachuca
Venido de Potosí
Venido de San Luis Potosí
Venido de Sombrerete
Venido de Zacatecas
Venido de Zimapán

Extraordinary Income

Derecho extraordinario de guerra
Extra y trueques de barras
Extraordinario de Real Hacienda
Extraordinario remisible
Extraordinario y restituciones
Extraordinarios de guerra

Carryover from Previous Years

Atesorado de cuentas anteriores
Caudal existente y agregado
Cobrado de valores año presente
Cobrado valores años anteriores
Deudas cobradas
Existencia
Existencia para soldados
Existencia ramo de novenos
Existencia ramo de sisa
Existencia ramo de tabacos
Recibido en la cuenta antecedente
Residuos y sobras de sueldos
Valores de años anteriores

Liquor, Wine, and Strong Drink

2% del vino y aguardiente
12.5 pesos cada pipa del vino
12.5% nuevo impuesto aguardiente
2 reales cada pipa del vino
4 pesos de aguardiente
12.5p pipa agte 6.25 vinagre
12.5p pipa del vino apl a Rl Hac
25p cada pipa agte 12.5p vgre RH

25p cada pipa agte 12.5p vinagre
25p cada pipa del vino de Rl Hac
25p p vino agte 12.5p vinagre RH
30 pesos en cada taberna
5% de una pipa de vino
Aguardiente
Aguardiente de caña
Aguardiente de Castilla
Aguardiente de Havana
Aguardiente del país
Aguardiente mescal
Arbitrios sobre pulque
Bebidas prohibidas
Caldos del reino
Cuartilla de vino
Cuatro pesos botija aguardiente
Der de 10% de aguardiente Havana
Desagüe carne y vino
Desagüe de Huehuetoca
Destilaciones de aguardiente
Empedrados
Imp pulque mil Querétaro Zelaya
Imposición vino aguard vinagre
Impuesto aguardiente de Parras
Impuesto de Tajamares
Impuesto para refacción asequia
Impuesto pulque comp de caminos
Impuesto pulque crimen lacordada
Impuesto pulque cuarteles ves mil
Impuesto pulque para cuarteles
Impuesto pulque para empedrados
Impuesto pulque vest milicia
Impuesto sobre el aguardiente
Impuestos
Indulto de aguardiente de caña
Nuevo arbitrio de aguardiente
Nuevo impuesto
Nuevo impuesto aguardiente vino
Nuevo impuesto de 12% aguardiente
Nuevo impuesto de aguardiente
Nuevo impuesto de chicha
Nuevo impuesto del 12.5%
Nuevo impuesto vino agte vinagre
Pulque blanco
Pulques

Pulques foraneas
Real de botija
Sisa de Tlaltenango
Sisa del aguardiente de caña
Sisa del vino debida
Sisa del vino vendido Guanajuato
Vino mexicano
Vino y aguardiente
Vinos mes lic extrac de ganados
Vinos mescales
Vinos mescales apl palacio Guada

Donations, Loans, Special Assesments, and Subsidies

Cesiones a Su Majestad
Cobrado para Su Majestad
Contr extra real en marco quinto
Contr extraord sobre sueldos
Contr para auxilio de metrópoli
Contr para soldados de Alto Perú
Contr sueldos Rl Con de Indias
Contrib extraord de guerra
Contrib extraord de sueldos
Contribución de 3%
Contribución de legados
Contribución de mantener soldados
Contribución extraordinaria
Contribución patriótica
Contribución provisional
Contribución subsidiaria
Contribución temporal
Contribución temporal de guerra
Donativo
Donativo a Su Majestad
Donativo antiguo
Donativo de los portugueses
Donativo de minería
Donativo del año 1622
Donativo del año 1625
Donativo eclesiástico
Donativo ejército del Alto Perú
Donativo en alhajas
Donativo extraordinario guerra
Donativo fábrica de bajeles

Donativo fábrica real palacio
Donativo gracioso
Donativo guerra con Francia
Donativo guerra con Inglaterra
Donativo para almacén de pólvora
Donativo para ayudar soldados esp
Donativo para Buenos Aires
Donativo para conf de oficios
Donativo para defensa del reino
Donativo para el reino
Donativo para fragata Leocadia
Donativo para la guerra
Donativo para la metrópoli
Donativo para la península
Donativo para la reina
Donativo para merced del oficio
Donativo para reponer en fragata
Donativo primero
Donativo reedificación Cartagena
Donativo San Lorenzo del Escorial
Donativo segundo
Donativo subs min consejo estado
Donativo tercero
Donativo voluntario
Donativos de haciendas
Emprestito defensa de B Aires
Emprestito forzoso
Emprestitos
Emprestitos de españoles
Emprestitos de indios
Emprestitos y trueques de barras
Gastos de la monarquía donativo
Imposición de capitales
Nueva imposición de capitales
Nuevo donativo
Nuevo donativo del año 1798
Nuevo real subsidio
Préstamo a Su Majestad
Préstamo al estado
Préstamo al herario público
Préstamo forzado
Préstamo patriótico
Préstamo patriótico antiguo
Préstamo patriótico de 20 million
Préstamo patriótico segundo

Préstamo primero
Préstamo segundo
Préstamo tercero
Préstamos
Préstamos ejércitos extra
Préstamos extraordinarios
Préstamos y servicios
Principal de censos
Real subsidio eclesiástico
Servicio y donativo gracioso
Subscripción patriótica
Subsidio
Subsidio caritativo
Subsidio eclesiástico
Subsidio eclesiástico antiguo
Subsidio eclesiástico de Puebla
Subsidio eclesiástico de Veracruz
Subsidio eclesiástico moderno
Subsidio eclesiástico nuevo
Subsidio eclesiástico primero
Subsidio eclesiástico segundo
Subsidio real
Subvención de guerra

Mercury Sales

4p cada quintal azogue rep laguna
25 pesos aum el quintal de azogue
5 pesos por quintal de azogue
5% de azogues atrasados
5% de debitos azogues atrasados
Afianzado de azogues
Aprovechamientos de azogues
Azogue fiado
Azogues
Azogues adm factores particulares
Azogues antiguos
Azogues atrasados
Azogues beneficiados del oro
Azogues de Alemania
Azogues de Bolaños
Azogues de Castilla
Azogues de China
Azogues de contado
Azogues de contado antecesores

Azogues de escrituras
Azogues de España
Azogues de Europa
Azogues de Filipinas
Azogues de Guarochiri
Azogues de Huancavelica
Azogues de los mineros
Azogues de montaño
Azogues de Perú y Alemania
Azogues de Potosí y cajas fueras
Azogues de Punitaqui
Azogues de Quebradilla
Azogues de rescate
Azogues de Su Majestad
Azogues debido de cobrar
Azogues del Almadén
Azogues del Perú
Azogues del Perú antiguos
Azogues del Perú y Castilla
Azogues en caldo
Azogues en rescate
Azogues en urcas
Azogues fiados
Azogues plata de rescates
Azogues rezagos de Huancavelica
Azogues venidos en la flota
Azogues y media anata
Azogues y papel sellado
Cobrado azogues debido de cobrar
Consumido de azogues
Consumido de azogues adm
Consumido de azogues mineros
Consumido y quinzeno azogues adm
Consumido y quinzeno azogues min
Consumido y quinzeno de azogues
Crecimiento de azogues
Debido de cobrar de azogues
Dependencias de azogues
Diezmos de azogues
Dos quintales de azogues
Especies reconocidas en azogue
Fletes de azogues de Alemania re
Fletes de azogues de Castilla re
Fletes de azogues del Perú rein
Fletes de azogues reintegros
Frascos de hierro colado

Maderas de azogues
Mermas de azogue
Mermas de azogue de Castilla
Mermas de azogue del Perú
Minas de Huancavelica
Productos de azogues
Quinzeno de azogues
Quinzeno de azogues adm
Quinzeno de azogues mineros
Receptores de azogues
Reintegros fletes de azogues
Remisible de azogues
Restos atrasados de azogues
Resultas de azogues
Sacado de mineros de N España
Vendido de azogues

Temporalidades

Depositos de temporalidades
Temporalidades
Temporalidades apl col Luis Gonz
Temporalidades para el seminario
Temporalidades y sus depositos

Real Hacienda en Común

Hacienda nacional en común
Real Hacienda
Real Hacienda en común

Deposits, Advances, Individual Deposits

Alcance de fundidor
Alcance de proveedor
Alcance líquido
Alcances de alcabalas
Alcances de azogue
Alcances de corregidores
Alcances de cuentas
Alcances de cuentas de alcabalas
Alcances de cuentas por reintegro
Alcances de cuentas por tributos
Alcances de doctrinas forasteras
Alcances de la visita
Alcances de mineros

Alcances de particular
Alcances de reales oficiales Rl H
Alcances de relación jurada
Alcances del tribunal de cuentas
Alcances dn Fernando de Portugal
Bienes de Aguilar Azebedo
Bienes de Andrés de Aramburu
Bienes de Diego de Salzedo
Bienes de difuntos
Bienes de Filipinas en Acapulco
Bienes de franceses
Bienes de fray M de Prado Ramírez
Bienes de Gonzalo M. de Zavala
Bienes de Hernando Pizarro
Bienes de indios rebeldes
Bienes de J Bautista de Magreda
Bienes de Jorge de Aranda
Bienes de Joseph de Victoria
Bienes de Juan de Gama
Bienes de Juan Rodríguez Countino
Bienes de la inquisición
Bienes de Manuel de Zavala
Bienes de particulares
Bienes de Pedro de Armentía
Bienes de Ruidíaz de Mendoza
Bienes embargados particulares
Bienes oidor M Gutiérrez Torre
Caudales de cajas del virreinato
Data de F de Salazar
Data de Melchor Legazpi
Data del tes Alonso de Santoyo
Data del tes Casasano
Data del tes Gerónimo López
Data del tes Juan de Ybarra
Data del tes Paredes
Data del tesorero
Deposito de novenos y vacantes
Depositos
Depositos de alcabalas
Depositos de azogues
Depositos de barras
Depositos de bulas de S Cruzada
Depositos de contrabando
Depositos de correos
Depositos de encomiendas
Depositos de guias

Depositos de la caja de Piura
Depositos de la visita
Depositos de limpia de acequias
Depositos de novenos reales
Depositos de particulares
Depositos de plata
Depositos de seguros traficantes
Depositos de sombrerete
Depositos de tributos
Depositos de vacantes ecles
Depositos del fondo de California
Depositos en especie
Depositos extr de temporalidades
Depositos extraordinarios
Depositos fábrica de iglesias
Depositos militares
Depositos pasados a rl caja
Depositos provisionales
Depositos y bulas
Depositos y multas
Diezmos en deposito
Ditas y rezagos
Fiador del escribano
Fiadores de B Albornoz
Fiadores de Mateo de Astogui
Fiadores de N Romero de Mella
Fianzas
Frascos de hierro en especie
Premio de depositos
Residuos
Residuos de ramos part de Rl Hac
Residuos para buenos efectos
Residuos y sobras de sueldos
Resultas
Resultas del tribunal de cuentas
Resultas por saldo
Resultas y alcance de 1 trozo
Resultas y alcance de 3 trozo
Resultas y alcances de cuentas
Rezagos
Sobras de sueldos
Sobras de sueldos de caciques
Sobras de sueldos de justicia
Sueldo del oidor Jimenez d Morot
Sueldos
Sueldos del real consejo

Sueldos en exceso
Venta de barras

Bulas de Santa Cruzada
y de Cuadragesimales

Recibido en la data no cobrado
Residuo de la cuenta año anterior
Resultas
Resultas de corregidores
Resultas de la cuenta
Sobras

Debts Uncollected

Abono en la cuenta anterior
Abono y no cobrado de almonedas
Cobrado y no cobrado cuenta ante
Cobrado y no cobrado esta cuenta
Debe de los naturales de Tuetalpa
Debe el virrey a la Real Hacienda
Debido cobrar cuentas anteriores
Debido cobrar de alcabalas atras
Debido cobrar de salinas
Debido cobrar ramos part y agenos
Debido cobrar y no cobrado
Debido de cobrar
Debido de cobrar almojarifazgos
Debido de cobrar comp extranjeros
Debido de cobrar esta cuenta
Debido de cobrar para el futuro
Debido de cobrar ramos varios
Debido de cobrar temporalidades
Debido de las almonedas
Deuda atrasada
Deudas
Deudas antiguas
Deudas antiguas y modernas
Deudas de Charcas
Deudas modernas

Specie and Products Held
in Royal Treasury

Alhajas
Alhajas y bulas cuad en especie
Azogue en especie

Azogues de Alemania en especie
Azogues de Castilla en especie
Azogues de Europa en especie
Bulas cuadra en especie b corrte
Bulas cuadra en especie b futuro
Bulas cuadra en especie b pasado
Bulas cuadragesimales en especie
Bulas cuadragesimales en especie
Bulas de S Cruzada en especie
Bulas de SC en especie b corrte
Bulas de SC en especie b futuro
Bulas de SC en especie b pasado
Bulas de SC y p sellado especie
Bulas SC y cuad en especie
Efectos en depósitos
Efectos y alhajas en depósito
Ferreterías en especie
Oro en especie
Papel sellado en especie
Papel sellado en especie b corrte
Papel sellado en especie b futuro
Papel sellado en especie b pasado
Tabaco en polvo

Expenditure Taxes Grouped
by Area of Activity

Commercial and
Agricultural Activity

1 peso un barril
1% de avería
1.5% del consulado
1.5% sobre efectos de comercio
2/3 de 1.5% y quinto y almo
25 pesos cada pipa de aguardiente
4% y 6% de receptores alcabalas
Aduana
Alcabala de 1.5% Armada de bar
Alcabala de 2%
Alcabala de 4%
Alcabala de 5%
Alcabala de 6%
Alcabala de 8%
Alcabala de cabezón y viento
Alcabala de Castilla y encabezón
Alcabala de efectos de Castilla

Alcabala de mar
Alcabala de mar de 6%
Alcabala de tarifa
Alcabala de tierra
Alcabala de tierra de 3%
Alcabala de tierra de 5%
Alcabala de tierra de 6%
Alcabala de viento
Alcabala del consulado
Alcabala del mar de 3%
Alcabala del mar de 5%
Alcabala del mar de 8%
Alcabalas
Alcabalas almos y pulperías
Alcabalas corrientes
Alcabalas de 3%
Alcabalas de aguardiente de caña
Alcabalas de asiento
Alcabalas de Castilla
Alcabalas de diezmo
Alcabalas de tarifa
Alcabalas de Valdivia y Panamá
Alcabalas de viento
Alcabalas del mar de 6% y 8%
Alcabalas devueltas
Alcabalas en administración
Alcabalas en arrendamiento
Alcabalas encabezadas
Alcabalas foraneas
Alcabalas reales
Alcabalas y almojarifazgos
Alcabalas y nuevo impuesto
Alcabalas y sisa del vino
Alcabalas y unión de armas
Almacenaje
Almirantazgo
Almo 10% mercaderías de Filipinas
Almojarifazgo de 15%
Almojarifazgo de 2.5%
Almojarifazgo de 3%
Almojarifazgo de 4%
Almojarifazgo de 5%
Almojarifazgo de 7%
Almojarifazgo de 30%
Almojarifazgo de entrada
Almojarifazgo de entrada de 1.25%

Almojarifazgo de entrada de 1.75%
Almojarifazgo de salida
Almojarifazgo de unión de armas
Almojarifazgo nuevo
Almojarifazgo viejo
Almojarifazgos
Almonedas extra de contrapartidas
Almonedas extra en libro común
Almonedas extraordinarias
Almonedas ordinarias
Anclaje
Ancoraje
Arbit. de grana tinta vainillas
Arbitrios extraord y temporal
Arrend. De pulperías
Arrend. Venta composición tierras
Arrendamiento de asientos
Arrendamiento de haciendas
Arrendamiento de puente
Arrendamiento de puertos
Arrendamientos
Asiento de Cailloma
Auxilio de buques
Avería
Avería de armada
Avería de negros bozales
Avería de Sevilla
Avería y armada 2% de entrada
Avería y armada 2% de salida
Azucar y cacao
Barco de Maule
Barco del Río Maule
Barcos de antigua
Bueyes que se compraron
Buques
Cabezones
Cacao de Guayaquil
Canal de Maipo
Cascarilla de Calisaya
Composición de caminos
Composición de cosecheros
Composiciones
Compra de xareza
Compras de cuerda
Cuatro novenos beneficiales
Cueros

Derecho de los barcos a California
Derecho de 10%
Derecho de apartado
Derecho de salida de Tabasco
Derechos de 10%
Derechos de 5% y 10%
Derechos de consumo y apartado
Derechos de entrada de 20%
Derechos de entrada de 3%
Derechos de entrada de 7%
Derechos de esclavos
Derechos de huacas
Derechos de salida de España
Descaminos de esclavos
Descaminos de mercaderías
Devuelto de almo de 5% de entrada
Devuelto por ramo oe alcabalas
Diezmos de almojarifazgos
Diezmos de especies
Diezmos reales
Diversos deudores
Efectos de Castilla
Estancias
Exlingaje
Fábricas
Fletes de plata y maíz
Fragata Venus
Fragata Victoria
Guardas de aduana
Guias
Guias de forasteros
Hacienda el Pochitocal
Impuesto de ganados
Impuesto del cacao
Impuesto del vino
Impuesto provincial en Tabasco
Impuestos generales
Lana de vicuña
Licencias y aduanilla de negros
Manifestaciones de esclavos
Marchamo
Noveno general de diezmos
Noveno mayor
Noveno para la amortización
Noveno y medio de cuentas pasada
Noveno y medio de esta cuenta

Noveno y medio del hospital
Noveno y medio hospital Chillán
Novenos atrasados
Novenos de diezmos
Novenos de diezmos cuentas pasad
Novenos del obispado de Oaxaca
Novenos integr para consolidación
Novenos nacionales
Novenos para la capilla real
Novenos reales
Novenos y hospital de la Plata
Nuevo impuesto del cacao
Nuevo impuesto por arbitrios
Nuevo noveno decimal
Nuevos arbitrios
Obrajes
Oficio de chancilleria
Pagado al comercio
Pagado de avería supl Armada de b
Peaje
Peaje y barcas
Pontazgo de Aconcagua
Propios de ciudades y villas
Propios y arbitrios de Campeche
Provision de almacenes
Pulperías
Pulperías foraneas
Receptor de alcabalas
Renta de aguardiente y vinagre
SC y novenos reales reh a Córdoba
Servicio de entrada
Sisa
Sisa de mulas
Substracción de alcabalas
Sumarios de carne
Tercero cabezón del consulado
Tercia encomienda y alcabala
Unión de armas
Venta de azo
Venta de libros

War and Defense

1% de Armada de barlovento
23 compañías de pardos
25p cada pipa vino supl a de bar

25p pipa aguar 12.5p vinagre a ba
4% de sueldos para la guerra
Aplicado para el fuerte
Arbitrio de 1%
Arbitrio de esta ciudad
Arbitrio para mantener tropas sud
Arbitrios de 4 rls cacao milicia
Arbitrios de milicias
Arbitrios extraordinarios guerra
Arbitrios y sisa
Armada
Armada de barlovento
Armada de barlovento de Rl Hac
Armada de China
Armada de Drake saquea Guatulco
Armas
Armas de Veracruz
Arrend de cuarteles y otras depen
Arsenal
Artillería
Artillería y compañía de pardos
Asamblea
Asambleas y milicias provinciales
Asentista de la real armada
Auxilio al ejército a Acapulco
Auxilio al ejército a Chile
Auxilio al ejército a Quito
Auxilio al ejército de Alto Perú
Auxilio al ejército de Montevideo
Ayuda contra los insurgentes
Bastamentos de Valdivia
Bastimientos armas municiones
Bastimientos de Valdivia
Buenas cuentas a la tropa
Campo formado de 30 hombres
Cañoneras
Capitanes de indios barqueros
Capitanía de Talcahuano
Capitanía general y estado mayor
Cavallería
Comisaría de artillería
Comisaría de guerra
Comisaría de guerra y artillería
Comisaría de marina
Comp presidiales volantes Apaches
Compañía de infantería de pardos

Compañías de guardia del virrey
Compra de pólvora
Compra de pólvora para las armas
Compras de bastimientos
Cond apl al fuerte de Acapulco
Conquista de negros cimarrones
Convoy
Costas de navíos
Cuartel de dragones
Cuarteles de tropas
Cuenta con pres San Fel Bacalar
Cuerdas de arcabuzes
Cuerpo de marina
Curenas de la fuerza otras casas
Data de murallas
Defensa y guerra
Der de armada vino aguar vinagre
Der de desfalcos de soldados
Destacamento de Nayarit
Destacamento voluntarios Cataluña
Destinados a Frontera de Mendoza
Dotación de Isla Juan Fernández
Dotación de la plaza y castillo
Dragones
Ejército acontanado de Jalapa
Ejército de la frontera
El galeon Santa Teresa de Jesús
Establecimientos fixos de marina
Estado de guerra
Estado mayor
Estado mayor de la plaza
Expedición
Expedición a Islas Malvinas
Expedición a Mattogrosso
Expedición a misiones
Expedición a mojos
Expedición a Uruguay
Expedición contra insurgentes
Expedición de Acayucán
Expedición de Papantla
Expedición de Pensacola
Expedición del Tiburón
Expediciones contra los indios
Extraordinario de real armada
Fábrica de artilleríía Ximena
Fábrica de galeones de Guayaquil

Fábrica de almacén
Fábrica de cuarteles
Fábrica del presidio Bacoachi
Factoría
Fletes de municiones
Fond de villas fronteras y repar
Fondo de los forzados
Fondo del ejército
Fondo para premios de militares
Fortificación
Fortificación antigua
Fortificación extraordinaria
Fortificación nueva
Fortificaciones de Portobelo
Forzados
Fuerte de Santa Barbara
Fuerte de Santa Teresa
Fuerte de Sn Felipe de Bacalar
Fuerte del Pongo
Gastado en la galeota
Gastos de Apaches
Gastos de armada
Gastos de armada del Callao
Gastos de armada y pres Callao
Gastos de artillería
Gastos de chichimecas
Gastos de costa de Patagonia
Gastos de cureña
Gastos de exp contra Walix
Gastos de exped en esta provincia
Gastos de expedición
Gastos de guerra
Gastos de guerra de chichimecas
Gastos de guerra en Veracruz
Gastos de guerra para N México
Gastos de la Paz
Gastos de lino y cáñamo
Gastos de milicias de la costa
Gastos de navíos
Gastos de negros de Santo Domingo
Gastos de paz de chichimecas
Gastos de plaza
Gastos de poblaciones y familias
Gastos de presidios
Gastos de prisioneros de guerra

Gastos de revolución del Perú
Gastos del ejército acantonado
Gastos del ejército de operación
Gastos extraordinarios de guerra
Gastos extraordinarios operacione
Gastos ord de guerra y pólvora
Gastos ord y extra de guerra
Gastos ordinarios de guerra
Gastos ordinarios y extra guerra
Gastos pacificación del Perú
Gratificación de hombres
Guardacostas
Guardia de a pie
Guerra
Guerra en Nueva Viscaya
Guerra extraordinaria
Guerra paz y correos
Guerra sueldos de la tropa
Guerra tropa y cuarteles
Guerra y paz
Impuesto pulque cuarteles ves mil
Impuesto pulque para cuarteles
Impuesto pulque para cuartillo
Impuesto pulque vestuario milicia
Infantería
Ingeniero para la guerra
Isla de Lobos
Lanchas cañoneras
Leña de soldados
Lona para nao de Filipinas
Luzes de la tropa
Luzes del cuerpo de guardia
Madera del construidor
Maestranza de artillería
Maestranza de guerra
Maestranza de herrería
Maestranza de la plaza
Manutención de prisioneros
Manutención reos insurgentes
Marina
Marina de Havana
Marina de Veracruz
Milicias
Municipal de guerra
Muralla de Lima

Navío de Filipinas
Negros auxiliares
Obras de muelles
Obras de murallas
Obras del campo santo
Obras del castillo
Obras extraordinarias
Obras provisionales
Oficialidad suelta
Pagado a calafates y carpenteros
Pagado a infantería socorro flota
Pagado a jornaleros carpintería
Pagado a los 24 soldados
Pagado a los calafates
Pagado a los presidios
Pagado a los soldados
Pagado a los soldados ir a N León
Pagado a Nuevo México
Pagado a rl f y soldados Acapulco
Pagado a rl fuerza ac castellano
Pagado a soldados campaña Parral
Pagado al pres de SF de conchos
Pagado al presidio de Cerro Gordo
Pagado al presidio de Cuencame
Pagado al presidio de Guaguila
Pagado al presidio de S Catharina
Pagado al presidio de S Sebastián
Pagado al presidio de San Antonio
Pagado al presidio de Sinaloa
Pagado al presidio de Sn Hipólito
Pagado al presidio de Tepeguanes
Pagado al presidio del Gallo
Pagado al soldado
Pagado al ten Tetela de Tonetla
Pagado en virtud órdenes sr com g
Pagado por cuenta Armada de barlo
Pagadoría de guerra
Pagadoría de la real armada
Panadería y bayuca del castillo
Piquetes sueltos
Plana mayor
Pólvora
Pólvora en especie
Premio de guerra
Presidio de Havana

Presidios y compañías volantes
Proveedoría
Proveedoría de guerra
Provisión de Lima
Raciones
Real fuerza de Acapulco
Real provisión
Real sala de armas
Reconicimiento de costa del norte
Refaccion de cuarteles
Refacción muralla de la Laguna
Refuerzo de navíos Mar del Sur
Registrado a Canarias
Registrado a Cartagena
Registrado a Providencia
Registrado subsistencia tropa rno
Rem a presidio Nra Sra de Pilar
Remesas de bulas Santa Cruzada
Remesas de papel sellado
Remisible a Havana
Remitido a Arispe
Remitido a California
Remitido a Campeche
Remitido a Guadalajara
Remitido a Guatemala
Remitido a Havana
Remitido a Laguna
Remitido a las Islas Barlovento
Remitido a Mapimí
Remitido a presidios barlovento
Remitido a rl caja de Veracruz
Remitido a San Blas
Remitido a Sonora
Remitido a Tabasco
Remitido a Texas
Remitido al presidio del Carmen
Reparo de las fuerzas reales
Reparo del castillo de Acapulco
Reparos del castillo
Resguardo
Sala de armas
Salario del alguacil de guerra
Salarios de lo pert a guerra
Salarios de ministros de guerra
Salarios de protectores veedores

Salarios doctrinas y guerra
Salarios y guerra
Sit del ministro de Nueva York
Sit pres del Carmen y Pensacola
Sit pres Sta Rosa Punta Sigüenza
Situado Bahia y presidio S Joseph
Situado de Buenos Aires
Situado de California
Situado de Cartagena
Situado de Chile
Situado de Chiloe
Situado de Cuba
Situado de Filipinas
Situado de Florida
Situado de Guatemala
Situado de Habana
Situado de la Concepción
Situado de Luisiana
Situado de marina de Havana
Situado de Maynas
Situado de Nueva Orleans
Situado de Panamá
Situado de Pensacola
Situado de presidios internos
Situado de Puerto Rico
Situado de San Blas
Situado de Santiago de Cuba
Situado de Santo Domingo
Situado de tierra de Havana
Situado de Trinidad
Situado de Valdivia
Situado de Ysla del Carmen
Situado de Yucatán
Situado extraordinario de Caracas
Situado la Florida S M de Galbe
Situado para Vizcocho
Situado presidio S Maria de Galbe
Situado y leva de soldados
Situados
Situados de Panamá y Valdivia
Situados ultramarinos
Situados varios
Socorro de Chile
Socorro de Chile extraordinario
Socorro de Valdivia

Socorro de Veracruz
Socorro Havana Acapulco S J Ullua
Soldados de Sinaloa
Sublevación de indios infieles
Sueldo comandante Sn F de Bacalar
Sueldo del teniente
Sueldos de armada
Sueldos de tropa de Colotlán
Sueldos fuerte Sn Fel de Bacalar
Sueldos milit y gastos de guerra
Sueldos militares
Sueldos militares pag a fin abril
Sueldos militares retenidos
Sueldos tropa de callao
Sueldos y gastos de guerra
Sueldos y gastos militares
Suplido a la tropa
Taller de armería
Tripulaciones
Tropa arreglada
Tropa de dragonas de España
Tropa de refuerzo
Tropa de tarma
Tropa suelta
Tropa veterana
Tropa veterana infantería y artil
Union de armas de Valparaiso
Utensilios
Vestuario de milicias
Vigías
Villas fronteras reparos y obras
Víveres
Yslas Mariannas

Administrative Expenses

2% de administración
6% de alcabalas
A la contaduría de Hendosa
Administración
Administración al 6%
Administración de 2%
Administración de bulas de SC
Agente fiscal
Arrendamiento de casas

Arrendamientos de casas reales
Audiencia de Cuzco
Audiencia de Lima
Bara del alguacil mayor
Bulas cuadragesimales en especie
Cajas reales del reino
Casa de la rl audiencia
Contador
Contaduría de tributos y otras
Contribución sueldos Rl C Indias
Corregidores alcaldes mayores ten
Corregidores y al mayores n órden
Cuartilla de real para defensor
Der de desfalcos de soldados
Emolumentos de balanzario
Emolumentos de oficinas
Emolumentos de Real Hacienda
Emolumentos escr mayor de R H
Emolumentos oficios contratación
Enterado por el cabildo
Estado de Real Hacienda
Estado político
Fabrica de casas reales
Gastos atenciones este destino
Gastos atrasados
Gastos comunes
Gastos comunes y generales
Gastos de caja y papel
Gastos de callanías
Gastos de contaduría y Rl Hac
Gastos de contratación
Gastos de escritorio
Gastos de expulsión de regulares
Gastos de justicia
Gastos de la real caja
Gastos de la secretaría
Gastos de la visita
Gastos de los alcaldes mayores
Gastos de matriculas
Gastos de oficina y correos
Gastos de oficinas
Gastos de Real Hacienda
Gastos de visita
Gastos del escritorio
Gastos extraordinarios

Gastos extraordinarios de la R H
Gastos generales
Gastos generales de Real Hacda
Gastos justicia y penas estrados
Gastos ord y extraordinarios
Gastos ordinarios de Rl Hacienda
Gastos y cargos generales
Impuesto pulque crimen lacordada
Indios canones
Intendentes tenientes y gastos
Intendentes y gobernadores
Libra y remez la aduana de Mendoza
Libra de oficiales r propietarios
Libros y papel
Ministerio de la Real Hacienda
Ministro de intendentes
Ministros de audiencia emigrados
Ministros de audiencias
Mitad de salario de caciques
Obras y reparos de esta ciudad
Obras y reparos de plazas
Oficiales y subalternos de r h
Pagado a la real audiencia
Pagado al adelantado
Pagado al corregidor
Pagado al gob de Nueva Vizcaya
Pagado al protector
Pagado al visitador
Papel entregado al sr governador
Papel para la caja de Jujuy
Papel suministrado al tente real
Penas de cámara
Penas de estrados
Penas de estrados gastos justicia
Pension de capellanes de Almadén
Premios
Protector de indios
Quitas vac corregidores a mayores
Ramos municipales la intendencia
Real audiencia y subalternos
Real fisco
Real tribunal de cuentas
Receptor de la villa de Tachall
Reditos prin de obras pias y cap
Residencia del gobierno

Revisitadores
Salario del agente fiscal
Salario del alcalde mayor
Salarios
Salarios de Acapulco y filipinas
Salarios de alcabalas
Salarios de caciques
Salarios de comisionada
Salarios de juezes de matrícula
Salarios de justicias
Salarios de la visita
Salarios de los alemanes
Salarios de los subdelagados
Salarios de ministros
Salarios de oficiales reales
Salarios de rl audiencia rls ofic
Salarios de tributos reales
Salarios del Real Consejo
Salarios del servicio rl de indio
Salarios gastos pensiones
Salarios guerra lim extra y rem
Salarios guerra limosnas extraord
Salarios limosnas y guerra
Salarios ord y extraordinarios
Salarios sínodos y limosnas
Salarios sínodos y pensiones
Salarios tributos reales y azogue
Salarios y gastos
Salarios y gastos de contaduría
Salarios y limosnas
Salarios y mercedes
Salarios y pensiones
Salarios y raciones
Salarios y sinodos
Secr y asesoría del virreinato
Secretaría del gobierno
Secuestro bienes duq de Monte Leó
Socorro del oidor
Subdelegados y preceptores
Sueldo y gast de mstr y empl R H
Sueldo alguacil executor rl caja
Sueldo de asesores de gobernador
Sueldo de corregidor de Paria
Sueldo del contador
Sueldo del escribano
Sueldo del tesorero

Sueldo oficial mayor de rl caja
Sueldos correg mojos y chuquitos
Sueldos de 6%
Sueldos de admin y resguardo rh
Sueldos de alquaciles mayores
Sueldos de caciques
Sueldos de corregidores
Sueldos de hacienda
Sueldos de intendencia
Sueldos de justicia
Sueldos de la real audiencia
Sueldos de los procuradores
Sueldos de ofic reales a Bs As
Sueldos de oficiales de corrtes
Sueldos de oficiales de indios
Sueldos de oficiales mayores R H
Sueldos de preceptores
Sueldos de real aduana
Sueldos de Real Hacienda
Sueldos de RH al fin de abril
Sueldos de sec del gobierno
Sueldos del tente gov esta ciudad
Sueldos del tes y recept de 6y2%
Sueldos intendencia y asesoría
Sueldos políticos
Sueldos supernumerarios
Sueldos varios
Sueldos y gastos de estado polít
Sueldos y gastos de intendencia
Sueldos y gastos de Real Hacienda
Sueldos y gastos del edo político
Sueldos y gastos exp metalúrgica
Sueldos y gastos extraordinarios
Sueldos y gastos generales
Sueldos y gastos temporalidades
Sueldos y gastos varios atrasados
Sueldos y pensiones
Sueldos y renta de tabacos
Sumarios de cruzada pasada
Superintendente y su secretaría
Tercios de salarios

Mercury Costs

Azogue de Huancavelica
Azogue remitido a los lamos

Azogues
Azogues de administración
Azogues de Alemania
Azogues de Alemania en especie
Azogues de Carangas
Azogues de Castilla
Azogues de Castilla en especie
Azogues de China
Azogues de contado
Azogues de escrituras
Azogues de Europa
Azogues de Europa en especie
Azogues de Guarochiri en especie
Azogues de Huancavelica
Azogues de Juan Pérez
Azogues de montaño
Azogues de Potosí y cajas fueras
Azogues de Punitaqui
Azogues de Su Majestad
Azogues debido de cobrar
Azogues del Almadén
Azogues del Perú
Azogues en especie
Azogues y papel sellado
Compra de azogues de Huancavelica
Conducción de azogue
Costas y fletes de azogues
Crecimiento de azogues
Cuenta con minas de Huancavelica
Fletes de azogue de los lamos
Fletes de azogues
Fletes de azogues bulas p sellado
Fletes de azogues de Castilla
Fletes de azogues del Perú
Fletes de azogues y bulas de SC
Fletes de azogues y papel sellado
Frascos de hierro colado
Gastos de fundición de azogues
Gastos de minas de Huancavelica
Maderas de azogues
Mitas de Huancavelica
Pagado al ensayador de azogues
Producto de azogues
Refacción y reparo mina Huancavel
Remisible de azogues
Resultas de azogues

Socorro de Huancavelica
Valor de azogues

Extraordinary Expenses

Derecho extraordinario de guerra
Extra y trueques de barras
Extraordinario y congregaciones
Extraordinario y Real Hacienda

Carryover Funds

Existencia
Existencia azogues Castilla
Existencia azogues Huancavelica
Existencia de ramos part de Rl H
Existencia para la tropa
Existencia para los presidios
Por resta de cuenta anterior
Real del ducado
Residuos
Rezagos
Sobras
Sobras de alcabalas
Sobras de salarios
Sobras de salarios de justicia

Real Hacienda en Común

Hacienda nacional en común
Real Hacienda
Real Hacienda en común
Real Hacienda general

Royal Monopolies, Excluding Liquor and Papal Bulls

Administración de sal
Alumbres
Amanuenses
Aumento de lim de bulas cruzada
Aumento de tasas bulas de cruzada
Barajas
Bienes corr en la dir de tabacos
Breas
Cobre
Cobre de labor

Coliseo de gallos
Comisos y nieve
Compra de estaño
Compra de salitre
Compra de tabacos pólvora y breas
Cordobanes
Depósitos de la renta del tabaco
Escrituras procedidas de sal
Estaño
Fletes de bulas de Santa Cruzada
Fletes de bulas y papel sellado
Fletes de libros de nuevo rezado
Fletes de papel sellado
Gastos de salinas de Peñol Blanco
Juego de gallos
Lastre
Lotería
Lotería auxiliar
Lotería forzosa
Minas de cobre
Naipes
Nieve
Papel común a rubricar
Papel gastado en esta real caja
Papel habilitado
Papel rubricado
Papel sellado
Papel sellado bienio corriente
Papel sellado bienio futuro
Papel sellado bienio pasado
Papel sellado consumido en caja
Papel sellado de Buenos Aires
Papel sellado devuelt por errado
Papel sellado en especie
Papel sellado en especie b futuro
Papel sellado en especie b pasado
Papel sellado sobrante
Papel sellado y amanuense
Plaza de toros
Plomo
Producto de papel sellado
Producto de tabaco en polvo
Quintos de estaño
Sal
Sal de S María y Peñol Blanco

Sal fiada
Sal fiada de Penól Blanco
Sal fiada de Santa María
Sal y fletes del mar
Salinas
Salinas de Acaponeta
Salinas de Chametla
Salinas de Culiacán
Salinas de la purificación
Salinas de Peñol Blanco
Salinas de Santa María
Sellos bienio futuro
Sellos bienio pasado
Solimán
Suplemento a renta de tabaco
Tabaco en polvo
Tabacos
Veinteabo de cobre

Donations, Loans, Special Assessments

Contr de sueldos extra a metrópol
Contrib extraord de guerra
Contrib extraord de sueldos
Contribución extraordinaria
Contribución patriótica
Contribución provisional
Contribución temporal de guerra
Contribución voluntaria de indios
Donativo
Donativo de Filipinas
Donativo de minería
Donativo eclesiástico
Donativo en alhajas
Donativo gracioso
Donativo para Ceuta
Donativo para conf de oficios
Donativo para el reyno
Donativo para fragata Leocadia
Donativo para la guerra
Donativo para la península
Donativo primero
Donativo segundo
Donativo tercero

Donativo voluntario
Emprestito defensa de B Aires
Emprestito forzoso
Emprestitos
Emprestitos y trueques de barras
Imposición de capitales
Nueva imposición de capitales
Nuevo donativo
Plata prestada
Premios de emprestitos
Prestado avería San Juan de Ullua
Prestado de avería de imposición
Prestado para reparo de Lagunas
Préstamo a Su Majestad
Préstamo al estado
Préstamo extraordinario
Préstamo forzado
Préstamo patriótico
Préstamo patriótico antiguo
Préstamo patriótico de 20 million
Préstamo patriótico primero
Préstamo patriótico segundo
Préstamos
Préstamos del tiempo de guerra
Préstamos y servicios
Venta de barras

Remittances to Castile

Asignaciones y reint para España
Consignaciones para España
Efectos remisibles a España
Enviado a Castilla y otras partes
Extraordinario remisible
Registrado a Castilla
Rem a Chihuahua presidios int
Remisible a otras tesorerías
Remisible de particulares
Remitido a Castilla b SC Guatemal
Remitido a Castilla b SC México
Remitido a Castilla bienes dif
Remitido a Castilla de Acapulco
Remitido a Castilla de Campeche
Remitido a Castilla de Caracas
Remitido a Castilla de Cumaná

Remitido a Castilla de Guatemala
Remitido a Castilla de Maracaibo
Remitido a Castilla de México
Remitido a Castilla de Pt Rico
Remitido a Castilla de Puebla
Remitido a Castilla de S Domingo
Remitido a Castilla de Soconusco
Remitido a Castilla de Tabasco
Remitido a Castilla de Veracruz
Remitido a Castilla de Yucatán
Remitido a Castilla der esclavos
Remitido a Castilla Guadalajara
Remitido a Castilla media anata
Remitido a Castilla o de Puebla
Remitido a Castilla p sellado
Remitido a Castilla particulares
Remitido a Rosario y Arispe
Remitido a Veracruz Armada de bar
Remitido a Veracruz condenaciones
Remitido a Veracruz media anata
Remitido a Veracruz n servicio
Remitido al duque Medina Sidonia
Remitido de rl caja de México

Alms, Charity, and Pious Foundations

15% de capellanías
3% del colegio seminario
3% para el colegio de Monterrey
3% para el seminario
3% para seminario de la Paz
4% sobre rentas del Escorial
5% de sínodos
5% de sínodos mojos y chuquito
5% para doctrineros de mdjos
A la universidad
Accesión del obispo
Aceite vino y cera
Aceite y vino
Administración del real hospital
Arbitrios
Arbitrios para el hospital
Artesanos de California
Auxilio de familias pobladas

Beaterio de Jesús María y Joseph
Bidimus e instrucciones de SC
Bulas cuadra en especie b corrte
Bulas cuadra en especie b futuro
Bulas cuadra en especie b pasado
Bulas cuadragesimales
Bulas cuadragesimales b corriente
Bulas cuadragesimales b futuro
Bulas cuadragesimales b pasado
Bulas cuadragesimales en especie
Bulas de carne
Bulas de cruzada otras tesorerías
Bulas de fierro
Bulas de indulto y cruzada
Bulas de s cruzada en especie
Bulas de s cruzada entregadas
Bulas de Santa Cruzada
Bulas de SC bienio corriente
Bulas de SC bienio futuro
Bulas de SC bienio pasado
Bulas de SC de otras tesorerías
Bulas de SC en especie b corrte
Bulas de SC en especie b futuro
Bulas de SC en especie b pasado
Bulas de SC esp b corrie pasado
Canal del Río Maypo
Capellanes
Capellanes de coro
Capellanías
Capilla real
Carnicerías y desague
Carros para religiosos a N México
Colegio de Ocapa
Colegio de San Carlos de Lima
Colegio de San Felipe de Lima
Colegio seminario
Colegio seminario de la Plata
Colegio seminario del Cuzco
Compra de casa real
Condenaciones obras esta ciudad
Condenaciones obras esta palacio
Congregaciones de indios
Conquistadores hijos nietos mujer
Consignaciones sit eclesiásticas
Construcción de aduana

Contribución al hospital
Conversiones colegio de Ocopa
Custodia del Parral
Desague de Huehuetoca
Doctrina forastera
Eclesiásticos
Edificio del convento S Sebastián
El colegio Na Sa Guadalupe Zac
Empedrados
Encomiendas y pensiones
Estado eclesiástico
Estipendios espirituales
Exigido para montepío de ministro
Exigido para montepío de oficinas
Expedición botánica
Expedición de historia natural
Expedición de la vacuna
Fábrica
Fábrica de casa de fund y ensaye
Fábrica de catedral
Fábrica de la casa de moneda
Fábrica de las iglesias
Fábrica del hospital
Fábrica del real palacio
Fiesta de N Snra del Rosario
Fondo de beneficios
Fondo de California y depósitos
Fondo de lacordada
Fondo piadoso de California
Fundacion piadosa de Zúñiga
Gastos de iglesia
Gastos de real hospital
Gastos indios en fron chichimeca
Gastos para curar los enfermos
Gastos religiosos env de Castilla
Hospital
Hospital de los indios de México
Hospital de San Andrés
Hospital de San Carlos
Hospital militar
Hospital real
Hospitalidades de la tropa
Iglesia catedral de Durango
Iglesia catedral de Guadalajara
Impuesto pulque para empedrados

Indulto quadragesimal
Indultos quadr en especie b pas
Indultos quadragesimales b corrte
Jornada y conversión de indios
Limosnas
Limosnas a conventos viejos de SF
Limosnas a conventos y religiosos
Limosnas a religiosos de San Fran
Limosnas a San Isidro
Limosnas de la santa bula
Limosnas de Santa Cruzada
Limosnas de vino aceite medicina
Limosnas hospital Santiago de Gal
Limosnas medicina vino aceite maíz
Limosnas Nra Sra de Guadalupe
Limosnas para las monjas de Chile
Limosnas San Gerónimo de Espeja
Limosnas San Lorenzo del Escorial
Limosnas vino cena aceite fr Guad
Limosnas de vino y aceite
Maiz para los indios Laltenango
Medio real de hospital
Medio real de ministros
Mejoramiento de la ciudad
Mercedes
Mercedes conventos SF Guadalajara
Mercedes conventos SF Zacatecas
Mercedes de indios
Mercedes y situaciones
Misiones
Misiones de la compañía de Jesús
Misiones de Ocopa
Monte pío
Monte pío cirujanos del ejército
Monte pío de batallones de marina
Monte pío de cirugía general
Monte pío de cirujanos
Monte pío de cirujanos de armada
Monte pío de cirujanos militares
Monte pío de ingenieros
Monte pío de la maestranza
Monte pío de las brigadas
Monte pío de ministros
Monte pío de oficiales del mar
Monte pío de oficinas

Monte pío de pilotos
Monte pío militar
Noveno al real seminario
Noveno y medio de fábrica
Novenos del hospital
Obispo del Paraguay
Obras de calada
Obras del cárcel
Obras pías
Obras pías y capellanías
Obras públicas
Obras reales de esta ciudad
Obras y reparos de casas reales
Ornamentos de iglesia de B Aires
Pagado a compañía de jesuitas
Pagado a curas Maloya y Parral
Pagado a los curas
Pagado a los curas doctrineros
Pagado a los indios
Pagado a los indios de Acaponeta
Pagado a los misiones Taraumara
Pagado a un militar retirado
Pagado al misionero
Pagado al obispo cabildos iglesia
Pagado indios en fron chichimeca
Papel sellado en especie b corrte
Pavellones pert a Su Majestad
Pensión capellán mayor de Su Maj
Pensión carolina
Pensión de coches
Pensión de la biblioteca
Pensión de lic para cavallos
Pensión de mitras y catedrales
Pensión de mojonazgo
Pensión de Universidad Salamanca
Pensión de viudas de ministros
Pensión del alguacil mayor de Méx
Pensión del obispo de Luisiana
Pensión del prin Clemente Saxonia
Pensión en favor de Juan Muñoz
Pensión en favor de Rafael Muñoz
Pensión militar
Pensión vitalicia
Pensiones
Pensiones de encomienda

Pensiones eclesiásticas
Pensiones y obras pías
Pensionistas
Plata entregada al colegio real
Puentes
Real hospital
Real palacio
Real seminario
Recepción del obispo
Rector del real colegio
Reedificación de esta plaza
Retención de las escuelas
Salarios de real hospital
San Lorenzo del Escorial
Santa iglesia catedral
Santos lugares de Jerusalem
Seminario
Seminario conciliar
Seminario de nobles
Sínodos
Sínodos de indios
Sínodos de misiones
Sínodos de Nayarit
Sínodos de curas
Situación de ant Ovando y la univ
Situación de María de Vargas
Situación Lorenzo Vaca de Silva
Situación M de Castro y a Ovando
Situaciones
Situaciones de la cuenta
Situaciones mercedes censos
Situaciones y consign ecles
Situaciones y obras pías
Socorro de viudas
Sueldos de vagos dest a Calif
Sueldos eclesiásticos
Sueldos y gast de cía de obreros
Temporalidades apl col Luis Gonz
Trigéssimo conciliar
Universidad de San Marcos
Vacantes de sínodos
Venta de bien raíz de obras pías
Vestuario
Vestuario de forzados

Censos and Juros (Mortgages)

16% de censos de indios
Censos
Censos de bienes mostrencos
Censos de indios
Censos de indios y 16%
Censos de la molina chapultepec
Censos de las molinas
Censos sobre renta de tabaco
Censos y arrendamiento de tiendas
Censos y capellanías
Censos y juros
Imposición a censo
Juros
Juros y censos
Principales a reditos
Principales de censos de indios
Reditos de censos de indios
Reditos de principales a censo
Reditos de principales y censos
Rendiciones de censos

Miscellaneous Expenses

.25 de comisos remisibles
1.5% reales del hospital
10% de encomiendas
10% de fincas
10% de salarios
10% del servicio pecuniario
15% amortización de principales
15% de amortización
15% de vales
15% de vales reales
15% sobre manos muertos
2% de amortiz nov r y vacantes
2% de los ramos de Real Hacienda
2% del valor de tierras realengas
2% sueldos
4% de sueldos para la guerra
4% de tributos
4% y 2% propios arbit bienes comu
5% de la traslación de Purén
5% de oficios

5% de salarios
5% que llamaron de consideración
6 panchos remitidos
6% de creditos
6% de salarios atrasados
A cuenta general por sello
Abonado por cargado dos vezes
Acrecentamientos salarios del rc
Acrecido falta cuenta
Aderezos de la real caja
Agasejos de indios
Al mayor minas de Charcas Havana
Alquiler casa para el tesoro
Amortización de vales
Amortización de vales pasados
Anata de corregidores
Anualidades
Anualidades eclesiásticas
Aplicado a los chasquis
Aplicado en la cuenta anterior
Aprovechamientos
Armamento
Arrendamiento cajones antiguos
Arrendamiento cajones de palacio
Arrendamiento cajones fierro viej
Arrendamiento de casas y tiendas
Arrendamiento de suertes
Arrendamiento de tiendas
Arrendamiento de tierras
Arrendamiento y venta de minas
Arrendamientos
Arrendamientos de indios
Asignaciones
Aumento de tributos no cobrado
Aumento en el peso de plata
Averiguar una muerte
Bajas
Banco de rescate
Banco nacional de San Carlos
Banco real
Bara alguacil mayor de Quenoxingo
Barreteras
Beneficiados
Beneficios de oficios

Bienes confiscados de insurgentes
Bienes de contrabando
Bienes de extranjeros
Bienes del obispo
Bosques y plantíos
Botes del rey
Brevarios
Buenas cuentas
Buenos efectos y residuos
Cabezones de haciendas
Caja de Coquimbo
Caja de la prov de Culiacán
Caja extinguido de Sana
Caja nacional
Caja Tineque
Cajones de fierro viejo
Cajones de palacio
Cajones de Rivera
Cajones para estaño
Caldos del reino
Capitales impuestos a censo de 4%
Cargas generales
Carros matos
Casa de contratación
Cascarilla de Loja
Cinco porciento de salarios
Ciudad de Ancón
Cobrado de cuentas anteriores
Cobrado en cuenta de dependencias
Cobrado en el tiempo esta cuenta
Cobrado gastos de almonedas
Cobrado por caja de Lima
Comisión de Pastrana
Comisión secreta de Havana
Comisiones de Martín Ribera
Comiso para ministro de Indias
Comisos
Comisos apl excmo sup gen de R H
Comisos apl Rl Cons de Indias
Comisos de ministros
Comisos del excmo sup general
Comisos del Rl Consejo de Indias
Comisos y extravíos
Composición de aduana

Composición de almacenes
Composición de caminos
Composición de capillas
Composición de Diego de Orejón
Composición de encomiendas
Composición de extranjeros
Composición de indios
Composición de obrajes
Composición de Pedro de Quiroga
Composición de pesos y presas
Composición de pulperías
Composición de tierra y aguas
Composición de tierras
Composición del camino Mextitlán
Composición y venta de tierras
Composiciones de la caja
Compra de bastimientos
Compra de jarcias
Compra de muebles
Compras de casas
Comunidades
Concursos
Condenaciones
Condenaciones de cámara
Condenaciones de guerra
Condenaciones de la S Cruzada
Condenaciones de la visita
Condenaciones de negros
Condenaciones de Pedro de Salas
Condenaciones de residencia
Condenaciones de San Luis Potosí
Condenaciones de tribunal cuentas
Condenaciones de tributos
Condenaciones del fuerte Callao
Condenaciones del oro S L Potosí
Condenaciones del real consejo
Condenaciones Pedro portugueses
Condenaciones rl aud Guadalajara
Condenaciones visita S Juan Ullua
Conducción de cargas
Conducción de cargas a Tucumán
Conducción de efectos de Catamarca
Conducción de lienzo remitido
Conducción de reos
Confiscaciones

Conmutaciones
Conmutaciones del maíz
Consignación
Consolidaciones
Construcción de cigarrillos
Consulado
Contr extraordinaria sobre sueldo
Contrabando
Contrapartidas almon oro ant cuen
Contrapartidas de almonedas
Contrapartidas de almonedas extra
Contribución
Contribución de 4%
Contribución de indios
Contribución de tiendas
Contribución general
Contribuciones herencias tras
Correos
Corveta
Cosecheros de la ciudad
Costas de rematados de tributos
Costos de retazas
Creditos activos
Creditos pasivos
Creditos pasivos Rl H
Cuarta arzobispal
Cuarta episcopal
Cuarta episcopal de Cuzco
Cuarta parte comisos min de Rl H
Cuarta parte comisos rl con de in
Cuenta almon extra de esta cuenta
Cuenta arzobispal
Cuenta con Havana
Cuenta con Laguna
Cuenta con Mérida
Cuenta con presidio del Carmen
Cuenta con Veracruz
Cuenta de real caja de Potosí
Cuenta episcopal del Cuzco
Cuenta general
Cuero y demás utensilios
Curuguati
Defaltas de doctrinas
Defectos efectos
Der de contaduría de media anata

Der de regulación de media anata
Derecho de mitas
Derecho del estado
Derecho del montado
Derechos de guerra temporal
Derechos de oficinas
Derechos de sucesión
Derechos de Tomás Razón
Derechos extraordinarios
Descamino de navío
Descaminos de plata
Descubierto de la caja
Descubierto de Pablo Agudo
Descubierto ministros suspensos
Descubrimiento yslas incognitas
Descuento a la tropa
Descuento de 6% de encomiendas
Descuento de sueldos
Descuento de suplemento
Descuento para consejo y secr
Descuento para presente guerra
Descuentos para España
Descuentos por contribución
Detenido para la minería en caja
Deudas se deben a Su Majestad
Devoluciones
Diezmos de conmutaciones del maíz
Diezmos de panuco
Diezmos de tributos
Diezmos eclesiásticos
Diferencia de ensaiado
Divisoria de límites
Donativo de haciendas
Dos meses de los corregidores
Efectos beneficiados
Efectos de Armada de barlovento
Efectos de la residencia
Efectos de la visita
Efectos del consulado de Sevilla
Efectos del Nuevo Reino de León
Efectos del Rl Consejo de Indias
Efectos remitidos almonedas rls
Efectos y alhajas en deposito
Embarcaciones
Embargo de encomiendas

Embargo de vacantes
Embargos de Real Hacienda
Emolumentos
Emolumentos cont de media anata
En 3 partidos
En 4 partidos
Encomiendas
Enter por libr de sres oficial r
Enterada contrapartida
Enterado a la minería
Enterado de ramos ajenos
Enterado en la caja
Enterado para los encomenderos
Enteros para libramientos
Entr a asentista cargas ent caja
Entradas del ramo de propios
Entregado a sres oficiales
Entregado al tesorero
Entregado de la caja
Envaces
Errores contra reales oficiales
Escrituras
Especies
Espolios
Estrados reales
Executorias de Consejo de Indias
Expedición
Expediciones
Falta en la cuenta
Ferreterías
Fiador del escribano
Fierro
Fierro corriente
Fincas
Fletes
Fletes al conductor
Fletes al trapisero
Fletes conducción cartas cuentas
Fletes de arrieros
Fletes de bulas SC de Guatemala
Fletes de caudal rem a los lamos
Fletes de caudales rem a Durango
Fletes de cobre
Fletes de estaño
Fletes de extraordinario

Fletes de plata remitido a México
Fletes de plata remitido Veracruz
Fletes del maíz
Fletes y aprovechamientos
Fletes y gastos de almonedas
Fondo de construcción de aduana
Fondo del banco vitalicio
Fondo general de tributos
Fondos del soberano congreso
Frascos de fierro
Futuras succesiones
Gastos de almonedas cuenta ante
Gastos de correos
Gastos de demarcación
Gastos de la monarchía
Gastos de materiales
Gastos de resello
Gastos extravagantes
Gastos reintegrables
Gobierno de Francisco Amusquibar
Gorriti
Gracias al sacar
Gran masa
Gratificaciones
Gratificaciones de la mesa
Guacas
Herencias transversales
Hierros
Holpatán o medio rl de ministros
Honras y obsequias de la reyna
Hospital de San Lázaro
Huarochiri
Imposición y avería
Imposiciones y rendiciones princ
Impuesto de taxamares
Impuesto patriótico
Impuestos de tajamares
Indulto de aguardiente de caña
Indulto del comercio
Indulto y diferentes bienes
Indultos
Indultos de tributos vacos
Ingenios de Tarapaya
Intereses
Inválidos

Inventario de la caja
Islas Malvinas
Jornada de Filipinas
Jornales de la real caja
Lana de vicuña en especie
Lanzas
Lanzas de titulos
Lanzas y arcabuzes
Legados herencias transversales
Legitimaciones
Librado en prov de tribunal cuen
Librado para pagar rl caja México
Libramientos de los sres reales
Libranzas
Libranzas en favor de Iznardi
Libranzas en favor J Enr de Otero
Libranzas en favor J M de Hervas
Libranzas generales
Libros de nueva recopilación
Libros del nuevo rezado
Licencias para herrar ganado
Liquido debido al desague
Lo metido en esta rl caja México
Lo que aplicado a sus generos
Lutos
Malvinas
Mandas de cruz conmut votos disp
Mandas forzosas
Manifestaciones de negros
Manifestaciones de Riacas
Mayor servicio
Mayorazgos
Media anata
Media anata anadida
Media anata antigua
Media anata de buques
Media anata de corregidores
Media anata de encomiendas
Media anata de la contaduría gen
Media anata de tierras
Media anata de Tucumán
Media anata eclesiástica
Media anata nueva
Media anata oficios del cabildo
Media anata para Buenos Aires

Media anata secular
Media anata y lanzas
Media tasa de indios
Medias anatas y mesadas ecles
Medias anatas y oficios vendibles
Medio porciento libranzas de Méx
Medio rl hospital indios de Méx
Mercaderías descaminadas
Merced del oficio
Mermas de plata
Mesadas de la flota
Mesadas eclesiásticas
Mesadas para la real capilla
Mesadas y media anata ecles
Minería
Mitad de encomiendas
Mitad de extravíos
Mitad de rentas
Mitad de salarios de corregidores
Mitad de tercios de sínodos
Mulas pert a Su Majestad
Multa del prior y los consules
Multas
Multas de la visita
Multas eclesiásticas
Multas militares
Multas y condenaciones
Multas y penas de cámara
Navío del Carmen
Novenos reales de amortización
Nuevo real subsidio
Nuevo servicio de Culiacán
Nuevo servicio pueblos encomen
Nuevo servicio pueblos rls indios
Nuevo servicio y unión de armas
Nuevos diezmos
Oficio del alquacil mayor
Oficio del factor
Oficio del tesorero Casa Moneda
Oficios beneficiados
Oficios de registros
Oficios del cabildo
Oficios suprimidos
Oficios suspendidos
Oficios vendibles y renunciables

Orden de Su Magestad
Ordenes superiores
Osadía
Otras contrapartidas extra
Otras contrapartidas ordinarias
Otras tesorerías
Pagado a diferentes personas
Pagado a la casa de contratación
Pagado a los indios
Pagado a los indios tepaguanes
Pagado a los indios tlaspiques
Pagado a Luis de Carreago
Pagado a ramos varios de Rl Hac
Pagado de cuenta de particulares
Pagado de la real caja
Pagado en Lima
Pagado en oro
Pagado en virtud de rls cédulas
Pagado por órden del sup gobiern
Pagado sin libranzas
Pagas hechas
Palios del marqués de Mancera
Papel sellado remitido otras tes
Partidas del libro común
Pasages del Río Itata
Patagonia
Penas de cámara de Sombrerete
Plata vuelta a la caja
Premio al 6 y 2%
Premios a los subdelegados
Premios de subdelegados
Presas
Producto de encomiendas
Producto de la inquisición
Producto indulto cuadragesimal
Propios remitido
Propios y arbitrios
Prorrata
Provisiones y mandamientos
Provistos por Su Magestad
Quarta comiso de ministro de ind
Quarta comiso de Su Magestad
Quarta comiso para Rl Consejo
Quarta comiso para sup Rl Hac
Quillacas y aconaques

Quince porciento de amortización
Quinto de indios
Quitas de oficios
Quitas de pueblos suprimidos
Ramos agenos
Ramos agenos y particulares
Ramos particulares
Ramos particulares y agenos
Ratas y desmontes
Real camara
Real de botija
Real del ducado
Real familia
Real rden de Carlos III
Real y Sup Consejo de Indias
Rebaja de efectos que se remiten
Rebaja de partidas
Rebaja de tributos
Recaudación de tributos
Recibido de debido de cobrar
Redención de cautivos
Reditos
Reditos géns de consolidación
Reditos pasivos pasados
Reditos principales impuesto a ca
Reditos temporalidades fon vitali
Reensaye de plata
Rehabilitación de un molino
Reint al ramo de oficios de R H
Reintegro a tesorería de B Aires
Reintegro a tesorería de Madrid
Reintegro de correos
Reintegro de depósitos
Reintegro de vacantes mayores
Reintegro para Lima
Reintegros
Reintegros a la Real Hacienda
Remijido en exceso
Remisible cuarta parte comisos
Remisible general
Remisible para población Florida
Remitido a Durango
Remitido a Maldonado
Remitido a Malvinas
Remitido a Mérida

Remitido a Mérida de Yucatán
Remitido a México de señoreage
Remitido por rezagos
Renta del estado
Rentas de encomenderos
Renunciaciones de oficios
Reparo de almacenes reales
Reparo de las casas reales
Repoblación de Osorno
Represalia
Represalia de los franceses
Represalia de los ingleses
Represalia de los portugeses
Represalia rl cía de Inglaterra
Residencia
Residuo del año anterior
Restituciones
Resultas
Resultas de tributos
Resultas del tribunal de cuentas
Resultas por saldo
Retención de sínodos
Retención de sueldos
Revisiones de cuentas de 2% y 4%
Robo de la real caja
Ropa de contrabando
Ropa manifiesta puerto Acapulco
Sacado de la caja sin libranzas
Sacado de rl caja forciblemente
Seguros de alcabalas
Sello real
Sequestros
Seceníssimo principe de Asturias
Servicio gracioso
Servicio nuevo de indios
Servicio por el colla del oro
Servicio real de indios
Servicio rl pueblos encomendados
Servicios
Sisa del agua
Sobrantes para pagar a Ocopa
Sobras de quintos
Sobras de tributos
Socorro de los mineros de Parral
Solares

Subscripción remisible
Subsidio eclesiástico
Subsidio eclesiástico moderno
Subsidio eclesiástico nuevo
Subsidio eclesiástico primero
Subsidio eclesiástico segundo
Subvención de guerra
Subvención remisible
Sumarios de indultos pasados
Sup general de Real Hacienda
Suple del juzgado de interesados
Suplemento a la real audiencia
Suplemento a la Rl Hacienda quart
Suplemento a la Rl Hacienda quint
Suplemento a Rl Hacienda segundo
Suplemento a Rl Hacienda tercero
Suplemento de la casa de moneda
Suplementos
Suplementos a otras tesorerías
Tablas de alerce
Tanto porciento de salarios
Temporalidades
Temporalidades y sus depósitos
Tercias partes del valor oficio
Tercias y situaciones encomienda
Tercio de aprovechamientos
Tercio de la secretaría
Tercios de encomiendas
Tercios de fuera
Tercios de Lima
Tercios de salarios
Tesorería general
Tesorerías de otros virreinatos
Testimon de efectos de Castilla
Tiendas mestizas
Tierras de comunidad de indios
Tierras realengas
Títulos de Castilla
Tlapisques y gastos mercaderías
Tomín de hospital
Traslación de Purén
Tres esclavos dados por comisos
Tres tanto
Trib sv rl pueblos encomendados
Tribs capilla de Univ de Lima

Tribs de parroquias de ciudad
Tribs lanzas Aullagas Uruquillas
Tribs lanzas Caquina y Picachuri
Tribs lanzas Chuquicota y Sabaya
Tribs lanzas Colque y Andamarca
Tribs lanzas Sabaya y Sacabaya
Tribs lanzas Santiago de Curia
Tribs lanzas Tacobamba Potobamba
Tribs lanzas Totora y Curaguera
Tribs lz Chuquicota Sabaya Sacaba
Tribs pls de Presto y Tarabuco
Tribs rls Aullagas y Uruquillas
Tribs rls de San Pedro de B Vista
Tribs rls degla guardia de apie
Tribs rls Lipes condes de Arabate
Tribs rls Quillacas y Asanaques
Tribs rls Yotala Quilaquila
Tribs yanaconas la Plata y distr
Tribs yanaconas Misque y Pocona
Tributos 1/3 parte de Chayanta
Tributos 2/3 parte de Chayanta
Tributos atrasados
Tributos cons de lanzas Aullagas
Tributos cons de lanzas Caracara
Tributos cons de lanzas Chaqui
Tributos cons de lanzas Chuquito
Tributos cons de lanzas Macha
Tributos cons de lanzas Sacaca
Tributos cons de lanzas Totora
Tributos cons de lanzas Visisa
Tributos consignaciones de lanzas
Tributos de encomiendas
Tributos de indios laborios
Tributos de lanzas
Tributos de Nueva España
Tributos de Nueva Galicia
Tributos de nuevas leyes
Tributos de nuevas leyes conqui
Tributos de vacantes
Tributos de yanaconas
Tributos en gallinas
Tributos foraneos
Tributos lanzas
Tributos lanzas debido de cobrar
Tributos negros y mulatos libres

Tributos para gastos de guerra
Tributos pueblos de adel montejo
Tributos reales de Atacama
Tributos reales de Capinota
Tributos reales de Caracara
Tributos reales de Carangas
Tributos reales de Chayanta
Tributos reales de Chichas
Tributos reales de Chuquito
Tributos reales de Cochabamba
Tributos reales de Curaguasi
Tributos reales de forasteros
Tributos reales de indios
Tributos reales de indios de Potosí
Tributos reales de indios de Yungas
Tributos reales de Jauja
Tributos reales de Lipes
Tributos reales de Misque
Tributos reales de Moromoro
Tributos reales de Mojos
Tributos reales de Paria
Tributos reales de Paucarcolla
Tributos reales de Pilaya
Tributos reales de Pocona
Tributos reales de Porco
Tributos reales de Puna
Tributos reales de Sacaca
Tributos reales de Sipesipe
Tributos reales de Tomina
Tributos reales de Totora
Tributos reales de Yamparaes
Tributos reales embargados
Tributos reales rezagos
Tributos rls condes de Arabate
Tributos rls Cualparocas de Guata
Tributos vacos
Tributos vacos y tribs de Jauja
Tributos y azogues
Tributos y de Jauja
Tributos y servicio real indios
Tributos yanaconas de Charcas
Tributos yanaconas de Cochabamba
Tributos yanaconas de la Plata
Tributos yanaconas de Pitantora
Tributos yanaconas de Porco

Tributos yanaconas de Potosí
Tributos yanaconas de Totora vaca
Tributos zapotecas
Túmulo
Única contribución
Única contribución de los indios
Vacaciones
Vacante de minas
Vacante de obispado depositado
Vacante de obispado remitido
Vacante del obispado de Tucumán
Vacantes
Vacantes de caciques
Vacantes de curatos
Vacantes de doctrinas
Vacantes de encom de particulares
Vacantes de encomiendas
Vacantes de justicia
Vacantes de obispados
Vacantes de obispados Filipinas
Vacantes de oficios
Vacantes de prebendas
Vacantes de salarios
Vacantes del obispo
Vacantes eclesiásticas
Vacantes embargadas
Vacantes mayores
Vacantes mayores y menores
Vacantes menores
Vacantes menores atrasados
Valería
Valimientos
Valimientos de 10% de salarios
Valimientos de 4% de salarios
Valimientos de 5%
Valimientos de renta
Valimientos embargo de encomienda
Valor del oficio de ensayador
Varios efectos y alhajas
Vasijas de azogues
Venta de fierro
Venta de minas
Venta de tierras
Ventas y arrendamientos de tierra
Ventas y composiciones de tierras

Vestuario de invalidos
Villa rica
Villas nuevas
Visita de Gonzalo Suárez
Visita de J Palafox y Ped Gálvez
Visita de Juan Palafox
Visita de la Real Hacienda
Visita de minas de azogue
Visita de Pedro de Gálvez
Visita general
Visitas y revisitas

Remittances to the Philippines

Derechos de las Islas Filipinas
Entr a maestre plata para Fil
Enviado a rls oficiales Filipinas
Fletes de Filipinas
Gastos de Filipinas
Gastos de religiosos y Filipinas
Gastos de una galleta
Gastos del nao de China
Gastos extra de Filipinas
Invernada de patache de Fil
Islas Filipinas
Pagado a doctrineros de Fil
Pagado a infanteria de Filipinas
Pagado a la gente del mar Fil
Registrado para las Filipinas
Remitido a Filipinas misiones
Remitido a Manila para sup gob
Salarios r ofs gente del mar Fil
Sueldos de resguardo
Suplemento de Filipinas

Mining and Minting

1% diezmos y señoreage de plata
1% y diezmos de plata
1.5% de cobos
1.5% de cobos y diezmos
1.5% de cobos y quintos
1.5% de plata
1.5% y diezmos de plata
1.5% y quinto de plata
1.5% y quinto del oro

3% del oro
Afinación
Alhajas
Alhajas en depósito
Alhajas previosas
Amonedación
Arrend de casa de moneda
Arrendamiento de la mina de Porco
Arrendamiento de minas
Aumento de señoreage de minería
Baja el ley
Bajas de metales
Balanza
Barras de plata
Bocados de plata rescate
Cambio de plata
Casa de fundición
Casa de moneda
Casa de moneda provisional
Cobos
Cobos y diezmos
Derecho de barajas
Derecho del más a más
Derechos de barras
Derechos de ensaye y fundición
Derechos de oro y plata
Diezmos de ensaye
Diezmos de oro
Diezmos de plata
Diezmos de plata labrada
Diezmos y quintos de plata
Ensaye
Extracción de metales
Extravíos
Fletes de buques
Fletes de la flota
Fletes de metales
Fletes de plata
Fletes de plata y oro flota 1584
Fletes de plata y oro flota 1585
Fletes de plata y oro flota 1586
Fletes de plata y oro flota 1587
Fletes de plata y oro flota 1588
Fomento de minería
Fundición

Gastos de ensaye y fundición
Gastos de fundición
Gastos de guardar moneda enviada
Gastos de minas y fundición
Gastos de real minas
Imposición de barras
Indultos de vajilla
Metales y perlas
Minas de la Corona
Moneda columnaria antigua
Moneda Macuquina
Obra de la casa de moneda
Oro
Oro de azogue
Oro de Carabaya
Oro de fuego
Oro de San Luis Potosí
Oro pasta
Pagado a los mineros
Piezas de plata labrada
Pinas de extravío
Plata
Plata con oro
Plata de azogue
Plata de fuego
Plata de rescate
Plata estaño
Plata labrada
Plata para vajilla
Plata pasta
Plata por moneda
Plata y oro abono en esta cuenta
Plata y oro flota Villavicencio
Plata y oro labrado
Platas de vocadas
Quinto de oro
Quinto de perlas
Quinto de plata labrada
Quinto oro barras y plata labrada
Quinto real
Quintos de oro
Real en marco de minería
Real en marco para socabón
Reales labrados de barras
Rescate de reales

Rescates de plata
Rescates del oro
Señoreage
Señoreage de minería
Señoreage de plata y oro
Señoreage real de casa de moneda
Socorros de mineros
Sueldos de ensayadores
Tres porciento del oro
Veintabo o quinto de cobre
Venta de ingenio
Yerros de mineros señalar plata

Uncollected Debts

Almonedas en generos no cobrados
Almonedas no cobradas
Contrapartidas debidas de cobrar
Cuartilla de vino
Debido a los difuntos
Debido cobrar alcabalas atrasada
Debido cobrar cuentas anteriores
Debido cobrar rmos part y ajenos
Debido cobrar y no cobrado
Debido de cobrar
Debido de cobrar comp extranjeros
Debido de cobrar cuentas ants
Debido de cobrar de almojarifazgo
Debido de cobrar der de esclavos
Debido de cobrar esta cuenta
Debido de cobrar para el futuro
Debido de cobrar ramos varios
Debido y no cobrado
Debitos atrasados
Del año pasado
Deuda atrasada
Deudas anteriores no cobradas
Deudas de este año no cobradas
Deudas gastos y otras cosas
Deudas modernas
Ditas y rezagos
Lo que debe en almonedas
Lo que metido pero no aplicado
No cobrado almonedas reales
No cobrado contrapartidas almon

Por cobrar tributos
Vacante mayor para cobrar

Advances, Deposits, Etc.

Ajustamiento de la cuenta
Alcance de la cuenta
Alcances bienes J Bautista Magred
Alcances de azogues
Alcances de corregidores
Alcances de cuenta relación
Alcances de cuentas
Alcances de cuentas de lanzas
Alcances de cuentas de salarios
Alcances de oficiales reales
Alcances de relación jurada
Alcances del obispo Larracha
Alcances del tribunal de cuentas
Alcances fuera del virreinato
Alcances reg Soria y Extremadura
Bienes de Aguilar Azebedo
Bienes de Andrés de Aramburu
Bienes de comunidades de indios
Bienes de Cristobal guilar
Bienes de Diego de Salzedo
Bienes de difuntos
Bienes de difuntos de Guatemala
Bienes de Hernando Pizarro
Bienes de indios rebeldes
Bienes de J Bautista de Magreda
Bienes de Jorge de Aranda
Bienes de la inquisición
Bienes de otros gobernadores
Bienes de particulares
Bienes de Pedro Vélez de Mediano
Bienes del arzo Alonso de Cuevas
Bienes del arzobispo
Bienes del gobierno
Bienes del obispado y gobierno
Bienes del obispo de Oaxaca
Bienes del obispo de Yucatán
Bienes del obispo Diego de Cimia
Bienes del obispo gobernador
Bienes embargados J de Salazar
Bienes embargados particulares

Bienes fut en la dir de tabacos
Bienes mostrencos
Bienes oidor M Gutiérrez
Cajas de comunidad
Cargas en todos ramos del anterior
Caudales de cajas del virreinato
Data abonada en esta cuenta
Data del tesorero
Depósito de bulas
Depósito de fábrica de iglesias
Depósito de novenos
Depósito de vacantes
Depósito extraordinario de Calif
Depósitos
Depósitos bulas de Santa Cruzada
Depósitos de alcabalas
Depósitos de barras
Depósitos de California
Depósitos de corregidores
Depósitos de correos
Depósitos de encomiendas
Depósitos de la real audiencia
Depósitos de la visita
Depósitos de particulares
Depósitos de plata
Depósitos de seguros traficantes
Depósitos de temporalidades
Depósitos de tributos
Depósitos en caudal
Depósitos en especie
Depósitos extra de temporalidades
Depósitos extraordinarios
Depósitos provisionales
Depósitos y multas
Depósitos y remis a Buenos Aires
Diezmos en depósito
Efectos y alhajas en depósito
Ferreterías en especie
Sobras de tribs de forasteros
Tributos reales de indios

Liquor, Wines, Etc.

25 pesos cada pipa del vino
25 pesos una pipa del vino

4% en bot de aguardiente
Aguardiente
Aguardiente de caña
Aguardiente de Castilla
Aguardiente del país
Aguardiente mescal
Arbitrios sobre pulque
Bebidas prohibidas
Destilaciones de aguardiente
Impuestos
Impuesto sobre aguardiente
Nuevo arbitrio de aguardiente
Nuevo impuesto
Nuevo impuesto agte vinagre
Nuevo impuesto de aguardiente
Nuevo impuesto de chicha
Nuevo impuesto del vino
Nuevo impuesto vino agte vinagre
Pulques
Sisa de aguardiente de caña
Sisa del vino
Sisa y nuevo impuesto
Vinos mes lic extrac de ganados
Vinos mescales
Vinos mescales apl palacio Guada

Remittances to Other Treasuries

Algodón remitido
Aumento en la remesa a México
Caja real de Arica
Caja real de Coquimbo
Caja real de Córdoba
Caja real de Cuzco
Caja real de la Paz
Caja real de Oruro
Caja real de Tucumán
Cuenta con Campeche
Cuenta con México
Cuenta con Tabasco
Cuenta de real caja de Arica
Librado por las cajas de Jujuy
Lienzo remitido
Media anata remitida a Lima
Pagado y remitido

Plata de Potosí Oruro y la Paz
Plata de rescate rem a Casa Mon
Plata entregada
Plata remitida a caja de Jujuy
Plata remitida a esta caja
Plata remitida a la caja
Ramos remisibles
Real hacienda por remesas
Rem de Guadalajara para rescate
Remesa a la real caja
Remesas generales
Remitido
Remitido a aduana de B Aires
Remitido a Buenos Aires
Remitido a Carangas
Remitido a cajas foraneas
Remitido a Chuquito
Remitido a ciudad de la Plata
Remitido a Concepción
Remitido a Cuzco
Remitido a Huancavelica
Remitido a Jujuy
Remitido a la casa de moneda Méx
Remitido a la real aduana
Remitido a Lima
Remitido a Lima de donativo
Remitido a Lima de papel sellado
Remitido a los lamos
Remitido a Mendoza
Remitido a Méx comp extranjeros
Remitido a Méx quinto dmo plata
Remitido a México 2% Armada barlo
Remitido a México alcances
Remitido a México bienes y ramos
Remitido a México bulas de sc
Remitido a México comp al mayor
Remitido a México comp de tierras
Remitido a México condenaciones
Remitido a México crec de azogues
Remitido a México de alcabalas
Remitido a México de azogues
Remitido a México de depósitos
Remitido a México de desfalcos
Remitido a México de donativo
Remitido a México de masa común

Remitido a México de media anata
Remitido a México de mercedes
Remitido a México de naipes
Remitido a México de novenos
Remitido a México de oficios vend
Remitido a México de valimientos
Remitido a México del oro
Remitido a México extraordinario
Remitido a México juego truecos
Remitido a México media anata nue
Remitido a México mesadas ecles
Remitido a México montepío de min
Remitido a México montepío de of
Remitido a México papel sellado
Remitido a México penas de cámara
Remitido a México por su rescate
Remitido a México sal de Culiacán
Remitido a México trib Rl Corona
Remitido a México tributos indios
Remitido a México vacantes obispo
Remitido a México y Veracruz
Remitido a Oruro
Remitido a otras tesorerías
Remitido a Potosí
Remitido a Potosí de azogues
Remitido a Potosí de bulas de SC
Remitido a Potosí de Cochabamba
Remitido a Potosí de monte pío
Remitido a Potosí situado B Aires
Remitido a Potosí y Chuquito
Remitido a Potosí y Huancavelica
Remitido a Potosí y la Plata
Remitido a rl caja de Guadalajara
Remitido a rl caja de México

Remitido a rl caja de Zacatecas
Remitido a Rosario
Remitido a C Cruz de la Sierra
Remitido a Salta
Remitido a Santiago de Chile
Remitido a tes pral de Córdoba
Remitido a tesorería general
Remitido a Trujillo
Remitido a Valdivia
Remitido de cajas arribas
Remitido de cajas de fuera
Remitido de Carabaya
Remitido de Carangas para Potosí
Remitido de Chachapoyas
Remitido de Jujui
Remitido de Lima
Remitido de Potosí
Remitido por azogues
Socorro del virrey
Tesorería menor de corrientes
Vacantes remitidas

Specie, Etc., Reposing in the Treasury

Caja de comunidadad de Arica
Caja real de Buenos Aires
Caja real de Huancavelica
Caja real de Lima
Caja real de Panamá
Remitido a Arequipa
Remitido a Arequipa de tributos
Remitido a Lima de azogues

Notes

Preface

1. See my essay "Structure and Profitability of Royal Finance in the Viceroyalty of the Rio de la Plata in 1790," *Hispanic American Historical Review* 53(3)(August 1973), and the more extensive version published as "Las finanzas del virreinato del Río de la Plata en 1790," *Desarrollo Económico* 50(julio–septiembre 1973). A discussion of the findings of this article appears in a series of essays by S. Amaral, J. Fisher, J. Cuenca, and T. Halperin Donghi, along with my own comments, in the May 1984 issue of the *Hispanic American Historical Review*.

2. See John J. TePaske and Herbert S. Klein, *Royal Treasuries of the Spanish Empire in America, 1580–1825*, 3 vols., Durham, NC: Duke University Press, 1982 (1: Peru, 2: Uppe Peru, 3: Chile and Río de la Plata), and by the same authors, *Ingresos y egresos de la Real Hacienda en Nueva España*, 2 vols., Mexico City: Instituto Nacional de Antropología e Historia, 1986, 1988.

3. See our several joint essays: "Revolutionary Wars and Public Finances: The Madrid Treasury, 1784–1807," *Journal of Economic History* 41(2)(June 1981), "Las prioridades de un monarca ilustrado: El gasto público bajo el reinado de Carlos III, 1760–1785," *Revista de Historia Económica* 3(3)(1985), and finally, "Recent Trends in the Study of Spanish American Colonial Public Finance," *Latin American Research Review* 23(1)(1988).

4. See our joint study "The Seventeenth Century Crisis in New Spain: Myth or Reality?" *Past and Present* 90(February 1981), and our "Rejoinder" to the critiques of J. Israel and H. Kamen, *Past and Present* 97(November 1982). My own subsequent studies have included "Rentas de la Corona y economía del Virreino de Nueva España," *Hacienda Pública Española* [Madrid] 87(Marzo–Abril 1984), "La economía de la Nueva España, 1680–1809," *Historia Mexicana* 29(4)(136) (abril–junio 1985), and "Las economías de Nueva España y Perú, 1680–1809: La visión a partir de las Cajas Reales," in Heraclio Bonilla, ed., *El sistema colonial en la América Española* (Barcelona: Editorial Crítica, 1991). It should be stressed here that I have revised several of the series used in these articles and that the numbers used in this volume supercede them. I have also surveyed the entire field of fiscal studies in my recent essay "Historia fiscal colonial: Resultados y perspectivas," *Historia Mexicana* 42(2)(166)(octubre–diciembre 1992).

Chapter 1

1. The relationship of taxation to the rise of the modern state is laid out in the original works by Gabriel Ardant on the sociology and history of taxation. See his two major works in this area: *Théories sociologique de l'impôt*, 2 vols. (Paris: S.E.V.P.N, 1965), and *Histoire de l'impôt* (Paris: Fayard, 1971).

2. I have surveyed this new research in two recent articles. See Herbert S. Klein and Jacques Barbier, "Recent Trends in the Study of Spanish American Colonial Public Finance," *Latin American Research Review* 23(1)(1988):35–62, and most recently, Herbert S. Klein, "Historia fiscal colonial: Resultados y perspectivas," *Historia Mexicana* 42(2)(166)(octubre–diciembre 1992): 261–307.

3. The best single introduction to the ideas behind the creation of the colonial fiscal system and its difference from that of the original Castillian model is the study of Ismael Sánchez-Bella, *La organización financiera de las Indias, siglo XVI* (Sevilla: Escuela de Estudios Hispano-americanos, C.S.I.C., 1968).

4. Ricardo Levene, for example, a highly regarded early twentieth century Argentine historian, used the annual accounts (the *tanteos, cartas cuentas,* or *relaciones juradas*) to reconstruct the economic development of the Río de la Plata region. Ricardo Levene, *Investigaciones acerca de la historia económica del Virreinato del Plata* (2d ed., Buenos Aires: El Ateneo, 1952). And he was joined by at least one North American luminary of the same vintage, Clarence H. Haring, who produced an early study of the *libros mayores,* one of the essential elements in the colonial accounting process. See Clarence H. Haring, "Los libros mayores de los tesoreros reales de Hispano-américa en el siglo xvi," *Hispanic American Historical Review* 2(May 1919):173–87, and "Early Spanish Colonial Exchequer," *American Historical Review* 23(July 1918): 779–96. From the same generation is Arthur Scott Aiton's, "Real Hacienda in New Spain under the First Viceroy," *Hispanic American Historical Review* (1926):232–45.

5. Alexander von Humboldt, *Essai politique sur le royaume de la Nouvelle-Espagne* (6 vols. Paris: F. Schoell, 1811).

6. On of the more extreme such statements is found in Henry Kamen, "Debate: The Seventeenth-Century Crisis in New Spain: Myth or Reality?," *Past and Present* 97 (November 1982):144–50. Even he con-

cedes some modest relationship between a few mining taxes and underlying economic trends.

7. Examples of this are found in John J. TePaske, "The Records of the King's Countinghouse: Problems and Pitfalls," *Latin American Economic History Newsletter* 1 (December 1991):5–8.

8. Sánchez-Bella, *La organización financiera,* 82, 84.

9. Kenneth J. Andrien, *Crisis and Decline: The Viceroyalty of Peru in the Seventeenth Century* (Albuquerque: University of New Mexico Press, 1985), p. 112

10. Marcello Carmagnani, "La produción agro-pecuaria chilena: Aspectos cuantitativos (1630–1830)," *Cahiers des Amériques latines* 3(1969):3–21. Also see Cecilia Rabell, *Los diezmos de San Luis de la Paz: Economía de una región del Bajío en el siglo xviii* (Mexico: Instituto de Investigaciones Sociales, Universidad Nacional Autónoma de México, 1986); Héctor Lindo-Fuentes, "La utilidad de los diezmos como fuentes para la historia económica," *Historia Mexicana* 30(2)(1980): 273–89; and the debate on "The Economic Cycle in Bourbon Central Mexico," in *Hispanic American Historical Review* 69(3) (1989):545–49. A recent study of agriculture in seventeenth and eithteenth century Peru is based on such records. See Kendall W. Brown, *Bourbons and Brandy: Imperial Reform in Eighteenth-Century Arequipa* (Albuquerque: University of New Mexico, 1985), chap. 2.

11. See Kenneth J. Andrien, "The Sale of Fiscal Offices and the Decline of Royal Authority in the Viceroyalty of Peru, 1633–1700," *Hispanic American Historical Review* 62(February 1982):49–71; and J. H. Parry, *The Sale of Public Office in the Spanish Indies under the Hapsburgs* (Berkeley: University of California Press, 1953).

12. Most of the sales for New Spain were over by the 1720s, with 85 percent coming before 1715. In the period from 1680 to 1715, all royal treasury offices were sold in the viceroyalty. Michel Bertrand, "Grandeur et misères de l'office: Les officiers de finances

de Nouvelle-Espagne XVIIe–XVIIIe siècles," (2 vols., PhD udiss., Université de Paris-I, 1995) 1:148.

13. Both Bertrand and Andrien stress that those who purchased offices were much less qualified than openly recruited officials, who usually had years of treasury experience. The only difference between New Spain and Peru seems to have been that most of the purchasers of Mexican offices were from Spain, while the majority purchasing offices in Peru were local. Ibid., 1:149; and Andrien, *Crisis and Decline*, 115ff.

14. See appendix 1 for how these averages were created.

15. One of the most judicious reviews of this issue is found in Zacarías Moutoukias, "Una forma de oposición: El contrabando," in Massimo Ganci and Ruggiero Romano, eds., *Governare il mondo: L'impero spagnolo dal XV al XIX secolo* (Palermo: Società Siciliana per la Storia Patria, 1991), 333–68. In another seminal essay, Moutoukias has argued that in fact a complex combination of government subsidies and semi-illegal contraband trade actually strengthened royal government in the outpost frontier of Buenos Aires in the seventeenth century. Zacarías Moutoukias, "Power, Corruption and Commerce: The Making of the Local Administrative Structure in Seventeenth-Century Buenos Aires," *Hispanic American Historical Review* 68(4)(1988):771–801.

16. Carlos Sempat Assadourian, *El sistema de la economía colonial: Mercado interno, regiones y espacio económico* (Lima: Instituto de Estudios Peruanos, 1982), 125.

17. Interview with Zacarías Moutoukias, Paris, November 14, 1995.

18. These have been analyzed in detail in Carlos Marichal, "Las guerras imperiales y los préstamos novohispanos, 1781–1804," *Historia Mexicana* 39(4)(1990). It was estimated that over half (or 289 million) of the 500 million reales that the government raised in extraordinary funds in 1792 to pay for war with revolutionary France came from American sources; and these mostly from the local corporate associations. Miguel

Artola, *La hacienda del antiguo régimen* (Madrid: Alianza Editorial, 1982), 325.

19. For the nature of the debt arrangements in terms of loans, juros, and vales, see Artola, *La hacienda*, 19.

20. Richard Herr, *Rural Change and Royal Finance in Spain at the End of the Old Regime* (Berkeley: University of California Press, 1989), 79.

21. Among the numerous studies on the so-called "consolidación de vales reales," which began in the American colonies in 1805, see Asunción Lavrin, "The Execution of the Law of 'Consolidación' in New Spain: Economic Aims and Results," *Hispanic American Historical Review* 53(1)(February 1973); Brian R. Hamnett, "The Appropriation of Mexican Church Wealth by the Spanish Bourbon Government—The 'Consolidación de Vales Reales', 1805–1809," *Journal of Latin American Studies* 1(2)(November 1969); and Margaret Chowning, "The Consolidación de Vales Reales in the Bishopric of Michoacán," *Hispanic American Historical Review* 69(3) (1989).

22. One of the more exotic of the new debt arrangements were the so-called *libranzas*, which were eventually turned into letters of credit on an American treasury, to be paid to neutral European lenders who were allowed to trade with America to collect their funds. These and other arrangements, generally with neutral foreign powers such as Portugal and the Netherlands, but sometimes even with England, brought a breakdown of the colonial customs union by the first decade of the nineteenth century. These themes are explored in a series of articles by Jacques Barbier, "Anglo-American Investors and Payments on Spanish Imperial Treasuries, 1795–1808," in Jacques A. Barbier and Allan J. Kuethe, eds., *The North American Role in the Spanish Imperial Economy, 1760–1819* (Manchester: Manchester University Press, 1984), 134–41, "Peninsular Finance and Colonial Trade: The Dilemma of Charles IV's Spain," *Journal of Latin American Studies* 12(1)(May 1980), and "Venezuelan 'Libranzas', 1788–1807: From Economic Nostrum

to Fiscal Imperative," *The Americas* 37(4)
(April 1981).

23. The accounts for the eighteenth century were kept in units of pesos a 8. This was
also the predominant unit of account for
most of the sixteenth and seventeenth centuries. But in the two first centuries, crown
officials also kept some of the accounts in
gold pesos and *pesos ensayados*, and even
sometimes reported income or expenditures
in individual taxes in several of these mone-
tary units. In the present work all the varying monies have been converted into standard pesos a 8 units and then summed
together to arrive at total figures for each
tax. The conversion equations used were as
follows: For gold pesos up to and including
1612, a multiplier factor of 2.0441 is used
to obtain the equivalent value in pesos a 8;
from 1613 up to and including 1642, the
multiplier is 2.1177; for the period from
1643 to 1688, the multiplier is 2.5. Finally,
after 1688, the number of gold pesos is
multiplied by 3.125. As for the peso ensayado, the multiplier at all times is 1.6544
to arrive at the requisite value in pesos a 8.
Though it does not appear in any colonial
accounts, the crown used a separate mone-
tary unit for its metropolitan taxes. This
was the *real de vellón*, with twenty reales de
vellón equal to one colonial peso a 8.

24. On what such a complete price study
would look like, see Herbert S. Klein and
Stanley Engerman, "Methods and Meanings
in Price History," in Lyman Johnson and
Enrique Tandeter, eds., *Growth and Integration in the Atlantic Economy: Essays on the
Price History of Eighteenth-Century Latin America* (Albuquerque: University of New Mexico
Press, 1990), 9–20.

25. See Richard L. Garner with Spiro E.
Stefanou, *Economic Growth and Change in
Bourbon Mexico* (Gainesville: University Press
of Florida, 1993), 27–36. Garner also estimated production figures and found that
while inflation ran at around half a percent
per annum in the eighteenth century, this
was less than half the annual rate of growth
in local production.

Chapter 2

1. Harry E. Cross, "South American Bul-
lion Production and Export, 1550–1750," in
J. F. Richards, ed., *Precious Metals in the Later
Medieval and Early Modern Worlds* (Durham,
NC: Carolina Academic Press, 1983), 403,
table 2.

2. Carlos Sempat Assadourian, *El sistema
de la economía colonial: Mercado interno, regiones y espacio económico* (Lima: Instituto de
Estudios Peruanos, 1982), especially chap. 4.

3. If mercury sales are included, the figure rises to between 70 percent and 76 percent of total revenues until 1740.

4. If mercury sales are included, the
rates for Mexico are around 30 percent and
for Peru it increased to between 15 and
19 percent.

5. These royal mine tax income figures
follow closely the estimate provided by John
TePaske of total mine production. The total
mine production of the two Perus began to
grow after 1750 and by the 1790s actually
surpassed the peak 1630s production figures.
For the growth of Lower Peruvian mining in
this period, see John Fisher, *Minas y mineros
en el Perú colonial 1776–1824* (Lima: Instituto de Estudios Peruanos, 1977).

6. Although the royal fifth had been reduced to a tenth of the value of total output in the Mexican mines by the middle of
the seventeenth century, such relief did not
come to the Andean miners until 1736.
Peter Bakewell, "Mining in Colonial Spanish
America," in Leslie Bethell, ed., *Cambridge
History of Latin America* (Cambridge: Cambridge University Press, 1984)2:134.

7. A detailed listing of all royal monopolies is found in Fabián de Fonseca and Carlos
de Urrutia, *Historia general de Real Hacienda*,
6 vols. (Mexico City: V. G. Torres, 1845–53)
2:119–486 (*pólvoro, naipes, lotería, tabaco*);
3:5–62, 338–427, 521–637 (*papel sellado,
gallos, pulque, cobre-estaño-plomo-alumbre*);
4:6–141, 319–32, 392–97 (*sal, cordobanes,
nieve*); and 5:60–90 (*lastre*). The important
pulque tax is studied in José Jesús Hernández
Paloma, *La renta de pulque en Nueva España,*

1663–1810 (Sevilla: Escuela de Estudios Hispano-Americanos, C.S.I.C., 1979); the gunpowder monopoly in Covadongo Villar Ortiz, *La renta de la pólvora en Nueva España (1569–1767)* (Sevilla: Escuela de Estudios Hispano-Americanos, C.S.I.C., 1988) and James A. Lewis, "The Royal Gunpowder Monopoly in New Spain (1766–1783): Case Study of Management, Technology and Reform under Charles III," *Ibero-Amerikanisches Archiv* 6(4)(1980):355–72; playing cards in María de los Ángeles Cuello Martinelli, *La renta de los naipes en Nueva España* (Sevilla: Escuela de Estudios Hispano-Americanos, C.S.I.C., 1966); and cockfights in María Justina Sarabia Viejo, *El juego de gallos en Nueva España* (Sevilla: Escuela de Estudios Hispano-Americanos, C.S.I.C., 1972). For the mercury monopoly, see M. F. Lang, *El monopolio estatal del mercurio en el México colonial (1550–1710)* (Mexico City: Fondo de Cultura Económica, 1977).

8. See chaps. 3 and 5 for a detailed discussion of the Renta de Tabaco.

9. While I have listed 6.2 million pesos as the total average monopoly income per annum in the decade of the 1780s for monopoly consumption receipts, this number should be treated with caution. Some 1.1 million pesos of this total is accounted for by two exceptional year listings for mercury receipts in the port of Veracruz, which in all its history had such receipts for a total of only five years; amounts for the other three years were insignificant. Such high totals for two years represent extraordinary incomes, which may in fact be double-counted receipts from other treasuries.

10. For recent detailed studies of tribute tax in the colonial period, see Herbert S. Klein, *Haciendas and Ayllus: Rural Society in the Bolivian Andes in the 18th and 19th Centuries* (Stanford: Stanford University Press, 1993).

11. Nicolás Sánchez-Albornoz, *Indios y tributos en el Alto Perú* (Lima: Instituto de Estudios Peruanos, 1978), 43n.

12. An excellent review of these special taxes, forced loans, and patriotic gifts, all of which drained capital from Mexico, is found in Carlos Marichal, "Las guerras imperiales y los préstamos novohispanos, 1781–1804," *Historia Mexicana* 39(156)(abril–junio 1990) 881–907. Also see Pedro Pérez Herrero, *Plata y libranzas: La articulación commercial del México borbónico* (Mexico City: Colegio de México, 1988). Finally the impact of the international wars and internal early nineteenth century rebellions on regular fiscal collections has been examined by John TePaske, "La crisis financiera del virreinato de Nueva España a fines de la colonia," *Secuencia* 19(enero–abril 1991); see also his analysis of the two principal regional cajas in "General Tendencies and Secular Trends in the Economies of Mexico and Peru, 1750–1810: The View from the Cajas of Mexico and Lima," in Nils Jacobsen and Hans-Jürgen Puhle, eds., *The Economies of Mexico and Peru during the Late Colonial Period, 1760–1810* (Berlin: Colloquium Verlag, 1986).

13. For a survey of the situado sent to the Philippines see, Leslie Bauzon, "Deficit Government, Mexico and the Philippines 'Situado' (1606–1804)," (Ph.D. thesis, Duke University, 1970).

14. Herbert S. Klein, "Structure and Profitability of Royal Finance in the Viceroyalty of the Río de la Plata in 1790," *Hispanic American Historical Review* 53(3)(August 1973):440–69.

15. It is quite conceivable, as O'Phelan has recently argued, that some of the increase in royal revenues in the second half of the eighteenth century may be due to the expansion of the tax base itself and the inclusion of Indians and other previously exempt groups. See Scarlett O'Phelan Godoy, "Las reformas fiscales borbónicas y su impacto en la sociedad colonial del Bajo y Alto Perú," in Jacobsen and Puhle, *The Economies of Mexico and Peru.*

16. For more details on the seventeenth century crisis as seen from these fiscal accounts, see John TePaske and Herbert S. Klein, "The Seventeenth Century Crisis in New Spain: Myth or Reality," *Past and Present* 90 (February 1981):116–35; and a "Rejoin-

der" to the critiques of J.Israel and H. Kamen appeared in *Past and Present* 97(November 1982):157–62.

17. Marichal, "Las guerras imperiales," 898–99.

18. Carlos Marichal, "La bancarrota del virreinato: Finanzas, guerra y política en la Nueva España, 1770–1808," in Josefina Zoraida Vázquez, ed., *Interpretaciones del siglo XVIII mexicano: El impacto de las reformas borbónicas* (Mexico: Nueva Imagen, 1992), 182.

19. This has been shown to have been the case for the income of 1804. See A. Brading, "Facts and Figments in Bourbon Mexico," *Bulletin of Latin American Research* 4(1)(1985):62–63.

20. See Pedro Pérez Herrero, "El México borbónico: ¿Un 'exito' fracasado?" in Zoraida Vázquez, ed., *Interpretaciones del siglo XVIII mexicano*, 127.

21. A judicious summation of this position is found in Marichal, "La bancarrota del virreinato," pp. 153–186.

22. Carlos Marichal and Matilde Souto Mantecón, "Silver and Situados: New Spain and the Financing of the Spanish Empire in the Eighteenth Century," *Hispanic American Historical Review* 74(4)(1994):594, 603.

23. See Jacques Barbier and Herbert S. Klein, "Revolutionary Wars and Public Finances: The Madrid Treasury, 1784–1807," *Journal of Economic History* 41(2)(June 1981): 315–39; and Miguel Artola, *La hacienda del antiguo régimen* (Madrid: Alianza Editorial, 1982).

Chapter 3

1. This is the latest estimate, taken from David Nobel Cook, *The Demographic Collapse: Indian Peru, 1520–1620* (Cambridge: Cambridge University Press, 1981), 114.

2. On the creation of the audiencia, see Josep M. Barnadas, *Charcas: Orígenes históricas de una sociedad colonial* (La Paz: Centro de Investigación y Promoción del Campesinado, 1973).

3. Carlos Sempat Assadourian, *El sistema de la economía colonial: Mercado interno, re-*

giones y espacio económico (Lima: Instituto de Estudios Peruanos, 1982), 111.

4. See chap. 4.

5. Between fifteen hundred and thirty-five hundred *mitayos*, or forced labor miners, were drafted annually to work these mines. Carlos Contreras, *La ciudad del mercurio, Huancavelica, 1570–1700* (Lima: Instituto de Estudios Peruanos, 1982), 43. Also see Guillermo Lohmann Villena, *Las minas de Huancavelica en los siglos XVI y XVII* (Sevilla: Escuela de Estudios Hispano-Americanos, C.S.I.C., 1949).

6. See John J. TePaske, "Bullion Production in Mexico and Peru, 1581–1810," unpublished ms., 1987, tables 3 and 4; John Fisher, *Minas y mineros en el Perú colonial, 1776–1824* (Lima: Instituto de Estudios Peruanos, 1977); and José Deustúa, *La minería peruana y la iniciación de la República, 1820–1840* (Lima: Instituto de Estudios Peruanos, 1986).

7. Cook, *Demographic Collapse*, 94, table 18.

8. Ibid., 215, 219.

9. Ibid., 151.

10. Kenneth J. Andrien, *Crisis and Decline: The Viceroyalty of Peru in the Seventeenth Century* (Albuquerque: University of New Mexico Press, 1985), 31.

11. A detailed description of the regional Andean economy as it developed in the second half of the sixteenth century is found in Sempat Assadourian, *El sistema de la economía colonial*, especially chap. 4.

12. On the seventeenth century crisis and its impact on Peru, see John J. TePaske and Herbert S. Klein, "The Seventeenth Century Crisis in New Spain: Myth or Reality," *Past and Present*, 90(February 1981):116–35. For a discussion of the political tensions generated by the crisis and the special problems of the Potosí *mita* during this century, see Luis Miguel Glave, *Trajinantes: Caminos indígenas en la sociedad colonial siglos XVI/XVII* (Lima: Instituto de Apoyo Agrario, 1989), chap. 4.

13. This is the argument presented by Andrien, based on his analysis of the complex evolution of the Peruvian economy in

the seventeenth century, which continued many of the trends toward import substitution and economic self-sufficiency noted by Assadourian for the late sixteenth century. See Andrien, *Crisis and Decline*, chap. 2; and L. A. Clayton, "Trade and Navigation in the Seventeenth-Century Viceroyalty of Peru," *Journal of Latin American Studies* 7(1)(May 1975):1–21. A recent review of this literature stressing the dependency model, which suggests that while the center collapsed the periphery expanded, is found in Pedro Pérez Herrero, *Comercio y mercados en América Latina colonial* (Madrid: Editorial Mapfre, 1992), chap. 3. For a recent review of the literature for Europe and America in the seventeenth century collapse, see Ruggiero Romano, *Coyunturas opuestas: La crisis del siglo XVII en Europa e Hispanoamérica* (Mexico City: Fondo de Cultura Económica, 1993).

14. For a detailed analysis of the seventeenth century decline in one region, see Kendall W. Brown, *Bourbons and Brandy: Imperial Reform in the Eighteenth-Century Arequipa* (Albuquerque: University of New Mexico, 1985), 29–43.

15. For a detailed analysis of changes in the royal treasury districts of Peru, see Gullermo Céspedes del Castillo, "Reorganización de la Hacienda virreinal peruana en el siglo XVIII," *Anuario de Historia del Derecho Español* 23(1953):339ff. He estimates that by the end of the eighteenth century, there were sixty-five full-time "oficiales reales" at the senior level in the Peruvian viceroyalty, absorbing a total salary of some 63,000 pesos. Ibid., 345.

16. These total revenue figures will include not only the major tax categories (which in Peru accounted for just over two-thirds of total revenues) but a host of special and extraordinary taxes and income that contributed to the whole, less incomes that were carryovers from previous years, uncollected funds, etc.

17. A detailed analysis of the financial history of the principal Lima treasury in the seventeenth century is found in Andrien,

Crisis and Decline, especially chap. 3. Andrien used actual raw figures and a different yearly breakdown from that used here, so that our numbers are usually not the same, though the ratios and patterns are similar.

18. Lima as late as the 1680s made up for 88% of total colonial income revenues. For Cuzco—whose books are missing for the decades going from 1610–1629, and again from 1630–69, the best decade prior to 1709 was the 1580s, when this southern treasury produced an estimated annual average income of 304,327 pesos. Trujillo, the major regional center of the North, reached its highest pre-1700 annual figure in the decade of the 1640s, when it averaged 45,121 pesos per year.

19. For the growth of Lower Peruvian mining in this period, see John Fisher, *Minas y mineros en el Perú colonial 1776–1824* (Lima: Instituto de Estudios Peruanos, 1977).

20. Spanish taxation on mines and their output is a complex subject, and there is no question that New Spain would have received far more concessions than did Peru or Charcas. Given the state's claim to all subsoil rights, it taxed mines heavily from the very beginning. From 1504 the royalty on production was fixed at one-fifth (the *quinto real*) and was supplemented by an assay charge of 1–1.5 percent. But to promote local mining, the crown often reduced this rate. New Spain miners as early as 1548 began to get rather broad concessions, which reduced the royalty tax on mining to 10 percent (the *diezmo*) at selected local mines; by the mid-seventeenth century, few Mexican miners were paying the higher 20 percent fee. But in Peru and Charcas, the quinto was maintained intact until 1724, and no local concessions were granted. The Bourbon reformers after 1770 went further in Mexico, eliminating even the diezmo on mine production in many areas, in order to promote production, and only began to charge 10 percent after initial costs were recovered. This was used to great effect in the Zacatecas mining district. Peter Bakewell, "Mining in Colonial Spanish America," in Leslie Bethell,

ed., *Colonial Spanish America* (Cambridge: Cambridge University Press, 1987), 252.

21. Guillermo Céspedes del Castillo, "La renta del tabaco en el virreinato del Peru," *Revista Histórica* (Lima) 21(1954):25. Though tobacco rents probably exceeded monopoly rents in Peru as they did in Mexico, they were nowhere near the enormous rents received by the crown in New Spain; see chap. 5.

22. For a recent study see Christine Hünefeldt, "Etapa final del monopolio en el virreinato del Peru: El tabaco de Chachapoyas," in Nils Jacobsen and Hans-Jürgen Puhle, eds., *The Economies of Mexico and Peru During the Late Colonial Period* (Berlin: Colloquim Verlag, 1986).

23. Nicolás Sánchez-Albornoz, *La población de América Latina desde los tiempos precolombianos al año 2000*, 2d ed. (Madrid: Alianza Editorial, 1977), 65.

24. Günter Vollmer, *Bevölkerungspolitik und Bevölkerungsstruktur im Vizekönigreich Peru zu Ende der Kolonialzeit (1741–1821)* (Bad Homburg: Gehlen, 1967), 285.

25. Ibid., 285, 265. The 1792 census figure included 244,000 mestizos, 41,000 free blacks and mulattoes, and 40,000 slaves. Whites numbered 136,000. The zone populated most heavily by Indians was Cuzco, with 159,000 Indians.

26. Nicolás Sánchez-Albornoz, *Indios y tributos en el Alto Perú* Lima: Instituto de Estudios Peruanos, 1978), 43. On eighteenth century reforms, see the two useful legal studies by Carlos J. Díaz Rementería: "El régimen jurídico del ramo de tributos en Nueva España y las reformas peruanas de Carlos III," *Historia Mexicana* 28(3)(1979):401–38, and "En torno a un aspecto de la política reformista de Carlos III: Las matrículas de tributarios en los virreinatos del Perú y del Río de la Plata," *Revista de Indias* 37(147–148) (enero–junio 1977):51–139.

27. See the discussion in chap. 4.

28. Comparing total income, as reported in the *carta cuentas*, and total expenditure (that is, making no allowance for carryover incomes, deposits, and uncollected debts) for the period from 1700 to 1809 (when there were no annual accounting problems), yields very high correlations between income and expenditure *by year* for the three principal regional treasuries: Trujillo, Lima, and Cuzco. In all three centers the correlations were highly significant, at .9887 (80 known years) for Trujillo in the north, .8760 (for 110 known years) for Lima in the center, and .9647 (72 years) for Cuzco. The non-Lima treasuries clearly exhibit extraordinarily high correlations, but even for Lima, given its special role as viceregal center with unusual expenditure problems, a .88 correlation is exceptionally high.

29. All these subsidies, known as *situados*, are listed in the grouping of war-related expenditures and are subsumed in the numbers in table 2.10.

30. On the increasing dispute for economic control between Lima and the rising Buenos Aires, see Guillermo Céspedes del Castillo, *Lima y Buenos Aires: Repercusiones económicas y políticas de la creación del virreinato del Plata* (Sevilla: Escuela de Estudios Hispano-Americanos, 1947).

31. Jacques Barbier and Herbert Klein, "Revolutionary Wars and Public Finances: The Madrid Treasury, 1784–1807," *Journal of Economic History* 41(2)(June 1981).

Chapter 4

1. These estimated early sixteenth century population figures are taken from Eduardo Arze Quiroga, *Historia de Bolivia . . . siglo XVI* (La Paz: Los Amigos del Libro, 1969), 15. A later estimate based on a partial census of 1683 found only some 250,000 Indians for most of the regions which then went to make up the Audiencia de Charcas. Brian M. Evans, "Census Enumeration in Late 17th Century Alto Peru: The Numeración General of 1683–1684," in David J. Robinson, ed., *Studies in Spanish American Population History* (Boulder, CO: Westview Press, 1985), 36. All agree that this severe decline of the Indian population in the late sixteenth and seventeenth centuries was due to the impact of European diseases new to Amerindian populations. By the end of the

colonial period, the region's Indian population had grown considerably and was estimated to be 800,000 in 1826, at which time there were 200,000 mestizos and whites. John Barclay Pentland, *Informe sobre Bolivia* (1826; Potosí: Editorial Potosí, 1975).

2. It is estimated that Potosí and associated Charcas mines would produce close to 60 percent of the world's total silver output in both the sixteenth and seventeenth centuries. Harry E. Cross, "South American Bullion Production and Export, 1550–1750," in J. F. Richards, ed., *Precious Metals in the Later Medieval and Early Modern Worlds* (Durham, NC: Carolina Academic Press, 1983), 403, table 2.

3. Arze Quiroga, *Historia de Bolivia*, 11

4. Traditional estimates cite a population of 150,000 persons by 1611. If this number is correct, Potosí would have been the largest city in the Americas at the time. For these standard estimates, see Luis Peñaloza, *Historia económica de Bolivia*, 2 vols. (La Paz: n.p., 1953) 1:197.

5. The classic description of this market is contained in Carlos Sempat Assadourian, *El sistema de la economía colonial: Mercado interno, regiones y espacio económico* (Lima: Instituto de Estudios Peruanos, 1982), chap. 4.

6. For a detailed analysis of the early mita, see Jeffrey A. Cole, *The Potosí Mita 1573–1700: Compulsory Indian Labor in the Andes* (Stanford, CA: Stanford University Press, 1985).

7. For estimates of the laboring population at this time, see Peter Bakewell, *Miners of the Red Mountain: Indian Labor in Potosí, 1545–1650* (Albuquerque: University of New Mexico Press, 1984), 111–12.

8. Oruro, whose mines did not come into full production until the end of the seventeenth century, was the last major city to be founded in Charcas. It was formally established in 1606. Arze Quiroga, *Historia de Bolivia*, 37.

9. The best recent survey of the seventeenth century economy of Charcas, with an emphasis on the mining economy, is the work by Clara López Beltrán, *Estructura económica de una sociedad colonial: Charcas*

en el siglo XVII (La Paz: CERES, 1988). For an analysis of early mining, see Gaston Arduz Eguía, *Ensayos sobre la historia de la minería altoperuana* (Madrid: Editorial Parainfo, 1985). The data on Potosí production (which appear in graph 4.1) are taken from Peter J. Bakewell, "Registered Silver Production in Potosí, 1550–1735," *Jahrbuch für Geschichte von Staat, Wirtschaft und Gesellschaft Lateinamerikas* 12(1975):92–97, table 1; and Lamberto de Sierra, *"Manfiesto" de la plata extraida del cerro de Potosí, 1556–1800* (publication of 1808 ms., Buenos Aires: Academia Nacional de la Historia, 1971).

10. In 1696, in a very uncommon and unusual manner, most of the treasury offices of Charcas decided to change their traditional fiscal year, which paralleled the calendar year, to one running from May until June. This innovation lasted in most of these cajas until 1769, when they shifted back to the calendar year for 1770. This created problems for the years 1696 and 1769 in most districts, leaving the former at sixteen months and the later at only eight months. Otherwise the cajas were relatively free of the complex multiyear problems found to be so common in seventeenth and even early eighteenth century New Spain. Given that correcting this minor discrepancy would entail separating the decadal averages into exact calendar years, I have left them as if these were calendar years for the whole period. The results do not significantly change the direction or size of the relevant numbers.

11. Mercury income figures are not very highly correlated with mine incomes. Thus for Potosí the correlation was .51 over a ninety-six-year period when the two incomes were both received; and only .44 for ninety-seven years in Oruro during the same eighteenth century period. While statistically significant, these correlations are not as high as might have been expected.

12. See Herbert S. Klein, *Haciendas and Ayllus: Rural Society in the Bolivian Andes in the 18th and 19th Centuries* (Stanford, CA: Stanford University Press, 1992).

13. The correlations between gross income and expenditures for the period after

1700 (when accounts were kept on an annual basis for all cajas) for Potosí were .952 (ninety-five years); for Oruro .899 (one hundred years); and .965 for La Paz (eighty-nine years). All correlations are significant. I have used gross income and expenditure figures here and in all other calculated correlations, because these were the figures most often used by the royal officials when analyzing trends.

14. See Herbert S. Klein, "Structure and Profitability of Royal Finance in the Viceroyalty of the Río de la Plata in 1790," *Hispanic American Historical Review* 53(3)(August 1973).

Chapter 5

1. Alexander von Humboldt, *Essai politique sur le royaume de la Nouvelle-Espagne*, 6 vols. (Paris: F. Schoell, 1811) 5:38–39.

2. The best recent review of all the economic literature on eighteenth century Mexico is found in Richard L. Garner with Spiro E. Stefanou, *Economic Growth and Change in Bourbon Mexico* (Gainesville: University Press of Florida, 1993).

3. Garner estimates that the total value of legal Mexican silver production went from 6.7 million pesos per annum in 1700 to 13.3 million pesos in 1810, representing an annual growth rate of 1.4 percent. Ibid., 21.

4. Ibid., 19, 21.

5. Ibid., 19. For the major role that the 1784–86 crisis played in the crucial Guadalajara region, see Eric Van Young, *Hacienda and Market in Eighteenth-Century Mexico: The Rural Economy of the Guadalajara Region, 1675–1820* (Berkeley: University of California Press, 1981), 94–103.

6. Population figures for the nineteenth century are much in dispute, though all agree that population doubled in the century. Brading estimates that in 1742 Mexico's population stood at 3.3 million persons, and by 1810 it had climbed to 6.1 million; D. A. Brading, *Merchants and Miners in Bourbon Mexico, 1763–1810* (Cambridge: Cambridge University Press, 1971), 14. Garner suggests that the Mexican population grew from between 2.5 and 3 million in 1700 to between 5 million and 5.5 million in 1800; Garner and Stefanou, *Economic Growth*, 11.

7. The best survey of all of the Mexican prices will be found in Garner with Stefanou, *Economic Growth and Change in Bourbon Mexico*; also see appendix 2 of the present work.

8. These "otras" funds were usually listed as situado in the sending treasuries. The most detailed secondary analysis of these intertreasury subsidies for Mexico is Carlos Marichal and Matilde Souto Mantecón, "Silver and Situados: New Spain and the Financing of the Spanish Empire in the Eighteenth Century," *Hispanic American Historical Review* 74(4) (1994).

9. Humboldt, *Essai* 3:265, 347; 4:290.

10. Ibid. 4:362–63.

11. Ibid. 3:346.

12. Ibid. 4:143–44.

13. Richard L. Garner, "Silver Production and Entrepreneurial Structure in 18th Century Mexico", *Jahrbuch für Geschichte von Staat, Wirtschaft und Gesellschaft Lateinamerikas* 17(1980), 177n.

14. Ibid., 160.

15. Humboldt (*Essai* 3:340) ranks the viceroyalty's mining districts in terms of mining output in the period 1785–89. Humboldt's ranking is compared below to that obtained from the treasury districts for the decade 1780–89:

Ranking of Viceregal Mining Districts by Output

	Humboldt's Ranking, 1785–89	Treasury Ranking, 1780–89
1. Guanajuato	(25%)	2 (12%)
2. San Luis Potosí	(16%)	3 (7%)
3. Zacatecas	(12%)	4 (6%)
4. Mexico	(11%)	1 (58%)
5. Durango	(9%)	5 (4%)
6. Rosario	(7%)	6 (3%)
7. Guadalajara	(5%)	7 (3%)
8. Pachuca	(5%)	9 (2%)
9. Bolanos	(4%)	8 (2%)
10. Sombrerete	(3%)	10 (1%)
11. Zimapán	(3%)	11 (1%)

16. Peter Bakewell, "Mining in Colonial Spanish America," in Leslie Bethell, ed., *Cambridge History of Latin America* (Cambridge: Cambridge University Press, 1984), vol. 2.

17. Garner, "Silver Production", passim.

18. Recently there has been a major increase of studies using the alcabala, or sales tax, as a source for charting local trade patterns in Mexico. See especially the recent work of Juan Carlos Garavaglia and Juan Carlos Grosso, *Las alcabalas novohispanas (1776–1821)* (Mexico City: Archivo General de la Nación, 1987), and their joint studies "De Veracruz a Durango: Un análisis regional de la Nueva España borbónica," *Siglo XIX*, 2(4)(1987), and "Estado borbónico y opresión fiscal en la Nueva España, 1750–1821," in Antonio Annino, ed., *America Latina: Dallo stato coloniale allo stato nazionale*, 2 vols. (Torino: Franco Angeli, 1987) 1:78–97. Also see Jorge Silva Riquer, *La administración de alcabalas y pulques de Michoacán, 1776–1821* (Mexico City: Instituto Mora, 1993); Antonio Ibarra, "Mercado urbano y mercado regional en Guadalajara, 1790–1811: Tendencias cuantitativas de la renta de alcabalas," in Jorge Silva Riquer, et al., *Circuitos mercantiles y mercados en latinoamérica: Siglos XVIII–XIX* (Mexico City: Instituto Mora, 1995), 100–135.

19. For a detailed analysis of the increasing bankruptcy of the metropolitan Spanish treasury due to European wars from 1779 to 1808, see Miguel Artola, *La hacienda del antiguo régimen* (Madrid: Alianza Editorial, 1982), chap. 5.

20. J. H. Fisher, "The Imperial Response to 'Free Trade': Spanish Imports from Spanish America, 1778–1796," *Journal of Latin American Studies* 17(1985):78, table D4. The year of 1796 was also the date of the foundation of the Veracruz consulado.

21. Javier Ortiz de la Tabla Ducasse, *Comercio exterior de Veracruz, 1778–1821* (Sevilla: Escuela de Estudios Hispanoamericanos, C.S.I.C., 1978), 250 cuadro 1.

22. New Spain's foreign trade was quickly wiped out in the three years from 1821 to 1823, following the region's declaration of independence. The basic statistics for the Veracruz trade are found in Miguel Lerdo de Tejada, *Comercio exterior de Mexico*, 2d ed. (Mexico City: Banco Nacional de Comercio Exterior, 1967), table 14; and Ortiz de la Tabla, *Comercio exterior de Veracruz*, 241–61. For a study of postindependence trade, see Inés Herrera Canales, *El comercio exterior de Mexico, 1821–1875* (Mexico City: Colegio de México, 1977), 79ff.; and Leandro Prados de la Escosura, "Comercio exterior y cambio económico de España (1792–1849)," in Josep Fontana, *La economía española al final del antiguo régimen*, 3 vols. (Madrid: Alianza Editorial, 1982) 3:171ff.

23. Garavaglia and Grosso have even argued, on relatively imprecise data, that alcabala income outpaced actual commerce in this period, and that the crown, by implication, was increasing financial pressure. See Garavaglia and Grosso, "Estado borbónico y presión fiscal."

24. For a recent review of the tobacco monopoly and its revenues, see Susan Deans-Smith, "The Money Plant: The Royal Tobacco Monopoly of New Spain, 1765–1821," in Nils Jacobsen and Hans-Jürgen Puhle, eds., *The Economies of Mexico and Peru During the Late Colonial Period, 1760–1810* (Berlin: Collquium Verlag, 1986), and her *Bureaucrats, Planters and Workers: The Making of the Tobacco Monopoly in Bourbon Mexico* (Austin: University of Texas Press, 1992).

25. Fonseca and Urrutia, *Historia general* 2:437. Deans-Smith estimates that actual profit was about 50 percent of gross income; Deans-Smith, *Bureaucrats*, 261–62. It should also be stressed that some 500,000 pesos per annum were usually sent to Cuba to purchase the annual Cuban tobacco crop for Mexican factories and that this was usually an important part of the situado paid by the Mexican treasury to Cuba. Depending on the level of war expenditures, it could comprise as much as half the subsidy; Marichal and Souto Mantecón, "Silver and Situados," 691–92, 694–95. The factories of Mexico by the end of the colonial period were produc-

ing some 15 million cigars and over 100 million cigarettes per annum; Deans-Smith, Bureaucrats, 266.

26. On the origins of the tributo in New Spain, see José Miranda, *El tributo indígena en la Nueva España durante el siglo XVI* (Mexico City: El Colegio de México, 1952); and José de la Peña Cámara, *El "tributo": Sus orígenes: Su implantación en la Nueva España: Contribución al estudio de la real hacienda indiana* (Sevilla: Inprenta de la Gavidia, 1934).

27. Jacques Barbier and Herbert S. Klein, "Las prioridades de un monarca ilustrado: El gasto público bajo el reinado de Carlos III, 1760–1785," *Revista de Historia Económica* (Madrid) 3(3)(1985).

28. In the interwar period from 1802 to 1804, American loans and taxes made up on average 21 percent of total metropolitan incomes (26 percent when loans are excluded), indicating that the Spanish economy itself was providing a slightly higher amount in loan funds than the colonies. Francisco Comín Comín, *Hacienda y economía en la España contemporanea (1880–1936),* 2 vols. (Madrid: Instituto de Estudios Fiscales, 1988) 2:95, cuadro 3.

29. According to an official listing, by 1817 the Royal Treasury of New Spain owed some 10 million pesos on outstanding loans from the miners and merchants guilds. Another 22.7 million pesos was owed to the church; there were 24.3 million in unpaid bills and another 5 million in miscellaneous funds borrowed from other treasuries; Biblioteca Nacional (Madrid), Sala de Manuscritos, # 19710–23. I am indebted to John TePaske for this citation.

30. See Carlos Marichal, "Las guerras imperiales y los préstamos novohispanos, 1781–1804," *Historia mexicana* 39(156) (abril–junio 1990); and Gulhermina del Valle Pavón, "Los recursos extraordinarios de la hacienda novohispana, la dueda del México independiente," paper presented at the coloquium "Finanzas y estado en la primera república federal mexicana, 1824–1835," El Colegio de Michoacán, Zamora, Mexico, November 13–14, 1995.

31. It has even been suggested by Carlos Marichal that the post-1790 figures are no longer as reliable as those produced before that date. Interview with Carlos Marichal, Mexico City, November 12, 1995.

32. The so-called Consolidación decree involved a direct attack on the major source of loan capital in the colony. This was the estimated 50–60 million pesos available from the church's Division of Pious Funds and Charities (Juzgado de Testamentos, Capellanías y Obras Pías). From 1805 to 1809 the crown took over most of this capital and forced the payment on principal of all outstanding loans that fell due during this period. By this much disputed act, the crown generated some 11 million pesos in gross revenues and in effect seriously weakened the national capital market. See Brian R. Hamnett, "The Appropriation of Mexican Church Wealth by the Spanish Bourbon Government: The 'Consoldación de Vales Reales,' 1805–1809," *Journal of Latin American Studies* 1(2) (November 1969); and Asunción Lavrin, "The Execution of the Law of Consolidación in New Spain: Economic Aims and Results," *Hispanic American Historical Review* 53(1)(February 1973).

33. A good survey of the late colonial crisis in the treasury administration is found in John J. TePaske, "La desintegración financiario del gobierno real de México durante la época de independencia, 1791–1821," *Secuencia* (Mexico) 21(1991).

34. Adolf Soetbeer, *Edelmetall-Produktion und Werthverhaltniss zwischen Gold und Silber* (Gotha: J. Perthes, 1879), 55, 58. One crude estimate of gross national product recently calculated New Spain's output at $438 million in 1800 (1950 U.S. dollars); $420 million in 1845; and $392 million in 1860. It then began to rise rapidly, and by 1877 reached $613 million dollars. John H. Coatsworth, "Obstacles to Economic Growth in Nineteenth Century Mexico," *American Historical Review* 83(1)(February 1978):82.

35. Claude Morin, *Michoacán en la Nueva España del siglo XVIII* (Mexico City: Fondo de Cultura Económica, 1979), 134–40. It is entirely possible that new tax collection procedures may have suddenly generated new

income in the place of stagnant receipts, but this could only have occurred for a short period of time without causing severe economic crisis.

36. Pedro Pérez Herrero, "El México borbónico: ¿Un 'éxito' fracasado?" in Josefina Zoriada Vázquez, ed., *Interpretaciones del siglo XVIII mexicano: El impacto de las reformas borbónicas* (Mexico City: Nueva Imagen, 1992), 109–53.

37. Juan Carlos Garavaglia and Juan Carlos Grosso, "Estado borbónico y opresión fiscal."

38. Carlos Marichal, "La bancarrota del virreinato: Finanzas, guerra y política en la Nueva España, 1770–1808," in Zoriada Vázquez, *Interpretaciones del siglo XVIII mexicano*, 153–86.

39. Marichal and Souto, "Silver and Situados," 594, table 2.

40. Interview with Carlos Marichal, Mexico City, November 12, 1995. Between 1781 and 1784, the crown collected some 840,000 pesos as donations and contracted Mexican loans worth 2.5 million pesos; Marichal, "Guerras imperiales," 893. This very impressive loan sum was paid off by the end of the decade, thus encouraging local merchants to reinvest in the new loans issued in the next decade.

41. Carlos Marichal, "La bancarrota del virreinato: finanzas, guerra y política en la Nueva España, 1770–1808," in Zoraida Vázquez, *Interpretaciones del siglo XVIII mexicano*, pp. 172–174.

42. Humboldt, *Essai* 3:283.

43. Fonseca and Urrutia, *Historia general*.

44. See for example Morin, *Michoacán*, 132.

45. Humboldt, Essai, 4:434.

46. For gross income and expenditures after 1700, the correlations between the two variables by year is again extremely high and statistically significant for the three major treasuries of the Viceroyalty of New Spain. For the central treasury of Mexico it is .9964 (107 years), for Veracruz .9976 (96 years), and for Zacatecas .9912 (for 107 years).

47. Luis Antonio Jáuregui, "La autonomía del Fisco Colonial: La estructura administrativa de la Real Hacienda Novohispana,

1786–1821," (Ph.D. diss., Colegio de México, 1994), 173a, cuadro 9; 175a, cuadro 10A; 188, cuadro 11. These data cover the period from 1773 to 1798. As he concludes, right up to the beginnings of the nineteenth century "the Real Hacienda novohispana continued being economically efficient" in terms of maintaining a low ratio of administrative costs. Ibid., 186.

48. Biblioteca Nacional de Mexico, manuscrito no. 1282, "Memoria instructiva y documentada del estado comparativo de los productos de la Real Hacienda del año de 1809 . . . ," Mexico, August 1813. Within this collection of materials is an "Extracto general de valores y gastos y líquidos de los ramos comunes y particulares de la Real Hacienda de Nueva España dedicado de un año común por el quinquenio corrido desde 1795 hasta el de 1799," dated 15 July 1810. I am indebted to Carlos Marichal for providing me with this document. The sum of 20 million pesos (which with the deletion of the *donativos de guerra* would come to 19.4 million pesos) is quite close to the estimated total of 17.7 million pesos I obtained by using just the major production, commercial, consumption, and population taxes.

49. Spain seized Florida, but failed in its attempts to retake Jamaica, the Bahamas, and Honduras. It also greatly reenforced its Louisiana possession. Moreover the amount of situado it sent from Veracruz to Havana between 1779 and 1783 (some 38 million pesos) was double the ordinary annual defense budget of the Madrid treasury. Marichal and Souto, "Silver and Situados," 594, 606–7.

50. "Extracto general," Folio 2.

51. Humboldt estimated that the situado to American and Asian provinces cost the viceregal treasury at its maximum some 3.6 million pesos in the 1780s, with 1.8 million of that sum going to Cuba. Humboldt, Essai, 5:32.

52. Some 10.5 million pesos on average went for internal administration and defense within the viceroyalty; ibid., 5:26.

53. Ibid., 4:451–52.

54. Barbier and Klein, "The Madrid Trea-

sury," table 1. For the estimate of metropoli-
tan Spain's population in the 1790s, see Jordi
Nadal, *La población española (siglos XVI a XX)*
(Barcelona: Ariel, 1973), p.16.

55. For a detailed survey of these reforms
see Enrique Florescano and Isabel Gil Sánchez, "La época de las reformas borbónicas y
el crecimiento económico, 1750–1808", in
Centro de Estudios Históricos, El Colegio de
México, *Historia general de México*, 4 vols.
(Mexico City: El Colegio de México, 1976)
2:203–31. For the most recent debates about
the meanings of these reforms see the excellent set of essays in Zoraida Vázquez, *Interpretaciones del siglo XVIII mexicana*.

Conclusion

1. Earl J. Hamilton, *American Treasure and
the Price Revolution in Spain, 1501–1650*
(Cambridge, MA: Harvard University Press,
1934).

2. Michel Morineau, *Incroyables gazettes et
fabuleux métaux: Les retours des trésors américains d'apres les gazettes hollandaises (XVIe–
XVIIIe siècles)* (Paris: Cambridge University
Press and Maison des Sciences de l'Homme,
1985), chap. 3.

3. See for example Woodrow W. Borah,
New Spain's Century of Depression (Berkeley:
University of California Press, 1951). For an-
other view see J. I. Israel, "Mexico and the
'General Crisis' of the Seventeenth Century,"
Past and Present 63(May 1974):33–57, and
his *Race, Class and Politics in Colonial Mexico,
1610–1670* (Oxford: Oxford University
Press, 1975).

4. Of course local regional studies, such
as the work of Peter Bakewell on Zacatecas,
already indicated problems with the traditional view of uniform Mexican decline; see
P. J. Bakewell, *Silver Mining and Society in
Colonial Mexico: Zacatecas, 1546–1700* (Cambridge: Cambridge University Press, 1971).

5. It has even been suggested, though not
proven, that there was a large quantity of
unminted Mexican silver in circulation in
both the local and international economies
in the sixteenth and seventeenth centuries.

See Pedro Pérez Herrero, *Plata y libranzas: La
articulación commercial del México borbónico*
(Mexico City: Colegio de México, 1988),
chap. 6.

6. See John J. TePaske and Herbert S. Klein,
"The Seventeenth Century Crisis in New
Spain: Myth or Reality?", *Past and Present*
90(1981):11635.

7. Interview with John TePaske, February 12, 1996.

8. This was the basic argument in Ken-
neth J. Andrien's *Crisis and Decline: The
Viceroyalty of Peru in the Seventeenth Century*
(Albuquerque: University of New Mexico
Press, 1985).

9. See table 2.10 and John J. TePaske,
"New World Silver: Castile and the Far East
(1590–1750)," in John F. Richards, ed., *Precious Metals in the Later Medieval and Early
Modern Worlds* (Durham, NC: Carolina Academic Press, 1983), 425–46.

10. The classic model is presented in
François Chevalier, *Land and Society in Colonial Mexico: The Great Hacienda* (Berkeley:
University of California Press, 1970); and
Woodrow Borah, *New Spain's Century of Depression* (Iberoamericana, 35; Berkeley: Uni-
versity of California Press, 1951). The major
critiques have come from a host of scholars,
beginning with Peter Bakewell's work on *Sil-
ver Mining and Society in Colonial Mexico: Za-
catecas, 1546–1700* (Cambridge: Cambridge
University Press, 1971); through that of
William B. Taylor, *Landlord and Peasant in
Colonial Oaxaca* (Stanford, CA: Stanford Uni-
versity Press, 1972); and Eric Van Young,
*Hacienda and Market in Eighteenth-Century
Mexico: The Rural Economy of the Guadalajara
Region, 1675–1820* (Berkeley: University of
California Press, 1981).

11. So powerful was this earlier critique
that Chevalier himself greatly revised his position in the second Spanish edition of his
own text. See the introduction to the second
edition in François Chevalier, *La formación
de los latifundios en Mexico: Tierra y sociedad
en los siglos XVI y XVII* (2d rev. ed., Mexico
City: Fondo de Cultura Económica, 1976).

12. For the findings on the seventeenth

century crisis in Spain, see I. A. A. Thompson and Bartolomé Yun, eds., *The Castillian Crisis of the Seventeenth Century* (Cambridge: Cambridge University Press, 1994).

13. For a recent restatement of this position, see Pedro Pérez Herrero, *Comercio y mercados en América Latina colonial* (Madrid: Editorial Mapfre, 1992), chap. 3.

14. See above, chap. 1

15. David A. Brading and Harry E. Cross, "Colonial Silver Mining: Mexico and Peru," *Hispanic American Historical Review* 52(4)(November 1972):545–79. For the most recent summaries, see Peter Bakewell, "Mining in Colonial Spanish America," in Leslie Bethell, ed., *The Cambridge History of Latin America* (Cambridge: Cambridge University Press, 1984) 2:105–51; and John J. TePaske, "New World Silver."

16. Carlos Sempat Assadourian, *El sistema de la economía colonial: Mercado interno, regiones y espacio económico* (Lima: Instituto de Estudios Peruanos, 1982).

17. For a detailed analysis of these trends, see Herbert S. Klein, "Las economías de Nueva España y Perú, 1680–1809: La visión a partir de las Cajas Reales," in Heraclio Bonilla, ed., *El sistema colonial en la América Española* (Barcelona: Editorial Crítica, 1991); John J. TePaske, "General Tendencies and Secular Trends in the Economies of Mexico and Peru, 1750–1810: The View from the Cajas of Mexico and Lima," in Nils Jacobsen and Hans-Jürgen Puhle, eds., *The Economies of Mexico and Peru During the Late Colonial Period, 1760–1810* (Berlin: Colloquium Verlag, 1986); John J. TePaske, "Economic Cycles in New Spain in the Eighteenth Century: The View from the Public Sector," in Richard L. Garner and William B. Taylor, eds., *Iberian Colonies, New World Societies* (n.p.: n.p., 1986); and John J. TePaske, "The Fiscal Structure of Upper Peru and the Financing of Empire," in Karen Spalding, ed., *Essays in the Political, Economic and Social History of Colonial Latin America* (Newark, DE: Latin American Studies Program, University of Delaware, 1982).

18. See above, chap. 5.

19. See for example Antonio Domínguez Ortiz, "Los Caudales de Indias y la política exterior de Felipe IV," *Anuario de Estudios Americanos* 12(1956):311–83; and the works of María Encarnación Rodríguez Vicente, "Los caudales remitidos desde el Perú a España por cuenta de la Real Hacienda: Series estadísticas (1651–1739)," *Anuario de Estudios Americanos* 21(1964):1–24; and Julián B. Ruiz Rivera, "Remesas de caudales del Nuevo Reino de Granada en el siglo XVII," *Anuario de Estudios Americanos* 34(1977):241–70.

20. See above, chap. 5, note 49.

21. Alexander von Humboldt, *Essai politique sur le royaume de la Nouvelle-Espagne*, 6 vols. (Paris: F. Schoell, 1811), vol. 4.

22. Barbier and Klein, "The Madrid Treasury," table 1. For the estimate of metropolitan Spain's population in the 1790s, see Jordi Nadal, *La población española (siglos XVI a XX)* (Barcelona: Ariel, 1973), 16.}

23. These calculations were provided by Carlos Marichal and are based on numbers in Peter Mathias and Patrick O'Brien, "Taxation in Britain and France, 1715–1810: A Comparison of the Social and Economic Incidence of Taxes Collected for the Central Governments," *Journal of European Economic History* 5(1976):601–53.

24. See D. A. Brading, *Miners and Merchants in Bourbon Mexico 1763–1810* (Cambridge: Cambridge University Press, 1971).

25. One of the first quantitative attempts to evaluate the question of Mexican growth or stagnation in the nineteenth century was the essay written in 1978 by John Coatsworth and reprinted in *Los orígenes del atraso* (Mexico: Alianza Editorial, 1990), chap. 4. Recent challenges to this model have included Margaret Chowning, "The Contours of the Post-1810 Depression in Mexico: A Reappraisal from a Regional Perspective," *Latin American Research Review* 27(2)(1992).

26. This is the conclusion reached in several studies, including Herbert S. Klein, "La economía de la Nueva España, 1680–1809: Un análisis a partir de las cajas reales," *Historia Mexicana* 34(4)(1985):561–609; John J. TePaske, "Economic Cycles in New Spain in

the Eighteenth Century: The View from the Public Sector," *Iberian Colonies, New World Societies: Essays in Memory of Charles Gibson*, ed. by Richard Gardner and William B. Taylor (n.p.:n.p., 1985), 19–141; and Klein, "Las economías de México y Perú en el siglo XVIII."

27. For peninsular income see Jacques A. Barbier and Herbert S. Klein, "Revolutionary Wars and Public Finances: The Madrid Treasury, 1784–1807," *Journal of Economic History* 41(2)(June 1981):315–37; and Jacques A. Barbier, "Peninsular Finance and Colonial Trade: The Dilemma of Charles IV's Spain," *Journal of Latin American Studies* 12(1)(May 1980):21–37. For data from the first half of the eighteenth century, see Jacques A. Barbier, "Towards a New Chronology for Bourbon Colonialism: The 'Depositaria de Indias' of Cadiz, 1722–1789," *Ibero-Amerikanisches Archiv* 6(4)(1980):335–53. It has been calculated that in the period 1761–1765, the crown collected in gross tax incomes an average annual 147 million reales de vellón from its fifty principal treasury offices in America and only 59 million from its Tesorería General in metropolitan Spain; Renate Pieper, *La Real Hacienda bajo Fernando VI y Carlos III (1753–1788)* (Madrid: Instituto de Estudios Fiscales, 1992).

28. For a somewhat variant view, see, Leandro Prados de la Escosura, "Comercio exterior y cambio económico en España (1792–1849)," in Josep Fontana Lázaro, ed., *La economía española al final del antiguo régimen: III—Comercio y colonias* (Madrid: Alianza Editorial, 1982), 171–249. For competition over the control of trade, see Jacques A. Barbier, "Imperial Policy towards the Port of Veracruz, 1788–1808: The Struggle between Madrid, Cadiz and Havana Interests," in Nils Jacobsen and Hans-Jürgen Puhle, *The Economies of Mexico and Peru During the Late Colonial Period* (Berlin: Colloquium Verlag, 1986), 240–51.

29. On the fleet see Jacques A. Barbier, "Indies Revenues and Naval Spending: The Cost of Colonialism for the Spanish Bourbons, 1763–1805," Jahrbuch für Geschichte

von Staat, Wirtschaft und Geselschaft Lateinamerikas 21(1984):171–88.

30. Aside from the sources cited in chap. 5, note 32, see Geoffrey A. Cabat, "The Consolidación of 1804 in Guatemala," *The Americas* 28(1)(July 1971):20–38; and Reinhard Liehr, "Staatsverschuldung und Privatkredit: Die 'Consolidación de Vales Reales' in Hispano-amerika," *Ibero-Amerikanisches Archiv* 6(2)(1980):149–85. On the complex credit schemes implemented in these last years, see the following articles by Jacques A. Barbier: "Anglo-American Investors and Payments on Spanish Imperial Treasuries, 1795–1808," in Jacques A. Barbier and Allan J. Kuethe, eds., *The North American Role in the Spanish Imperial Economy, 1760–1819* (Manchester: Manchester University Press, 1984), 134–41; "Peninsular Finance and Colonial Trade: The Dilemma of Charles IV's Spain"; "Venezuelan 'Libranzas', 1788–1807: From Economic Nostrum to Fiscal Imperative," *The Americas* 37(4)(April 1981):457–78; and "Towards a New Chronology for Bourbon Colonialism: The 'Depositaria de Indias' of Cadiz, 1722–1789." See also Masae Sugawara H., ed., *La deuda pública de España y la economía novohispana, 1804–1809* (Mexico City: Instituto Nacional de Antropología e Historia, SEP, 1976); John Alexander Jackson, Jr., "The Mexican Silver Schemes: Finance and Profiteering in the Napoleonic Era, 1796–1811" (Ph.D. diss., University of North Carolina at Chapel Hill, 1978).

31. A good summary of their use for Mexico is found in Sherburn F. Cook and Woodrow Borah, *Essays in Population History*, 3 vols. (Berkeley: University of California Press, 1971–79). A leading example of this application for Peru is the work by Nobel David Cook, *The Demographic Collapse: Indian Peru, 1520–1620* (Cambridge: Cambridge University Press, 1981). I have just finished a similar work for Alto Peru-Bolivia; see Herbert S. Klein, *Haciendas and Ayllus: Rural Society in the Bolivian Andes in the 18th and 19th centuries* (Stanford, CA: Stanford University Press, 1993).

32. See for example Juan Carlos Gara-

vaglia and Juan Carlos Grosso, "La region de Puebla/Tlaxcala en la Nueva España del siglo XVIII," *Historia Mexicana* 25(4)(1986), as well as their volume *Las alcabalas novohispanas (1776–1821)* (Mexico City: Archivo General de la Nación, 1987); Enrique Tandeter, et al., "El mercado de Potosí a fines del siglo XVIII," in Olivia Harris, et al., *Participación indígena en los mercados surandinos: Estrategias y reproducción social, siglos XVI–XX* (La Paz: CERES, 1987); and Enrique Tandeter, "Crisis in Upper Peru, 1800–1805," *Hispanic American Historical Review* 71(1)(February 1991). Also see Jorge Silva Riquer, *La administración de alcabalas y pulques de Michoacán, 1776–1821* (Mexico City: Instituto Mora, 1993); Antonio Ibarra, "Mercado urbano y mercado regional en Guadalajara, 1790–1811: Tendencias cuantitativas de la renta de alcabalas," in Jorge Silva Riquer, et al., *Circuitos mercantiles y mercados en latinoamérica: Siglos XVIII–XIX* (Mexico City: Instituto Mora, 1995), 100–135.

33. An early study was that conducted by Pierre Chaunu and Hughette Chaunu, *Séville et l'Atlantique (1504–1650)*, 9 vols. (Paris: A. Colin, 1955–60). More recent is Lutgardo García Fuentes, *El comercio español con América (1650–1700)* (Sevilla: Escuela de Estudios Hispano-Americanos, C.S.I.C, 1978); Antonio García-Baquero González, *Cádiz y el Atlántico (1717–1778)*, 2 vols. (Sevilla: Escuela de Estudios Hispano-Americanos, C.S.I.C, 1976); Carlos Martínez Shaw, *Cataluña en la carrera de Indias, 1680–1756)* (Barcelona: Editorial Crítica, 1981). Only Veracruz in America has received such a detailed treatment of its Atlantic trade; see Javier Ortiz de la Tabla, *Comercio exterior de Veracruz, 1778–1821* (Sevilla: Escuela de Estudios Hispano-Americanos, C.S.I.C, 1978).

34. See for example Woodrow Borah, *Early Colonial Trade and Navigation between Mexico and Peru* (Berkeley: University of California Press, 1954); Eduardo Arcila Farias, *Comercio entre Venezuela y Mexico en los siglos XVII y XVIII* (Mexico City: Colegio de México, 1950); W. Schurz, *The Manila Galleon* (New York: E.P. Dutton & Co., 1939); Carmen

Yuste López, *El comercio de la Nueva España con Filipinas, 1590–1785* (Mexico City: Instituto Nacional de Antropología e Historia, 1984); Sergio Villalobos, *Comercio y contrabando en el Río de la Plata y Chile, 1700–1811* (Buenos Aires: Editorial Universitaria de Buenos Aries, 1965); and Javier Cuenca, "Comercio y hacienda en la caída del imperio español, 1778–1826," in Josep Fontana Lázaro, ed., *La economía española al final del antiguo régimen: III—Comercio y Colonias* (Madrid: Alianza Editorial, 1982), 389–453.

35. The classic work on trade, but with an almost entirely institutional focus, is that of C. H. Haring, *Trade and Navigation between Spain and the Indies in the Time of the Hapsburgs* (Cambridge, MA: Harvard University Press, 1918). See also Guillermo Céspedes del Castillo, *La avería en el comercio de Indias* (Sevilla: Escuela de Estudios Hispano-Americanos, C.S.I.C, 1945).

36. See sources cited in chap. 5, note 24.

37. See for example the detailed reconstruction of some three years done by Samuel Amaral, "Public Expenditure Financing in the Colonial Treasury: An Analysis of the Real Caja de Buenos Aires Accounts, 1789–1791," *Hispanic American Historical Review* 64(2) (May 1984):287–95; and my own comments on these revisions, Herbert Klein, "Robbing Peter to Pay Paul: The Internal Transfers Problem in the Royal Treasury Accounts," *Hispanic American Historical Review* 64(2)(May 1984):310–12. This type of critique is very different from a global rejection of the research enterprise, as exemplified in D. A. Brading, "Facts and Figments in Bourbon Mexico," *Bulletin of Latin American Research* 4(1)(1985):61–64. For a rejoinder to Braiding's extreme position, see Richard Garner, "Further Considerations on 'Facts and Figments in Bourbon Mexico,'" *Bulletin of Latin American Research* 6(1)(1987):55–63.

Appendix 1

1. An estimate of the missing data for the cajas of South America is provided in B. H. Slicher van Bath, *Real Hacienda y eco-*

nomía en Hispanoamérica, 1541–1820 (Amsterdam: EDLA, 1989).

2. In a few cases, again mostly concerning the New Spain treasuries, this chaotic situation extended into the first decade of the eighteenth century. These have equally been corrected in the following tables.

3. Unfortunately in some of my initial studies of this material, I did not fully take these discrepancies into account. Thus the figures appearing in this volume supersede the numbers I gave on Mexico in my essay "La economía de la Nueva España, 1680–1809," *Historia Mexicana* 34(4)(136)(abril–junio, 1985) and those that appeared in my preliminary essay "Las economías de Nueva España y Perú, 1680–1809: La visión a partir de las Cajas Reales," in Heraclio Bonilla, ed., *El sistema colonial en la América Española* (Barcelona: Editorial Crítica, 1991).

4. In 1970 an early model based on modern accounting techniques was suggested to deal with the crown's multitudinous war expenditures; see Paul E. Hoffman, "The Computer and the Colonial Treasury Accounts: A Proposal for a Methodology," *Hispanic American Historical Review* 50(4)(November 1970): 731–40. In the same period, I suggested a new categorization of all the ramos in light of modern economic historical concerns and categories; Herbert S. Klein, "Structure and Profitability of Royal Finances in the Viceroyalty of the Río de la Plata in 1790," *Hispanic American Historical Review* 53(3)(August 1973):440–69.

5. See Gaspar de Escalona Agüero, *Gazofilacio real del Peru*, 4th ed. (La Paz: Editorial del Estado, 1941); and Fabián de Fonseca and Carlos de Urrutia, *Historia general de Real Hacienda*, 6 vols. (Mexico City: V.G. Torres, 1845–53).

6. A listing of the individual taxes that made up these groups is found in an appendix table in Herbert S. Klein, "La economía de la Nueva España, 1680–1809," 601–9.

Appendix 2

1. On what such a complete price study would look like, see Herbert S. Klein and Stanley Engerman, "Methods and Meanings in Price History," in Lyman Johnson and Enrique Tandeter, eds., *Growth and Integration in the Atlantic Economy: Essays on the Price History of Eighteenth-Century Latin America* (Albuquerque: University of New Mexico Press, 1990), 9–20.

2. These price data are found in: Cecilia Rabell Romero, *Los diezmos de San Luis de la Paz: Economía en una región del Bajío en el siglo XVIII* (Mexico City: Universidad Nacional Autónoma de México, 1986); Enrique Florescano, *Precios del maíz y crisis agrícolas en México (1708–1810): Ensayo sobre el movimiento de los precios y sus consecuencias económicas y sociales* (Mexico City: El Colegio de México, 1969); Richard L. Garner with Spiro E. Stefanou, *Economic Growth and Change in Bourbon Mexico* (Gainesville: University Press of Florida, 1993), appendix 2; and Nathan Wachtel and Enrique Tandeter, "Prices and Agricultural Production, Potosí and Charcas in the Eighteenth Century," in Lyman Johnson and Enrique Tandeter, eds., *Essays in the Price History of Eighteenth Century Latin America* (Albuquerque: University of New Mexico Press, 1990), table 4.

3. Earl J. Hamilton, *War and Prices in Spain, 1651–1800* (Cambridge, MA: Harvard University Press, 1947), 172–73, table 11.

4. Garner with Stefanou, *Economic Growth and Change in Bourbon Mexico*, 48.

Bibliography

Unpublished Materials

Biblioteca Nacional (Madrid) Sala de Manuscritos, #19710-23.

Biblioteca Nacional de México, Manuscrito no. 1282, "Memoria instructiva y documentada del estado comparativo de los productos de la Real Hacienda del año de 1809 . . . ," Mexico City, August 1813; and "Extracto general de valores y gastos y líquidos de los ramos comunes y particulares de la Real Hacienda de Nueva España dedicado de un año común por el quinquenio corrido desde 1795 hasta el de 1799," dated July 15, 1810.

Bauzon, Leslie. "Deficit Government, Mexico and the Philippines 'Situado' (1606–1804)." Ph.D. diss., Duke University, 1970.

Bertrand, Michel. "Grandeur et misères de l'office: Les officiers de finances de Nouvelle-Espagne XVIIe–XVIIIe siècles." 2 vols. Ph.D. diss., Université de Paris-I, 1995.

Interview with Zacarías Moutoukias, Paris, November 14, 1995.

Interview with Carlos Marichal, Mexico City, November 12, 1995.

Interview with John TePaske, Durham, NC, February 12, 1996.

Jackson, John Alexander, Jr. "The Mexican Silver Schemes: Finance and Profiteering in the Napoleonic Era, 1796–1811." Ph.D. diss., University of North Carolina at Chapel Hill, 1978.

Jáuregui, Luis Antonio. "La autonomía del Fisco Colonial: La estructura administrativa de la Real Hacienda novohispana, 1786–1821." Ph.D. diss., Colegio de México, 1994.

TePaske, John J. "Bullion Production in Mexico and Peru, 1581–1810." Unpublished ms., 1987.

Published Studies

Aiton, Arthur Scott. "Real Hacienda in New Spain under the First Viceroy." *Hispanic American Historical Review* (1926):232–45.

Amaral, Samuel. "Public Expenditure Financing in the Colonial Treasury: An Analysis of the Real Caja de Buenos Aires Accounts, 1789–1791." *Hispanic American Historical Review* 64(2)(May 1984):287–95.

Andrien, Kenneth J. *Crisis and Decline: The Viceroyalty of Peru in the Seventeenth Century.* Albuquerque: University of New Mexico Press, 1985.

———. "The Sale of Fiscal Offices and the Decline of Royal Authority in the Viceroyalty of Peru, 1633–1700." *Hispanic American Historical Review* 62(February 1982):49–71.

Arcila Farías, Eduardo. *Comercio entre Venezuela y México en los siglos XVII y XVIII.* Mexico City: El Colegio de México, 1950.

Ardant, Gabriel. *Histoire de l'impôt.* Paris: Fayard, 1971.

————. *Théories sociologique de l'impôt.* 2 vols. Paris: S.E.V.P.N., 1965.

Arduz Eguía, Gaston. *Ensayos sobre la historia de la minería altoperuana.* Madrid: Editorial Parainfo, 1985.

Artola, Miguel. *La hacienda del antiguo régimen.* Madrid: Alianza Editorial, 1982.

Arze Quiroga, Eduardo. *Historia de Bolivia . . . siglo XVI.* La Paz: Los Amigos del Libro, 1969.

Bakewell, Peter J. *Miners of the Red Mountain: Indian Labor in Potosí, 1545–1650.* Albuquerque: University of New Mexico Press, 1984.

————. "Mining in Colonial Spanish America." In Leslie Bethell, ed., *The Cambridge History of Latin America,* vol. 2. Cambridge: Cambridge University Press, 1984.

————. "Registered Silver Production in Potosí, 1550–1735." *Jahrbuch für Geschichte von Staat, Wirtschaft und Gesellschaft Lateinamerikas* 12(1975).

————. *Silver Mining and Society in Colonial Mexico: Zacatecas, 1546–1700.* Cambridge: Cambridge University Press, 1971.

Barbier, Jacques. "Anglo-American Investors and Payments on Spanish Imperial Treasuries, 1795–1808." In Jacques A. Barbier and Allan J. Kuethe, eds., *The North American Role in the Spanish Imperial Economy, 1760–1819.* Manchester: Manchester University Press, 1984, 134–41.

————. "Imperial Policy towards the Port of Veracruz, 1788–1808: The Struggle Between Madrid, Cadiz and Havana Interests." In Nils Jacobsen and Hans-Jürgen Puhle, eds., *The Economies of Mexico and Peru During the Late Colonial Period.* Berlin: Colloquium Verlag, 1986), 240–51.

————. "Indies Revenues and Naval Spending: The Cost of Colonialism for the Spanish Bourbons, 1763–1805." *Jahrbuch für Geschichte von Staat, Wirtschaft und Gesellschaft Lateinamerikas* 21(1984):171–88.

————. "Peninsular Finance and Colonial Trade: The Dilemma of Charles IV's Spain." *Journal of Latin American Studies* 12(1)(May 1980):21–37.

————. "Towards a New Chronology for Bourbon Colonialism: The 'Depositaria de Indias' of Cadiz, 1722–1789." *Ibero-Amerikanisches Archiv* 6(4)1980):333–53.

————. "Venezuelan 'Libranzas', 1788–1807: From Economic Nostrum to Fiscal Imperative." *The Americas* 37(4)April 1981):457–78.

Barbier, Jacques, and Herbert S. Klein. "Las prioridades de un monarca ilustrado: El gasto público bajo el reinado de Carlos III, 1760–1785." *Revista de Historia Económica* 3(3)(1985):473–95.

————. "Revolutionary Wars and Public Finances: The Madrid Treasury, 1784–1807." *Journal of Economic History* 41(2)(June 1981):315–39.

Barnadas, Josep M. *Charcas: Orígenes históricas de una sociedad colonial.* La Paz: Centro de Investigación y Promoción del Campesinado, 1973.

Borah, Woodrow W. *Early Colonial Trade and Navigation between Mexico and Peru.* Berkeley: University of California Press, 1954.

————. *New Spain's Century of Depression.* Iberoamericana 35. Berkeley: University of California Press, 1951.

Brading, D. A. "Facts and Figments in Bourbon Mexico." *Bulletin of Latin American Research* 4(1)(1985):61–64.

————. *Miners and Merchants in Bourbon Mexico, 1763–1810.* Cambridge: Cambridge University Press, 1971.

Brading, David A., and Harry E. Cross. "Colonial Silver Mining: Mexico and Peru." *Hispanic American Historical Review* 52(4)November 1972):545–79.

Brown, Kendall W. *Bourbons and Brandy: Imperial Reform in the Eighteenth-Century Arequipa.* Albuquerque: University of New Mexico Press, 1985.

Cabat, Geoffrey A. "The Consolidación of 1804 in Guatemala." *The Americas* 28(1)July 1971):20–38.

Carmagnani, Marcello. "La produción agro-pecuaria chilena: Aspectos cuantitativos (1630–1830)." *Cahiers des Amériques latines* 3(1969):3–21.

Céspedes del Castillo, Guillermo. *La avería en el comercio de Indias.* Sevilla: Escuela de Estudios Hispano-Americanos, C.S.I.C, 1945.

———. *Lima y Buenos Aires: Repercusiones económicas y políticas de la creación del virreinato del Plata.* Sevilla: Escuela de Estudios Hispano-Americanos, C.S.I.C, 1947.

———. "La renta del tabaco en el virreinato del Perú." *Revista Histórica* (Lima) 21(1954).

———. "Reorganización de la Hacienda virreinal peruana en el siglo XVIII." *Anuario de Historia del Derecho Español* 23(1953).

Chaunu, Pierre, and Hughette Chaunu. *Seville et l'Atlantique (1504–1650).* 9 vols. Paris: Librairie Armand Colin, 1955–60.

Chevalier, François. *La formación de los latifundios en México: Tierra y sociedad en los siglos XVI y XVII.* 2d rev. ed. Mexico City: Fondo de Cultura Económica, 1976.

———. *Land and Society in Colonial Mexico: The Great Hacienda.* Berkeley: University of California Press, 1970.

Chowning, Margaret. "The Consolidación de Vales Reales in the Bishopric of Michoacán." *Hispanic American Historical Review* 69(3)(1989).

———. "The Contours of the Post-1810 Depression in Mexico: A Reappraisal from a Regional Perspective." *Latin American Research Review* 27(2)(1992).

Clayton, L. A. "Trade and Navigation in the Seventeenth-Century Viceroyalty of Peru." *Journal of Latin American Studies* 7(1)(May 1975):1–21.

Coatsworth, John H. "Obstacles to Economic Growth in Nineteenth Century Mexico." *American Historical Review* 83(1)(February 1978):80–100.

———. *Los orígenes del atraso.* Mexico City: Alianza Editorial, 1990.

Cole, Jeffrey A. *The Potosí Mita 1573–1700: Compulsory Indian Labor in the Andes.* Stanford, CA: Stanford University Press, 1985.

Comín Comín, Francisco. *Hacienda y economía en la España contemporanea (1880–1936).* 2 vols. Madrid: Instituto de Estudios Fiscales, 1988.

Contreras, Carlos. *La ciudad del mercurio, Huancavelica, 1570–1700.* Lima: Instituto de Estudios Peruanos, 1982.

Cook, David Nobel. *The Demographic Collapse: Indian Peru, 1520–1620.* Cambridge: Cambridge University Press, 1981.

Cook, Sherburn F., and Woodrow Borah. *Essays in Population History.* 3 vols. Berkeley: University of California Press, 1971–79.

Cross, Harry E. "South American Bullion Production and Export, 1550–1750." In J. F. Richards, ed., *Precious Metals in the Later Medieval and Early Modern Worlds.* Durham, NC: Carolina Academic Press, 1983, 397–423.

Cuello Martinelli, María de los Ángeles. *La renta de los naipes en Nueva España.* Sevilla: Escuela de Estudios Hispano-Americanos, C.S.I.C, 1966.

Cuenca, Javier. "Comercio y hacienda en la caída del imperio español, 1778–1826." In Josep Fontana Lázaro, ed., *La economía española al final del antiguo régimen: III—Comercio y colonias.* Madrid: Alianza Editorial, 1982, 389–453.

Deans-Smith, Susan. *Bureaucrats, Planters and Workers: The Making of the Tobacco Monopoly in Bourbon Mexico*. Austin: University of Texas Press, 1992.

———. "The Money Plant: The Royal Tobacco Monopoly of New Spain, 1765–1821." In Nils Jacobsen and Hans-Jürgen Puhle, eds., *The Economies of Mexico and Peru During the Late Colonial Period*. Berlin: Colloquium Verlag, 1986.

Del Valle Pavón, Gulhermina. "Los recursos extraordinarios de la hacienda novohispana, la dueda del México independiente." Paper presented at the colloquium "Finanzas y estado en la primera república federal mexicana, 1824–1835." El Colegio de Michoacán, Zamora, Mexico, November 13–14, 1995.

De Sierra, Lamberto. *"Manfiesto" de la plata extraida del cerro de Potosí, 1556–1800*. rep. ed. of 1808 ms. Buenos Aires: Academia Nacional de la Historia, 1971.

Deustúa, José. *La minería peruana y la iniciación de la República, 1820–1840*. Lima: Instituto de Estudios Peruanos, 1986.

Díaz Rementería, Carlos J. "En torno a un aspecto de la política reformista de Carlos III: Las matrículas de tributarios en los virreinatos del Perú y del Río de la Plata." *Revista de Indias* 37(147–48)(enero–junio 1977):51–139.

———. "El régimen jurídico del ramo de tributos en Nueva España y las reformas peruanas de Carlos III." *Historia Mexicana* 28(3)(1979):401–38.

Domínguez Ortiz, Antonio. "Los Caudales de Indias y la política exterior de Felipe IV." *Anuario de Estudios Americanos* 12(1956):311–83.

Escalona Agüero, Gaspar de. *Gazofilacio real del Perú*. 4th ed. La Paz: Editorial del Estado, 1941.

Evans, Brian M. "Census Enumeration in Late 17th Century Alto Peru: The Numeración General of 1683–1684." In David J. Robinson, ed., *Studies in Spanish American Population History*. (Boulder, CO: Westview Press, 1985).

Fisher, John. "The Imperial Response to 'Free Trade': Spanish Imports from Spanish America, 1778–1796." *Journal of Latin American Studies* 17(1985):35–78.

———. *Minas y mineros en el Perú colonial, 1776–1824*. Lima: Instituto de Estudios Peruanos, 1977.

Florescano, Enrique. *Precios del maíz y crisis agrícolas en México (1708–1810): Ensayo sobre el movimiento de los precios y sus consecuencias económicas y sociales*. Mexico City: El Colegio de México, 1969.

Florescano, Enrique, and Isabel Gil Sánchez. "La época de las reformas borbónicas y el crecimiento económico, 1750–1808." In Centro de Estudios Históricos, El Colego de México, *Historia general de México*. 4 vols. Mexico City: El Colegio de México, 1976, 2:203–31.

Fonseca, Fabián de, and Carlos de Urrutia. *Historia general de Real Hacienda*. 6 vols. Mexico City: V. G. Torres, 1845–53.

Garavaglia, Juan Carlos, and Juan Carlos Grosso. *Las alcabalas novohispanas (1776–1821)*. Mexico City: Archivo General de la Nación, 1987.

———. "De Veracruz a Durango: Un análisis regional de la Nueva España borbónica." *Siglo XIX* 2(4)(1987):9–52.

———. "Estado borbónico y opresión fiscal en la Nueva España, 1750–1821." In Antonio Annino, ed., *America Latina: Dallo stato coloniale allo stato nazionale*. 2 vols. Torino: Franco Angeli, 1987, 1:78–97.

———. "La región de Puebla/Tlaxcala en la Nueva España del siglo XVIII." *Historia Mexicana* 35(4)(1986):549–600.

García-Baquero González, Antonio. *Cádiz y el Atlántico (1717–1778)*. 2 vols. Sevilla: Escuela de Estudios Hispano-Americanos, C.S.I.C., 1976.

García Fuentes, Lutgardo. *El comercio español con América (1650–1700)*. Sevilla: Escuela de Estudios Hispano-Americanos, C.S.I.C., 1978.

Garner, Richard L. "Further Considerations on 'Facts and Figments in Bourbon Mexico.'" *Bulletin of Latin American Research* 6(1)(1987):55–63.

———. "Silver Production and Entrepreneurial Structure in 18th Century Mexico." *Jahrbuch für Geschichte von Staat, Wirtschaft und Gesellschaft Lateinamerikas* 17(1980):157–85.

Garner, Richard L., with Spiro E. Stefanou. *Economic Growth and Change in Bourbon Mexico*. Gainesville: University Press of Florida, 1993.

Garner, Richard L., and William B. Taylor, eds. *Iberian Colonies, New World Societies*. State College, PA: n.p., 1986.

Glave, Luis Miguel. *Trajinantes: Caminos indígenas en la sociedad colonial siglos XVI/XVII*. Lima: Instituto de Apoyo Agrario, 1989.

Hamilton, Earl J. *American Treasure and the Price Revolution in Spain, 1501–1650*. Cambridge, MA: Harvard University Press, 1934.

———. *War and Prices in Spain, 1651–1800*. Cambrdige, MA: Harvard University Press, 1947.

Hamnett, Brian R. "The Appropriation of Mexican Church Wealth by the Spanish Bourbon Government—The 'Consolidación de Vales Reales', 1805–1809." *Journal of Latin American Studies* 1(2)(November 1969):85–113.

Haring, C. H. "Early Spanish Colonial Exchequer." *American Historical Review* 23(July 1918):779–96.

———. "Los libros mayores de los tesoreros reales de Hispanoamérica en el siglo XVI." *Hispanic American Historical Review* 2(May 1919):173–87.

———. *Trade and Navigation between Spain and the Indies in the Time of the Hapsburgs*. Cambridge, MA: Harvard University Press, 1918.

Hernández Paloma, José Jesús. *La renta de pulque en Nueva España, 1663–1810*. Sevilla: Escuela de Estudios Hispano-Americanos, C.S.I.C., 1979.

Herr, Richard. *Rural Change and Royal Finance in Spain at the End of the Old Regime*. Berkeley: University of California Press, 1989.

Herrera Canales, Inés. *El comercio exterior de México, 1821–1875*. Mexico City: El Colegio de México, 1977.

Hoffman, Paul E. "The Computer and the Colonial Treasury Accounts: A Proposal for a Methodology." *Hispanic American Historical Review* 50(4)(November 1970):731–40.

Humboldt, Alexander von. *Essai politique sur le royaume de la Nouvelle-Espagne*. 6 vols. Paris: F. Schoell, 1811.

Hünefeldt, Christine. "Etapa final del monopolio en el virreinato del Perú: El tabaco de Chachapoyas." In Nils Jacobsen and Hans-Jürgen Puhle, eds., *The Economies of Mexico and Peru During the Late Colonial Period*. Berlin: Colloquium Verlag, 1986.

Ibarra, Antonio. "Mercado urbano y mercado regional en Guadalajara, 1790–1811: Tendencias cuantitativas de la renta de alcabalas." In Jorge Silva Riquer, Juan Carlos Grosso, and Carmen Yuste, *Circuitos mercantiles y mercados en Latinoamérica: Siglos XVIII–XIX*. Mexico City: Instituto Mora, 1995, 100–135.

Israel, J. I. "Mexico and the 'General Crisis' of the Seventeenth Century." *Past and Present* 63(May 1974):33–57.

———. *Race, Class and Politics in Colonial Mexico, 1610–1670*. Oxford: Oxford University Press, 1975.

Kamen, Henry. "Debate: The Seventeenth-Century Crisis in New Spain: Myth or Reality?" *Past and Present* 97(November 1982):144–50.

Klein, Herbert S. "La economía de la Nueva España, 1680–1809: Un análisis a partir de las cajas reales." *Historia Mexicana* 34(4)(136)(abril–junio 1985):561–609.

————. "Las economías de Nueva España y Perú, 1680–1809: La visión a partir de las cajas reales." In Heraclio Bonilla, ed. *El sistema colonial en la América Española.* Barcelona: Editorial Crítica, 1991, 154–217.

————. "Las finanzas del virreinato del Río de la Plata en 1790." *Desarrollo Económico* 50(julio–septiembre 1973):369–400.

————. *Haciendas and Ayllus: Rural Society in the Bolivian Andes in the 18th and 19th Centuries.* Stanford, CA: Stanford University Press, 1993.

————. "Historia fiscal colonial: Resultados y perspectivas." *Historia Mexicana* 42(2)(166) (octubre–diciembre 1992):261–307.

————. "Rentas de la Corona y economía del Virreino de Nueva España." *Hacienda Pública Española* (Madrid) 87(marzo–abril 1984):107–34.

————. "Robbing Peter to Pay Paul: The Internal Transfers Problem in the Royal Treasury Accounts." *Hispanic American Historical Review* 64(2)(May 1984):310–12.

————. "Structure and Profitability of Royal Finance in the Viceroyalty of the Río de la Plata in 1790." *Hispanic American Historical Review* 53(3)(August 1973):440–69.

Klein, Herbert S., and Jacques Barbier. "Recent Trends in the Study of Spanish American Colonial Public Finance." *Latin American Research Review* 23(1)(1988):35–62.

Klein, Herbert S., and Stanley Engerman. "Methods and Meanings in Price History." In Lyman Johnson and Enrique Tandeter, eds., *Growth and Integration in the Atlantic Economy: Essays on the Price History of Eighteenth-Century Latin America.* Albuquerque: University of New Mexico Press, 1990, 9–20.

Lang, M. F. *El monopolio estatal del mercurio en el México colonial (1550–1710).* Mexico City: Fondo de Cultura Económica, 1977.

Lavrin, Asunción. "The Execution of the Law of Consolidación in New Spain: Economic Aims and Results." *Hispanic American Historical Review* 53(1)(February 1973):27–49.

Lerdo de Tejada, Miguel. *Comercio exterior de México.* 2d ed. Mexico City: Banco Nacional de Comercio Exterior, 1967.

Levene, Ricardo. *Investigaciones acerca de la historia económica del virreinato del Plata.* 2d ed. Buenos Aires: El Ateneo, 1952.

Lewis, James A. "The Royal Gunpowder Monopoly in New Spain (1766–1783): Case Study of Management, Technology and Reform under Charles III." *Ibero-Amerikanisches Archiv* 6(4)(1980):355–72.

Liehr, Reinhard. "Staatsverschuldung und Privatkredit: Die 'Consolidación de Vales Reales' in Hispanoamerika." *Ibero-Amerikanisches Archiv* 6(2)(1980):149–85.

Lindo-Fuentes, Héctor. "La utilidad de los diezmos como fuentes para la historia económica." *Historia Mexicana* 30(2)(1980):273–89.

Lohmann Villena, Guillermo. *Las minas de Huancavelica en los siglos XVI y XVII.* Sevilla: Escuela de Estudios Hispano-Americanos, C.S.I.C., 1949.

López Beltrán, Clara. *Estructura económica de una sociedad colonial: Charcas en el siglo XVII.* La Paz: CERES, 1988.

Marichal, Carlos. "La bancarrota del virreinato: Finanzas, guerra y política en la Nueva España, 1770–1808." In Josefina Zoraida Vázquez, ed., *Interpretaciones del siglo XVIII mexicano: El impacto de las reformas borbónicas.* Mexico City: Nueva Imagen, 1992, 153–86.

————. "Las guerras imperiales y los préstamos novohispanos, 1781–1804." *Historia Mexicana* 39(4)(136)(abril–junio 1990):881–907.

Marichal, Carlos, and Matilde Souto Mantecón. "Silver and Situados: New Spain and the Financing of the Spanish Empire in the Eighteenth Century." *Hispanic American Historical Review* 74(4)(1994):587–613.

Martínez Shaw, Carlos. *Cataluña en la carrera de Indias, 1680–1756.* Barcelona: Editorial Crítica, 1981.

Mathias, Peter, and Patrick O'Brien. "Taxation in Britain and France, 1715–1810: A
     Comparison of the Social and Economic Incidence of Taxes Collected for the Central
     Governments." *Journal of European Economic History* 5(1976):601–53.
Miranda, José. *El tributo indígena en la Nueva España durante el siglo XVI*. Mexico City: El
     Colegio de México, 1952.
Morin, Claude. *Michoacán en la Nueva España del siglo XVIII*. Mexico City: Fondo de Cultura
     Económica, 1979.
Morineau, Michel. *Incroyables gazettes et fabuleux métaux: Les retours des trésors américains
     d'apres les gazettes hollandaises (XVIe–XVIIIe siècles)*. Paris: Cambridge University Press
     and Maison des Sciences de l'Homme, 1985.
Moutoukias, Zacarías. "Power, Corruption and Commerce: The Making of the Local
     Administrative Structure in Seventeenth-Century Buenos Aires." *Hispanic American
     Historical Review* 68(4)(1988):771–801.
————. "Una forma de oposición: El contrabando." In Massimo Ganci and Ruggiero Romano,
     Governare il mondo: L'impero spagnolo dal XV al XIX secolo. Palermo: Società Siciliana
     per la Storia Patria, 1991, 333–68.
Nadal, Jordi. *La población española (siglos XVI a XX)*. Barcelona: Ariel, 1973.
O'Phelan Godoy, Scarlett. "Las reformas fiscales borbónicas y su impacto en la sociedad
     colonial del Bajo y Alto Perú." In Nils Jacobsen and Hans-Jürgen Puhle, eds., *The
     Economics of Mexico and Peru During the Late Colonial Period, 1760–1810*. Berlin:
     Colloquium Verlag, 1986.
Ortiz de la Tabla Ducasse, Javier. *Comercio exterior de Veracruz, 1778–1821*. Sevilla: Escuela de
     Estudios Hispano-Americanos, C.S.I.C., 1978.
Parry, J. H. *The Sale of Public Office in the Spanish Indies under the Hapsburgs*. Berkeley:
     University of California Press, 1953.
Peña Cámara, José de la. *El "tributo": Sus orígenes: Su implantación en la Nueva España:
     Contribución al estudio de la Real Hacienda indiana*. Sevilla: Imprenta de la Gavidia, 1934.
Peñaloza, Luis. *Historia económica de Bolivia*. 2 vols. La Paz: n.p., 1953.
Pentland, John Barclay. *Informe sobre Bolivia, 1826*. Potosí: Editorial Potosí, 1975.
Pérez Herrero, Pedro. *Comercio y mercados en América Latina colonial*. Madrid: Editorial Mapfre,
     1992.
————. "El México borbónico: ¿Un 'exito' fracasado?" In Josefina Zoriada Vázquez, ed.,
     Interpretaciones del siglo XVIII mexicana: El impacto de las reformas borbónicas. Mexico
     City: Nueva Imagen, 1992, 109–52.
————. *Plata y libranzas: La articulación commercial del México borbónico*. Mexico City: El
     Colegio de México, 1988.
Pieper, Renate. *La Real Hacienda bajo Fernando VI y Carlos III (1753–1788)*. Madrid: Instituto
     de Estudios Fiscales, 1992.
Prados de la Escosura, Leandro. "Comercio exterior y cambio económico en España (1792–
     1849)." In Josep Fontana Lázaro, ed., *La economia española al final del antiguo régimen:
     III—Comercio y colonias*. Madrid: Alianza Editorial, 1982, 171–249.
Rabell Romero, Cecilia. *Los diezmos de San Luis de la Paz: Economía en una región del Bajío en el
     siglo XVIII*. Mexico City: Universidad Nacional Autónoma de México, 1986.
Rodríguez Vicente, María Encarnación. "Los caudales remitidos desde el Perú a España por
     cuenta de la Real Hacienda: Series estadísticas (1651–1739)." *Anuario de Estudios
     Americanos* 21(1964):1–24.
Romano, Ruggiero. *Coyunturas opuestas: La crisis del siglo XVII en Europa e Hispanoamérica*.
     Mexico City: Fondo de Cultura Económica, 1993.
Ruiz Rivera, Julián B. "Remesas de caudales del Nuevo Reino de Granada en el siglo XVII."
     Anuario de Estudios Americanos 34(1977):241–70.

Sánchez-Albornoz, Nicolás. *Indios y tributos en el Alto Perú*. Lima: Instituto de Estudios Peruanos, 1978.

――――. *La población de América Latina desde los tiempos precolombianos al año 2000*. 2d ed. Madrid: Alianza Editorial, 1977.

Sánchez-Bella, Ismael. *La organización financiera de las Indias, siglo XVI*. Sevilla: Escuela de Estudios Hispano-Americanos, C.S.I.C., 1968.

Sarabia Viejo, María Justina. *El juego de gallos en Nueva España*. Sevilla: Escuela de Estudios Hispano-Americanos, C.S.I.C., 1972.

Schurz, W. L. *The Manila Galleon*. New York: E.P. Dutton & Co., 1939.

Sempat Assadourian, Carlos. *El sistema de la economía colonial: Mercado interno, regiones y espacio económico*. Lima: Instituto de Estudios Peruanos, 1982.

Silva Riquer, Jorge. *La administración de alcabalas y pulques de Michoacán, 1776–1821*. Mexico City: Instituto Mora, 1993.

Slicher van Bath, B. H. *Real Hacienda y economía en Hispanoamérica, 1541–1820*. Amsterdam: EDLA, 1989.

Soetbeer, Adolf. *Edelmetall-Produktion und Wertverhaltniss zwischen Gold und Silber*. Gotha: J. Perthes, 1879.

Sugawara H., Masae, ed. *La deuda pública de España y la economía novohispana, 1804–1809*. Mexico City: Instituto Nacional de Antropología e Historia, SEP, 1976.

Tandeter, Enrique. "Crisis in Upper Peru, 1800–1805." *Hispanic American Historical Review* 71(1)(February 1991):35–71.

Tandeter, Enrique, Vilma Milletich, María Matilde Ollier, and Beatriz Ruibal, "El mercado de Potosí a fines del siglo XVIII." In Olivia Harris, Brooke Larson, and Enrique Tandeter, eds., *La Participación indígena en los mercados surandinos: Estrategias y reproducción social, siglos XVI–XX*. La Paz: CERES, 1987.

Taylor, William B. *Landlord and Peasant in Colonial Oaxaca*. Stanford, CA: Stanford University Press, 1972.

TePaske, John J. "La crisis financiera del virreinato de Nueva España a fines de la colonia," *Secuencia* 19(enero–abril 1991):123–40.

――――. "La desintegración financiera del gobierno real de México durante la época de independencia, 1791–1821." *Secuencia* (Mexico) 21(1991):106–24.

――――. "Economic Cycles in New Spain in the Eighteenth Century: The View from the Public Sector." In Richard Gardner and William B. Taylor, eds., *Iberian Colonies, New World Societies: Essays in Memory of Charles Gibson*. n.p.: n.p., 1985.

――――. "The Fiscal Structure of Upper Peru and the Financing of Empire." In Karen Spalding, ed., *Essays in the Political, Economic and Social History of Colonial Latin America*. Newark, DE: Latin American Studies Program, University of Delaware, 1982.

――――. "General Tendencies and Secular Trends in the Economies of Mexico and Peru, 1750–1810: The View from the Cajas of Mexico and Lima." In Nils Jacobsen and Hans-Jürgen Puhle, eds., *The Economies of Mexico and Peru During the Late Colonial Period, 1760–1810*. Berlin: Colloquium Verlag, 1986.

――――. "New World Silver: Castile and the Far East (1590–1750)." In John F. Richards, ed., *Precious Metals in the Later Medieval and Early Modern Worlds*. Durham, NC: Carolina Academic Press, 1983, 425–46.

――――. "The Records of the King's Countinghouse: Problems and Pitfalls." *Latin American Economic History Newsletter* 1(December 1991):5–8.

TePaske, John J., and Herbert S. Klein. *Ingresos y egresos de la Real Hacienda en Nueva España*. 2 vols. Mexico City: Instituto Nacional de Antropología e Historia, 1986, 1988.

――――. "Rejoinder" [to the critiques of J. Israel and H. Kamen]. *Past and Present* 97(November 1982):157–62.

———. *Royal Treasuries of the Spanish Empire in America, 1580–1825.* 3 vols. Durham, NC: Duke University Press, 1982.

———. "The Seventeenth Century Crisis in New Spain: Myth or Reality." *Past and Present,* 90(February 1981):116–35.

Thompson, I. A. A., and Bartolomé Yun, eds. *The Castillian Crisis of the Seventeenth Century.* Cambridge: Cambridge University Press, 1994.

Van Young, Eric. *Hacienda and Market in Eighteenth-Century Mexico: The Rural Economy of the Guadalajara Region, 1675–1820.* Berkeley: University of California Press, 1981.

Villalobos, Sergio. *Comercio y contrabando en el Río de la Plata y Chile, 1700–1811.* Buenos Aires: Editorial de la Universidad de Buenos Aires, 1965.

Villar Ortiz, Covadongo. *La renta de la pólvora en Nueva España (1569–1767).* Sevilla: Escuela de Estudios Hispano-Americanos, C.S.I.C., 1988.

Vollmer, Günter. *Bevölkerungspolitik und Bevölkerungsstruktur im Vizekönigreich Peru zu Ende der Kolonialzeit (1741–1821).* Bad Homburg: Gehlen, 1967.

Wachtel, Nathan, and Enrique Tandeter. "Prices and Agricultural Production, Potosí and Charcas in the Eighteenth Century." In Lyman Johnson and Enrique Tandeter, eds., *Essays in the Price History of Eighteenth Century Latin America.* Albuquerque: University of New Mexico Press, 1990.

Yuste López, Carmen. *El comercio de la Nueva España con Filipinas, 1590–1785.* Mexico City: Instituto Nacional de Antropología e Historia, 1984.

Zoraida Vázquez, Josefina, ed. *Interpretaciones del siglo XVIII mexicana: El impacto de las reformas borbónicas.* Mexico City: Nueva Imagen, 1992.

Index

Note: The reader will also want to consult the List of Tables in the front matter and the appendixes which follow the text for supporting data and methodological discussions.

About the Book and Author

The American Finances of the Spanish Empire
Royal Income and Expenditures in Colonial Mexico, Peru, and Bolivia, 1680–1809
Herbert S. Klein

This volume is the first to use treasury records to analyze and interpret the evolution of royal income and expenditure in Mexico, Peru, and Bolivia during the eighteenth century. These official statistics are invaluable for defining the economic evolution of Spanish America. Understanding the economic history of these key regions helps delineate long-term trends in everything from government revenues and expenditures to the growth and decline of regional economies.

The records Klein taps were the king's private source of information and his guarantee that his taxes were being collected and his accounts paid. From Klein's study emerge tentative answers to a series of questions basic to understanding the history of Spanish America: Were the colonists overtaxed? Was the seventeenth century an era of crisis and depression? Did Bourbon imperial policy lead to economic stagnation and hence create the seeds of independence? What were the respective costs and benefits of colonialism?

Herbert S. Klein is professor of history at Columbia University.